ALONE AGAINST
The SEA

ALONE AGAINST
The SEA

and other true adventures

By JON BOWERMASTER

THE LYONS PRESS
Guilford, Connecticut
An imprint of The Globe Pequot Press

The Lyons Press is an imprint of The Globe Pequot Press.

10 9 8 7 6 5 4 3 2 1

Printed in the United States of America

ISBN 1-59228-547-3

Library of Congress Cataloging-in-Publication Data is available on file.

For Barry Tessman (1959–2001),
who was along for many of these rides,
and a bunch more.

CONTENTS

ACKNOWLEDGMENTS

Most of these stories would never have made it to any page without the nod of approval, bankroll, and crafting of one admired editor or another. It is with great pleasure that I thank them here. I would single out my longtime editor and friend John Rasmus, the founding editor of *National Geographic Adventure.* More than one third of these pieces were written at magazines he was running—*Outside, Men's Journal* or *Adventure.* I take comfort in knowing that as long as J.R. has a job, I'll have a place to write.

Thanks also to Bill Allen, John Atwood, Richard Bangs, Keith Bellows, Graham Boynton, Mark Bryant, Karen Dane, David Dunbar, Hal Espen, Don George, Jon Gluck, John Harlin, Mark Jannot, Terry McDonnell, Adam Moss, Peter Miller, Tom Passavant, Scott Stuckey, Lisa Tabb, Ann Treistman, and Tom Wallace.

INTRODUCTION

My tongue is chapped, and the inside of my mouth and nostrils are badly burned, thanks to six continuous weeks hunted by fierce, non-stop altiplano winds and sun. How bad is it? My lips are so raw that when I sleep they seal shut and pulling them apart each morning I can literally hear new skin ripping.

Aaaah, adventure!

With a team of three others I've just completed a four-thousand-kilometer circuit by foot, sea kayak and 4x4 through the driest place on earth, a loop through northern Chile, northern Argentina and southern Bolivia. On assignment for *National Geographic,* we went looking for, of all things, water—which may seem silly, even pointless here where in some places a single drop of rain has never been recorded.

It proved not as far-fetched as it may sound. This high plain studded by chains of tall volcanoes—the Andes being the highest and most continuous mountain range outside the Himalayas—is where the sea used to be. We found reminders of the ocean everywhere. The payoffs to this search, to this adventure, were stumbling onto grand salt flats, high mountain lakes and trickles of forgotten rivers that kept reminding us that even in this most dry place, water is the key to life.

Payoff. That's what we were after. It's what makes this life, my life—and the stories that follow—so rewarding. (For me, at least.) In each adventure—whether rafting an unscouted river in Tibet, sailing on the

Atlantic, pulling sleds across Antarctica, or living off brambles and whiskey in Wales—there is always a powerful, if occasionally incalculable reward. During nearly twenty years of a life lived mostly on the road mine has been richly shaped by each of these adventures and the wide variety of bizarre and captivating people met along the way. When it comes to pay-off and reward we're not talking cash here, but rather the wealth that comes from a charmed meeting or simply surviving that unpredictable bend in the river.

Which brings me to an important distinction. I am a writer, first and foremost. Which makes these stories, and their sharing, the most valuable part of my wanderings. I am a writer who travels. And I travel for one reason. I am curious. About everything.

During the past two decades one label I've run from with the speed of a hurricane wind is that of "travel writer," a label I consider close to an epithet. Though a voracious reader of books about both the exotic and the routine corners of our world, none of my favorites have been written by anyone who would have accepted that moniker.

To me, "travel writer" comes with an image of pale-faced hacks on holiday, hosted by some high-end beachside cabana club, sucking up freebies, complaining all the way, and writing (maybe) an eight-hundred-word puff piece for the local paper, city magazine, or special interest publication about their "adventure." These people are not curious about anything, except when their bag will be picked up from outside their room, and where's their schwag. Any writing that emerges from such trips is not about traveling.

My take is that writers who travel create the very best of the travel-and-adventure writing genre, which has existed and evolved for centuries.

My definition of what qualifies as travel-and-adventure writing has an individual stamp. A list of my favorite books would include reporting at its highest level, a few semi-autobiographies, sociological inspections (and introspections), with visits to the grandest heights of adventure and exploration along the way. But you do not have to go halfway around the world to write an absorbing travel book. Around the corner can be sufficient, if you go with eyes wide open. It's all about exploring a new world and telling a good story.

Adventure stories can—and should—include political, environmental, and/or economic backgrounds. But the single most important link in the evolutionary chain of such writing is something often gone amiss these days: Narrative. Tell a good story. Show us a way of life, a way of thinking, we didn't know before. That's my goal in my pieces, collected here.

Most of these stories were written for some of the best editors at some of the best magazines published. The versions of the stories here are my takes, which means they may differ slightly—or greatly—from the stories that ended up in the magazines, which are often changed/altered/edited for space and other reasons unrelated to "the story."

I am privileged here to have the opportunity to let them run on a bit, like wild horses over the hills, and to share them, again.

JON BOWERMASTER
San Pedro de Atacama, Chile
December 2003

ALONE AGAINST
The SEA

A SHAGBAG'S JOURNEY

Our escape from Nairobi was plotted at a seedy bar called the Hurlingham. Planted on a busy four-lane highway on the outskirts of the sprawling capital city, the small hotel has the distinct air of better days gone by. Its bar—the air choked with cigarette smoke, the carpet lumpy from years of spills—is littered day and night with an international crowd of remittance chums and wanderers, many of them literally paid by their families to stay in Africa, to stave-off god knows what future embarrassment.

To a man, every one of the dozen or so regulars claims to be on the make for a way out of the city, anxious for any excuse to escape back into the bush, ostensibly the lure that dragged them first to Kenya however many years before. The reality is that most of these creepers are hardly comfortable staggering more than a half dozen steps away from their bar stools. They spend their afternoons and evenings drinking, arguing, insulting each other, then making up, their lives determined by whatever war is currently playing on CNN.

Ian Cameron differs from the rest of the hangers-on, in that he actually still make forays into the wilds. He uses the Hurlingham and its pay phone as his office when in Nairobi. At the moment his business is exotic camel safaris into the far reaches of Kenya's stark desert known as the Northern Frontier District, the NFD. Part bushman, part con man, in recent years he's worked his way back and forth across East Africa in a variety of jobs—from safari cook to UN population counter—always keeping one eye peeled for his idea of paradise: a big shade tree to camp under, fresh running water, abundant wildlife, friendly natives, and as few white folks as possible. A throwback to the Eurocolonials who first came to Africa at the turn of the century, Ian is a born raconteur, always looking for the next adventure, usually just a step ahead of an angry husband, irate African, or indebted shop keeper.

We loaded Ian's aging Range Rover near midnight. The impetus for our late-night departure is a rumor that Ian's twenty camels are soon to become dinner if he doesn't reappear soon and pay off back wages to the young Samburus who guard them. Since the camels are the only equity Ian has to show for five years of bumming around the wilds of Kenya, he doesn't dare lose them. Soon after the rumor hit his ears, Ian began scouring the Hurlingham for a couple suckers, er, investors to help him pay off his debts in return for a personally guided tour of the NFD, one of the planet's real remaining wild places. Me, I was desperately tired of CNN and the Hurlingham's dank cynicism so volunteered $500 to cover gas and food for a ten-day adventure.

Ian's old friend Willie Nocker put up the same amount, enough to cover Ian's bills at the local *dukas* (stores), his bar tab at the Hurlingham and back wages for the natives. We each had disparate reasons for throwing in together. Ian simply needed the cash and a reinvigorating dose of wilderness. Willie, just beginning a two-month sabbatical from his job with the UN in the Sudan, was coming along out of a kind of familial obligation. In an only-in-Kenya fashion, he and Ian are related: Each had fathered a child by the same spirited woman in Mombasa. They had long ago made a loose pledge to look out for each other.

My motives were more selfish. Sub-Saharan Africa grew more destabilized by the day. Just to our north Somalia was still wracked by civil war. The Sudan threatened to explode any day. Rwanda had imploded. Zaire was crumbling from a by-now familiar African disease: official corruption and greed, incompetence, neglect, and decay. By comparison, Ethiopia came off like a paradise, despite its tens of thousands of starving.

"Modern" Africa is a none-too-pretty sight. Too many people, too many *kombis* (cars), too much cement. Given the booming human population across the continent there will very soon no longer be room for four-legged animals. Africa's current population of five hundred twenty million will be more than a billion in less than twenty-five years; Kenya's population is now about thirty million and expected to more than double by 2020. Famine will inevitably increase, habitat will decrease, thus wildlife—and wild places—will disappear. Hardly a savior, AIDS is wracking the continent. Of the roughly fifteen million people infected with HIV, ten million live in Africa; and two million of the three million who have died of AIDS are Africans.

As for Kenya, once Africa's proudest democracy, I'd been here five months and the country was proving itself as nasty as any place the continent had yet created. I saw in Ian a guide to a last glimpse of the "old," un-modernized Africa. He promised a look at one of Africa's last hidden wildernesses, a quasi-secret place he knew high in the Mathews Mountains, in the middle of the NFD. Downing a last Tusker beer at the Hurlingham, he insisted the "real" Africa still exists, if you just knew where to look.

Though I know in advance he is part con, I haven't yet figured out which part. For now, I trust him. So, with money in pocket, we are off.

• • •

We leave Nairobi in the black of night, hurrying over the pocked tarmac, overtaking dozens of overloaded lorries struggling uphill. Several times we are stopped by police roadblocks, manned by dark men in long coats armed with Soviet Kalishnikovs. At each blockade the asphalt is spiked to make sure smugglers and overloaded lorries don't try and make a run for it. Prostitutes prowl each stop, hoping to snare truckers bedding down for the night.

We speak to the police first in English, then Swahili. It is baldly obvious they are looking for bribes and we worry they will "fine" us for bald tires or lack of a rear license plate light. Or the fact that we have affixed an outdated tax sticker from a Datsun to the Range Rover's windshield. At each stop Ian badgers the police just enough that they let us pass at no cost.

As the sun rises we pass vast wheat fields stretching for miles. (Farming is so good in these equatorial highlands they cull two crops a year.) Climbing the last hill before descending to the desert floor, we overtake a makeshift funeral car, a Land Rover with red ribbons tied off its back door. The mourners are crammed into the back of the jeep, squeezed on both sides and atop the pine casket, which juts out the rear. Neat white letters on the door of the vehicle identify the car's owner: "USAID—Population Control."

Easing off the flanks of Mt. Kenya into the desert the temperature climbs to more than one hundred degrees. Within forty minutes we drop from almost nine thousand feet to three thousand feet, from rolling wheat fields and verdant forests of mountain cedar to thirsty thornbush country, where red-robed nomads tend scrawny cattle and camels.

The pavement is soon replaced by a heavily corrugated, washboard road that runs through the mean desert all the way to Egypt. (Surprising to most, two-thirds of Kenya is desert; the booming population is crowded into the other third.) The NFD is raw country, the venue for wandering nomads, *shifta* (robbers), man-eating lions, and intrigue. Ian loves this part of Africa and blends in quickly when we pull into the border town of Isiolo, barking at the bangle hagglers, schmoozing with the border guards. (When you enter the NFD they make you sign out; in case you don't return they at least know who has been lost.) Isiolo is the gateway to the Greater Shag, as the NFD is known, filled with a randy mix of types and tribes. Somalis live on the north edge of town, Kikuyu and Meru on the southern border. In between are neighborhoods of Turkana, Borani, and Samburu. Like all of Kenya, one of the fastest-growing countries in the world, land is becoming increasingly precious. Wild animals in these parts are a thing of the past; now people are crowding out people.

We stop for breakfast and provisions. The breakfast room fronts a shabby courtyard hotel. A warm desert wind flutters lacy, tattered curtains and a radio murmurs in the background. "Bone Soup" and "Passion Juice" are the daily specials. A sign on the wall cautions: "What you see here, what you do here, what you hear here, what you learn here, please leave it here." A rooster crows and curious young Meru boys whisper "jambo" (hello) from just outside the door.

At the market stunning smooth-skinned women, heads wrapped in silky scarves, offer mangoes and passion fruit. We buy tomatoes, corn, bags of tobacco, maize, bhang, rosemary, and bundles of *mirra* (the natural amphetamine natives from Ethiopia to South Africa are addicted to).

As Ian shops I watch the car. This is the first light by which I am able to inspect the ten-year-old Range Rover we would be driving into the unforgiving desert. When Ian returns I ask, as innocently as I can, why his car has no mirrors, few working gauges or windows, no insurance, and why you must hammer the passenger door with the full weight of your body to open it. He locks me with a grimace and does not reply. "It's the Cameronian System," interjects Willie, standing beside his friend. "That's all. Don't ask."

• • •

The concept of safari (from the Arabic "safara," to travel) has changed greatly since the days when Philip Percival, Denys Finch Hatton, and Bror Blixen roamed these same plains. Though marked by persistent ordinariness, even the best safari can be hard to describe. A true safari, though, is not something you buy out of a catalog.

Throughout the early twentieth century the rich and famous made Kenya their African playground and the safari mystique was born. Idealized in literature and film, the glamorous figure of the white hunter— fearless, independent, cultivated, yet cynical, hard-drinking, irresistible to women—became an icon of modern African mythology. The romance of safari, with its quasi-military paraphernalia and hint of danger, remains rooted in the hunt. Thousands of Europeans were attracted by this growing mystique: undercapitalized farmers, indolent cadet sons of aristocratic families, bourgeois wanderers with a romantic streak, writers, con men, missionaries, amusement seekers weary or cast out from other climes or other countries, misfits, and neurasthenics. Most were of great breeding and charm, bounders like Josslyn Hay of *White Mischief* fame, described by associates as "a first class fellow, like a lot of those who never had anything to do. Clever, always had a brain, always an answer."

Ian and Willie are heirs to those pioneers. The differences between them though are many. The turn-of-the-century characters saw themselves as redeemers, as saviors. These latter-day white men understand that they are in Africa as guests, not conquerors. The turn-of-the-century settlers were often quaintly ignorant about Africa, its history, the tribal distinctions, and the wild animals. Ian knows the people, beasts, trees, flowers, and birds better than most Africans. Willie is a graduate of London's School of African studies and speaks many of Swhahili's dialects fluently.

Unfortunately for them, this modern-day pair is consumed by a quest to search out the last remaining vestiges of the wild life, a passion spawned in each at a young age. Willie's mother took him camping along the Uaso Nyiro River before he could walk; Ian grew up in the shadow of Mt. Kenya, where he learned to hunt and fish before he was ten. Though born in Kenya, they are heirs to a legacy that disappeared with independence in 1963 and the end of hunting in 1977. Fifty years ago Ian and Willie would have been among Kenya's leading gamesman—literate chasers of fun, beauty, and adventure. Today they understand they are just trespassers, in a place they will never truly be accepted. They admit they are just on one big, extended "camping trip."

"I'm just a tourist, man," says Ian, "like every other white man on the continent."

He promises to be an intriguing escort. When you look into the eyes of someone who has lived in isolation in the bush you are often met by a kind of raptness, an absent stare. The rangy, forty-two-year-old Scotsman has that look. The skin around his eyes is sallow and fallen like that of an aging elephant, encouraged by a young lifetime of hard living. Equal parts raconteur and naturalist, he could be gentle or gruff, often both simultaneously. One night I saw him slit a goat's throat from ear to ear while telling a joke and mixing a drink. An unexplained butterfly tattoo decorates his left elbow.

Born in Nanyuki in 1948 to a retired British military man, he spent his youth roaming Kenya's midsection. In his teens he was sent to England for schooling, followed by a four-year stint as a paratrooper. Though he visited Kenya during his twenties, he stayed primarily in England. For more than a decade he tried to toe the status quo of a young urban man on the make. He ran a small interior decorating business, lived in a nice flat in London, had a string of girlfriends, and took proper vacations. He returned to Kenya five years ago on holiday. At the time he had fallen into a love-hate relationship with a variety of pharmaceuticals, illicit and otherwise, and hoped that three weeks trout fishing at Mt. Kenya would stem his desires. He caught more than fish though; his childhood love for Africa retook him. He called his business partner, told her to sell the car and the typewriter and send him his half. Ever since he has spent his days involved in a kind of spiritual redemption, refamiliarizing himself with the wildernesses he had forsaken as a boy, aching for the days when game was plentiful and humans sparse. Sadly for Ian, he was fifty years too late.

When he decided to make Kenya his home, he vowed to drive every dirt track in search of a paradise he could call his own. When he crossed the Mathews range for the first time and stumbled upon the Kitich Valley—where we are now headed—he knew he'd found it. He made camp beneath a three-hundred-foot-tall fig tree overlooking the Ngeng River. His stash of bhang lasted a week, the booze ten days. After three weeks he was down to just beans. He stayed two months. Today it is his place away from civilization, a place few *mzungus* (whites) have seen.

Ian's frequent visits to the Mathews have gained him family status with the Samburu; recently he was granted the honor of serving as a "bubba" in a circumcision ceremony, which entailed holding one young boy from behind while the "doctor" whittled away. He is a throwback to an earlier day: He can name most birds on the fly, identify the quickest land animal, and trade jives in Swahili with locals. He proudly lives a life of "shiftless irresponsibility," a lifestyle choice he was reminded of on a recent visit with his elderly parents in England. His father asked him when he was going to settle down. "I have Dad, I have, don't you see," Ian tried to explain. He is, says his friend Willie, a creature of the night, the ultimate rogue.

Red-headed Willie, far better book-educated, is an equally skilled bushman. A trained botanist, anthropologist, naturalist, African historian, and poet, he lives in a small mud hut in the Sudan, where he grows his own vegetables and marijuana and is guarded at all times by four armed local soldiers. His job is supervising water-boring operations and the installation of hand pumps. "It is much different country there," he explains as we drive. "You expect a bullet in your back at any moment. They still kill people just for the sake of killing, burn whole villages, drive people into the desert where there is no water, take their cattle. That's just the nature of life."

"In the town where I live you still meet naked men walking down the street. They're just cruising and feel completely normal. They notice that others are wearing clothes, but I don't think they care.

"Of course all the educated Sudanese think it's utterly monstrous. Their word for these people means 'wild'—as if they were 'wild' animals. In truth they are just living in their own world of awareness. They have good manners, are incredibly fit, incredibly self-sufficient. The men are brave, the women have a lot of healthy children. It's a good life, but the world is changing fast around them."

Born outside Nairobi, educated in the United Kingdom, Willie is just thirty-two. He hasn't been back to England in ten years. His grandfather, who moved to Kenya from England in the forties, had this testimonial carved on his gravestone: "He was a great naturalist." Willie says he'd be happy if his read simply, "He planted trees." He's brought an Australian ficus to plant in the Mathews.

• • •

By late afternoon our first day in the NFD Ian grew increasingly irritable as the kilometers clicked by. Eyes locked on the horizon, hands at ten and two, he hunches over the steering wheel, an incessant Crown Bird cigarette dangling from his lips. We are racing along a narrow dirt path that leads across the desert; every fifteen minutes the Range Rover's temperature needle plunges deep into the red and we are forced to stop, throw open the bonnet, shoulder a five-gallon jerrican of water, and pour coolant into the leaking radiator. The bigger problem is that we are fast running out of water. Thankfully, after the tenth stop to top-off the radiator (and after covering the distributor with plastic and retightening every bolt and screw in sight, then dumping in a bottle of hot mustard as a "sealant") the Rover began keeping its cool.

Ian was made irritable by the overheating, but he was more nervous about the reception he would receive in the Mathews. Word had filtered back via human telegraph to him in Nairobi that his Samburu camel jockeys had threatened to shove a spear in him next time he showed his face . . . and part of him believes it true. Willie does little to help ease the tension by goading Ian with nonstop questions. "So, old chap, how many camels do you have? Where did you get them? How much did you pay for each?" Ian responds to this line of questioning with growls and har-rumphs. He was not in a good mood.

As we bumped across the acacia-studded desert toward the Mathews the horizon changes spectacularly. In the distance we see thundershowers and lightning followed by a wondrous rainbow, then intensely indigo skies and scudding cottonball autocumulus. The one constant breaking the flat-ness is the solitary cone-shaped mountain known locally as Stephanie Powers' Tit. Just beyond it, the Mathews rises like a wall and disappears into the distance. The range extends for forty miles and then merges with the N'doto hills, stretching as far as the South Horr Gap, to the very fringe of Lake Turkana. Otherwise the desert of the NFD has an apocalyptic quality, utterly stark and relieved only by the stumps of worn-out volca-noes. It is not only one of the hottest and driest places in the world (tem-peratures in the middle of the desert can literally reach boiling point), but when the wind picks up the sand it can be one of the most violent. The impression it leaves is that of an uninhabited corner of hell. For me, see-ing this landscape for the first time, it is as if we were traveling in a surreal bubble, the three of us sharing the same dream.

Several hours out of Isiolo we began to glimpse the first signs of the Samburu—herds of cows and goats and an occasional lone figure silhou-etted against the horizon. Their desert-colored *manyatta*s (grass huts) blended into the horizon and thin *commiphora* (brush). The tribe's young *moran*—or "warriors"—begin to appear in twos and threes along the road-side. Done up in red *kikois* (cloth skirts), hair died red with ochre, ears stretched, and beads wrapping their chests, necks, arms, and foreheads, each carries a knife, a club, and a seven-foot-long spear. Ian and a parcel of German missionaries are the only white men they know. We're not yet sure if they're glad to see us.

As the sun enters its final throes we pull into Ian's favorite stomping grounds. Samburu of all ages migrate to our vehicle and Ian's eyes search the gathering throng for those he owes money. "I have to remind them I'm a tough guy," he says nervously as he steps out of the car.

First to approach is a thin man in his thirties dressed in blue jeans and pullover. He was introduced as Shapiro. Ian leases a mud shack from him along the river, and owes him four months' back rent. Next, a young boy who watches Ian's pair of burros and two horses steps out of the crowd, palm extended. As Ian rolls shillings off a sizable roll he looks relieved. So far, no spears; Ian's equity seemed safe. The animals—and their tenders— are the linchpin of his only money-making scheme going, that is taking paying customers on two- and three-week-long foot safaris around the Mathews and into the nearby desert. From what I've been told by others, the trips are original and astounding and he is anxious not to lose the keys to his small but growing enterprise. Ian occasionally accompanies the trips, but most often sends travelers out in the capable and intriguing hands of his most trusted Samburu moran.

Back in the car we set out in search of Ian's other debtees, the now-cool Range Rover skillfully roaring up and down the green hills. We pull alongside dung-and-acacia shacks and Ian distributes the maize, tobacco and *kimbo* (cooking oil) he brought for the families. Snot-nosed kids and bone-thin *mzees* wrapped in brown blankets gather around us when we stop and women climb to the roofs of their huts and shout hello. As daylight fades we drive faster and faster, from grass home to grass home, searching for any last native who might bear a grudge. When we reach the peak of the mountains the view beyond is magnificent. Idyllic, soft green hills fade into a seemingly eternal desert. From atop the Mathews the frontier plains stretch toward Ethiopia, a boundless expanse of sand and lava dust, broken only by the wrecks of ancient volcanoes. The overpowering silence induces a serenity found in few places on the planet, not dissimilar from the quietude of the white plains of Antarctica's interior, where no man lives. We sit, surrounded by Samburu talking softly in Swahili, dazed by the long drive and the mountain's aura. An old man carrying a batch of freshly plucked honeycomb offers us a chunk. It is so sweet our mouths go numb, as if they'd been shot full of novocaine.

It is getting dark as we race back downhill, through windshield-tall grass, along a path only Ian could follow, especially at forty miles an hour. We cross dry riverbeds and thin streams, then roar up hills that are little more than slivers of riven dirt bordered on both sides by ten-foot ditches. It begins to rain as we finally plunge through the last thicket of grass to the foot of a three-hundred-foot-tall fig tree. We stop inches from a cliff overlooking the Ngeng River and set up camp in a drizzle. After grilled steaks and several rounds of scotch, sleep—on the ground, under thin blankets—comes quickly.

· · ·

We awake in a bower of euphoria, surrounded by a trio of dandy young Samburu splayed across the hood of the Range Rover. Bodies wrapped in yellow and red cloths, feathers dangle from their ochre-dyed hair. Strings of beads wrap around torsos, foreheads, arms, legs, and necks. Ivory spools stretch their lower ears; each wears a cheap plastic watch. They preen and stretch as they wait for us to rise. Aged fifteen to twenty-five, they are the tribe's "warriors" and cattle-watchmen. They come of age together, are circumcised together, then taken out into the fields and taught how to hunt and slaughter for food. They live in the bush, away from their families during this period of servitude. Like the Masai, the teenage moran crop their hair extremely close and plaster themselves with brick-red ochre and stand with one leg curled around the other, leaning on their spears. The next step is junior elder, when they can marry. Power in the tribe is held by the old men, who have as many wives as they can afford. A young wife costs twenty dollars; the primary payment is usually in cattle, though honey and beer are also valuable wife-buying commodities.

Ian's protégé, Lemolio, is the leader of the trio visiting us. A fine featured and gangly seventeen-year-old, it was he whom Ian held during his circumcision just four months before. He speaks pretty good English— learned from Ian—softly, effeminately. A string of blue-and-white beads runs from one pierced ear, beneath his chin, to his opposite ear. It has as its tip an old artillery shell scavenged from a nearby army practice range. "Very good when thrown," he says.

Ian greets his friends gruffly. "The word came back that my staff was going to put a spear in my back," he says to Lemolio in Swahili. "Was that true?" The moran get a big chuckle out of the boss's obvious discomfort. "Nobody is going to do such a thing," Lemolio smiles devilishly, spitting a white glob onto the ground and errantly swatting at flies on his legs and shoulders.

They have come to take us on a search for a pair of rhino, mother and son, who have recently been spotted nearby. When we set off the Ngeng Valley is shrouded in late morning clouds. As we climb ten miles uphill, paralleling the river, we dodge tree spiders, red ants, and cannabis stingers. By midday the clouds dissipate, yielding bright azure skies. Near the mountain's top we cross the river and swim in a deep cool pool.

The grounds north of Isiolo were once prime Masai grazing lands. When the British pushed them south of the Mombasa-Uganda rail line, the Samburu were left behind in the desert. Today roughly twenty thousand Samburu live in a fifty-square-kilometer area of the Mathews. They are pastoralists, raising mostly cattle and some camels. Like the Masai, they are exceptionally good-looking, arrogant, and lazy. Condemned to a life of incessant wandering they take their leisure seriously, existing for days on the principle of least effort.

They live in nomadic "subdivisions," scattered around the tops of the lush mountains. During the days that followed we would visit many hilltop manyattas, shopping for the best deal on a goat, buying empty paint cans filled with fresh honey. Each family compound, or hut, is surrounded by an acacia-branch fence; houses are made of mud, dung, and sticks, weirdly and colorfully highlighted by the occasional plastic tarp or bleach bottle. Tin cans tied into the fence scare off curious wildlife. They live in family units, and each compound comprises six to ten huts—for mom, dad, grandparents, children, goats, cattle, chickens. When too many flies or vermin take over, they torch their homes and move to the next hilltop. Their basic diet is milk mixed with camel blood, augmented occasionally by goat meat, honey and butter.

When Ian first came here there was one duka, a nursery school, and a primary school. In just three years another four more dukas and a health center have been added, built by a pair of competing churches and a German aid group. Ian is concerned by the rapid development, but knows it is inevitable. He insists that if the Samburu are going to survive they must make an effort to blend in with the burgeoning western society swallowing all of Africa. "They're going to change, that's not the issue. What disturbs me so much about the change is that they are so ill-prepared. They are like innocent children and it's a big bad civilization out there waiting."

It is midday and hot. We sit, naked, sunning on riverside rocks. Ian is holding forth. "They must get some of their own people to guide their destiny or they will come to grief. Young men must go away, get educated, and come back. Otherwise they will be fatally corrupted."

He has tried on his visits to help the Samburu manage the transition. For example, two years ago a pair of American school teachers visited the local school. It isn't much to look at—a tin roof with mud walls, plank benches, no blackboard, few pens or pencils, two textbooks. After returning home the Americans sent the headmaster $200 with the instructions to give it to "Mr. Cameron" to use for the school.

"The first list of 'supplies' the headmaster presented me with was for an end-of-term party," says Ian. "They wanted me to bring them six cases of soda, one carton of cigarettes and one case of beer. I went up to the school on the given day, empty-handed. I said, 'What is this . . . beer, cigarettes? That money was meant to help the school.' I said, 'Listen mate, we're talking pencils, paper, chalk, blackboards, or bits of wood, and fucking paint. If I bring you nails, I want to see you bang them into wood, I don't want them going home. I thought they got the message.

"A few days later I got called before the 'school committee'"—the assistant chief and eight mzees. They said, 'The committee has decided we should take charge of this money.' I said, 'Forget it, I'm not giving it to you. The deal was I would purchase what you needed.' 'Okay, we give in,' they said. I used the $200 for two blackboards and a lifetime supply of chalk."

• • •

The afternoon is spent trailing through the bush. Though we find no sign of rhino, mounds of fresh buffalo scat litter the narrow trail and an abundance of birdlife soars overhead—fish eagles, harrier hawks, crested francolins, emerald cuckoos, a variety of turacos, cinammon-chested bee-eaters, hornbills and barbets and weavers of all sorts. Above us is woven a dense thicket of ficus, podocarpus, junipers, cordia, croton, *Olea capensis,* hibiscus, acacia, and jasmine trees. Butterflies, thousands of little green-and-white insects, flutter over us like chains of flowers, rising in showers from the pools of chocolate-colored mud and resettling, quivering.

I spend most of the day talking with the young Samburu, who are curious about America. How many blacks are in the United States? Do they speak Swahili? Are there any Samburu? Incredibly, they ask about Bill Clinton and Saddam Hussein. Fifteen-year-old Jackson (the missionaries are prolific, even in this remoteness) is the most curious. Like many his age he is torn between leading the bush life of the *moran,* or devoting himself to school. It is a hard choice, in part because he is an accomplished bushman. One-inch ceremonial scars band his chest and stomach. The middle tooth of his lower jaw was pulled when he was circumcised; his lower ears are stretched by ivory spools. Point to a fish that's just slid beneath a rock and he stabs it in seconds with a sharp stick. Gesture to a butterfly and he snatches it between bare finger and thumb before you finish asking. He is currently in eighth grade and during the week trades in his loincloth for schoolbooks. But he hasn't decided to give up the life of the *moran* for good, at least not yet.

Lemolio, on the other hand, finished elementary school, and called it quits. "Now I am in the school of life," he pronounces, a motto most assuredly picked up from one of Ian's safari clients.

As our hike takes us back downhill we rarely stop and stand in one place, for when we do our ankles are instantly covered by army ants, the most formidable insects in Africa. It's claimed that if a horse is left tethered among these ants it will be eaten and left a skeleton where it stands. True desert nomads, army ants have no permanent nests, pausing only long enough every thirty or forty days to raise their young. They never settle down, an outstanding example of a society that has defied the law that says that no large association of individuals can exist exclusively as carnivores. For us, they are great impetus not to dawdle.

All day long my itinerant white pals traipse just behind, sounding from a distance less like road warriors than a pair of hip ornithologists."

Oh look, Willie, a kingfisher"

"Oh really? Really?"

"Yes quite, a pgymy."

"No, not really? Really? Superb! Is it small, with an orange head?"

"Yes, exactly, do you see it?"

"Quite. A pygmy kingfisher! Superb"

"Willie?"

"Yes, Ian?"

"Pass me the joint."

• • •

Two days later Ian is off negotiating for the continued safety of his animals; Willie and I set out to climb a granite face above our camp. Our intent is to find buffalo, so we head straight into the tall grass, perfect buffalo-feeding territory. Big droppings are all around. It begins to rain as we climb, making the granite extremely slick. Rather than risk a fall we take refuge in a cave—a leopard's cave. Willie enters first—after all, he's the one that studied at London's School of African Studies. I assumed they'd taught him the appropriate way to enter a leopard's lair. Inside it is warm, dry, and dark, littered with bones and porcupine quills. Perched on the lip of the cave, peering through a misty rain we spot a solitary elephant working his way up the opposite slope. Three antelope browsed in a clearing, but we see no buffalo. When the rain stops we scramble back downhill. When we near the flats the brambles are so thick we are forced to crawl on hands and knees. Acacia thorns rip at skin and cloth. Once on the valley's floor buffalo droppings are everywhere. Slightly concerned that one might actually be just around the next bush we agree to talk loudly in order to alert them to our presence. Willie suggests we review our favorite and least favorite movies about Africa. Willie gives thumbs down to *Mountains of the Moon* ("No historical veracity," he claims) and thumbs up to *Out of Africa,* which I discount as biased since he worked on the film, as Barkley Cole's stand-in.

• • •

At sunrise the next morning, the three of us in the Range Rover climb a grassy hill to have a look across the valley for signs of beasts. We are optimistic. Late the previous evening we had gone for a short drive and spotted oryx, gerenuk, Grant's gazelles, Grevy's zebras, and reticulated giraffes in meadows not far from where we'd camped. The grass is dewy and slick, the otherworldliness of the view amplified by the morning mist. Near the top of the hill we stop. Sitting atop the car we watch the haze lift, but there is no sign of big animals. Then, just as we are about to give up and head back for breakfast, we spot tusks gleaming in the early morning light as a sizable elephant munches its way through the acacias. Willie sights the big beast first, near the wedge where the valley and the river intersect. "Oh say, Ian, there's our jumbo." A cuckoo sings above our heads.

"My, Willie, you're absolutely right," Ian whispers, reaching with one hand for his binoculars, the other deftly lighting a Crown Bird. "That's the old bull I've seen before, in the same area." Happy for the sighting, we sit nearly rigid for thirty minutes. Ian's "Man Friday," Rendille, assures us the elephant we're watching is known as Macor. (Only about twenty elephants live in the valley and the natives know each by name.) This one is renowned as a mean-spirited bull with a reputation for harassing both cattle and cattle drivers. After an hour of watching the ellie eat, just as we begin to tire of the watch, to its left we hear a rumbling. At first it appears a half dozen black buffalo are headed downhill, on a path leading them directly for the elephant. Macor hears them too and looks up, big ears extended, keyed into their mooing and bellowing. But soon we can see it is not a half-dozen buffalo, more like one hundred, wending their way to the river for a drink. As they cross through the dense thicket they come and go from our view masked by the compacted forest.

The elephant, not wanting a confrontation, lumbers downhill, out of their way. Exactly how long such beasts will casually roam these hills is uncertain. This land is forest preserve; if it were a park, under the jurisdiction of the Kenya Wildlife Service, it would be patrolled by rangers and four-wheel drives and the wildlife that remains thus offered some protection from poachers. Without such protection, if these buffalo and elephants head east out of the boxed valley, they walk straight into the sites of waiting Somalis and Wambas armed with AK-47s. Just two months before poachers had taken a half dozen elephants and three rhinos from this region. Unfortunately, it is unlikely that the cash-strapped, occasionally corrupt KWS will ever try and protect the Mathews range. As a result, these hard-to-reach hills will never be filled with tourists, nor will they for much longer be home to such a variety of wildlife.

Enthused by the morning's sightings we move camp to a grassy meadow farther downriver, a place known for heavy elephant and buffalo traffic. After breakfast of eggs, toast, beans and red chilis, pineapple, and tea we lie back with smokes and books, under thin Ugandan blankets to stave off the tsetses and hornets, waiting for the day to heat up. Within the hour we hear an elephant trumpeting, just over a thick hedge of acacias separating the meadow from the river.

Ian is again gone most of the afternoon, settling up accounts and advising his helpmates on upcoming camel trips. He is gone long enough that we wonder if perhaps he hasn't gotten speared after all. Just before dark he returns, in one piece. The Range Rover was full of young Samburu, their spears ripping away at the vehicle's already-shredded interior. They quickly set about slaughtering the goat Ian bought off an old mzee for $8. "Inflation has reached the Mathews," he announces. "Two years ago that goat would have cost just five bucks."

Within the hour we are feasting. Heart-spleen-kidney-stomach soup, a liver appetizer, blood sausage made from the small intestine and packed with fat, onions, mushrooms, green peppers, chilis, and warm blood. For a sorbet we suck on fresh *popo* fruit; cocktails are rum and passion fruit sundowners, and an "energy" drink of blood and goat milk, shaken and frothy. The main course is roasted leg, held by the hoof over the fire, and grilled avocado. The goat's skin is hung over the bushes to dry, its head stares at us from atop the cooler. When we are finished eating, the Africans set the head in the fire for half an hour, split it in two and eat the brains. It begins to rain and, sated, we crawl into a hastily assembled tent and fall asleep to the sound of laughing hyenas.

It is a fitful sleep, though. The night sounds were just wild enough to keep us turning. Just beyond the hedge we can make out the rumblings of one very loud elephant, several buffalo, and the bark of bush buck. By morning the goat's remains, which we'd left scattered around the fire, have been devoured by hyenas.

• • •

After a peaceful ten days in the bush we pack to return to Nairobi. The first part of our drive away from the Mathews focuses on our good fortune; we'd seen elephants, buffalo, tracks of leopards and lions, drank from clean, clear streams, eaten well. Such idyllic days are numbered, even in the Mathews. It is inevitable, given Kenya's ever-expanding population, these lush hills will fill with man. The big animals will be gone within the next decade or two, to poachers and hungry families. We were fortunate to see the place as we did. Halfway to Isiolo we stop in Archer's Post, a desolate outpost smack in the middle of the NFD. Prostitutes and young men prowl the boardwalk outside the tiny restaurant where we munch hot rolls and tea. Outside the window we watch minivans loaded with tourists cruise down the dusty street, headed for the luxury lodges in nearby Samburu Park. Looks of disbelief mask the pale faces of the tourists as they gawk at the knotted bunches of Africans lining the sidewalk. We are surprised by the traffic. Even in Archer's Post, not so long ago the definition of nowhere, civilization is coming.

As we head back down the rough dirt road toward Isiolo, I try to pin Willie and Ian down on their definition of "safari" in the nineties. Willie, as is his wont, sounds optimistic, as if such opportunity would be afforded him as long as he sought it. "To me," says Willie, "it is going out and seeing, hearing, smelling, and feeling Africa. There is no other place like it, none. And if someone were to tell me tomorrow I'd never see Mt. Kenya again, life wouldn't be worth living." Ian, lost in thought, doesn't respond. Fifteen minutes goes by. "For me, the saddest thing is that, try as I might, I'll never really be an African. The only way is to die here, be buried here. That's the only way I'll really become part of Africa."

DESERT WANDERINGS

Abdul picked us out within sight of the Marrakech airport, chasing our rent-a-jeep with practiced precision, following and waving. When we zoomed past our hotel, slightly lost, momentarily confused . . . he smelled blood.

"You looking for nice hotel?" he asked, pulling his push-start scooter up to my open window. Hearing the English and French spoken inside the car, his rapid questions came at us in both languages (besides his mother-tongue Arabic, he also spoke pretty good Spanish and Italian).

"How about I show you to the town?"

We declined in every language we knew as we lugged our bags up the red-brick drive into the Hotel Tichka. The hotel was a beautiful oasis, marked by a bored elegance similar to many expatriate and monied-tourist hangouts around the Mediterranean. The parking lot was filled with dusty four-wheel drives, in from the southern desert. Heavy wooden furniture filled the cool, tiled lobby and small rooms off the mezzanine. It was easy to envision shady deals being conducted in the darkened bar. Around the blue-tiled pool stood tall palms, figs, and ficus. Pink flowers bloomed from dark green hedges. Guests reclined on the lawn, languorously smoking and whispering atop soft white towels provided by a hunky pool boy. All these topless women, most of them French, must be a titillating shock (pleasure?) to the Muslim towel boys; it's probably a much sought-after job.

When we emerged from the hotel three hours later, after a swim, lunch, and a petite siesta, Abdul was still there, astride his bike, waiting.

We—Brigitte and I, bent on a two-week driving tour of Morocco—held a brief consultation. Here we were, in the heart of Islam, the religion of surrender, whose followers believe that in order to be happy, you must cease striving and admit you are powerless. Why not go with the flow? I like to think we *chose* to follow Abdul. Plus, we had no idea where we were going.

After a fifteen-minute drive across the city, following close on his brakelight, Abdul guided us to a parking space in the midst of an empty lot adjacent to the Place Djemaa el Fna, an open plaza swarming with people and cars. Our eyes glued to the back of Abdul's closely cropped head, we followed into the heart of the labyrinthine marketplace, irresistible and impossible to navigate without a guide. We pushed through a gaggle of Berbers—skullcaps on their heads and *djellabas* (the robelike cloak worn in public by most men) barely cloaking long daggers—just arrived by camel from the Sahara to sell and trade and buy everything from rice to silk. We passed shops hawking ceramics, musical instruments, earthenware bowls, necklaces, kaftans, kohl boxes, brooches, pewter, brass, gold, cakes, and biscuits. Exotic, the smells were enveloping, ranging in no order from mint to dead cats, incense to donkey shit.

As we might have predicted, one of our first stops was a rug market ("government-sanctioned," Abdul assured, and most likely owned by one of his relatives) where we drank pots of sweet mint tea and viewed dozens of rugs and kilms. We heard and immediately forgot everything there is to know about warps, weaves and knots and finally succumbed, buying a pair of magnificent if not exactly cheap Berber rugs.

When we finally left the shop it was dark. One of Abdul's "cousins" had appeared with a broken-down Toyota, to ferry us back to our car. Our guides appeared worried, and not only about the Toyota, which barely ran.

"We must hurry," warned Abdul, almost under his breath. "It is possible they may have taken your car."

"What?" we asked incredulously. Our guide of three hours was telling us we may have "lost" our car. Why did I smell scam?

As we ping-ponged our way through the increasingly crowded streets, the driver plunging without hesitancy into the hordes now bustling through the narrow streets and filling the torch-lit plaza, the car stalled whenever we slowed, requiring us to jump out and push.

As we closed in on where our car should have been, the pavement now crawling with incense dealers and sidewalk-pharmacists trading in everything from headache powders to potions to cure infertility, it became apparent that Abdul's—and our—worst fears were true. The rent-a-jeep was gone. We'd driven it less than ten miles.

"*Merde,*" said we.

"Shit," muttered the Muslim.

• • •

Dépaysement is the French word for the feeling of being totally out of place when you travel to a country that is nothing like home. That's what we sought by coming to Morocco—and that's what we found. Instantly. Stepping off the plane into the midday heat, the blood-red Moroccan flags whipping in the wind, a sheet of sand blew across the runway. I felt like I'd stepped onto a movie set. Maybe that was because my initial interest in coming to see the Sahara had been sparked by the cinema, most recently, Bertolucci's film of the Paul Bowles book *Sheltering Sky* and, years before, Orson Welles's film version of *Othello*. Both were set against backdrops of tall white sand dunes and rose-colored kasbahs. But it was hardly an original voyage—the romance, light, and very exoticness of Morocco has attracted legions of writers and painters, ne'er-do-wells and idyll-seekers for hundreds of years, from Matisse to Bowles, J. Paul Getty to Yves Saint Laurent, Winston Churchill to Richard Nixon.

I was most interested in seeing the desert, the Berbers, maybe a Blue Man or two. But with more than twenty-two hundred miles of Atlantic and Mediterranean coastline, ridges of tall mountains, and the widest range of climates across North Africa, Morocco offers a medley of escapes. There are trails to suit all desires, whether your preference is city, sea, or desert, whether your preferred manner of travel be foot, mountain bike, horse, camel, or four-wheeler.

Many come here for some kind of enlightenment, cultural, spiritual, or otherwise. That's because Morocco is such a blend of old and new, weighted toward the old. It was less than one hundred years ago that sultans controlled only the coastal ports and the regions around the imperial cities of Fez, Marrakech, Rabat, and Meknès. The rest of Morocco—the Rif, the three Atlas mountain ranges, the vast Saharan desert—was populated almost exclusively by nomadic Berber tribesmen. Today, if you want a glimpse of what North Africa was like centuries ago, Morocco may be the last safe bet, since fundamentalist Islamics bent on economic havoc as a means to their end have made the rest of northern Africa—Algeria, Libya, the Sudan, even Egypt—hazardous for visitors. Here it is still easy to have a quixotic desert adventure.

Be forewarned, though. The biggest drawback to visiting Morocco may be the guides, who, especially in the cities, are a necessary evil. Given the complexities of the souks—the overcrowded markets that dominate the big cities—it's nigh impossible to avoid them. And they know it. You can't live without them, and you can't shoot them. It's hardly a new complaint. In an oft-told anecdote, British civil servant and writer Peter Mayne, who lived in Morocco during the 1940s and 1950s, once said angrily to a guide in Tangier, "I am a mad person who does not think it strange to be alone and to know nothing, and within a few minutes I shall be gone from here, and I am praying that where I am going I shall find a world where guides are born with the mark on them, so that they can be identified by their mamas and strangled."

• • •

Enlisting the aid of Abdul's "brother-in-law"—a stocky man with a mustache, dressed in kaftan, sunglasses, and Fila™ slip-ons, who stepped from the shadows as soon as we arrived where the rent-a-jeep had been—we set out on the trail of our lost vehicle.

At this point I have to admit to having more than certain trepidations, based on both experience and stereotype. Here we were, six hours into Morocco, stuffed into the backseat of an ill-running car with three big Arabs. The door handles were busted off both back doors, making them impossible to open from inside. Maybe this was the oldest scam in the books: Now they drive us to the fringe of town, rob us, and leave us, two more silly tourists taken for an easy ride. As we drove along dark, narrow streets we passed a police blockade. I considered yelling out the window, but had second thoughts both for reasons of appearing foolish and concern that the big guy squeezed next to me just might be carrying a dagger.

My faith that this was an honest mistake came from my knowledge that Morocco's king, Hassan II (or "Deux" as he's known locally), is renowned for meting out brutal punishment to citizens found guilty of messing with tourists. Tourism is the country's biggest economy and the king does everything in his power to eliminate troublemakers from his kingdom (especially religious fundamentalists bent on derailing his peace). More importantly, everything in Morocco operates through baksheesh—tips and kickbacks. It was very likely there would be some bribes to pay along the way to retrieving our jeep.

The trio took us first to a junkyard ten miles from the plaza. A uniformed policeman sat indifferently inside a small wooden shack, on a plywood bed covered with a Berber blanket. Once we proved it was our car we paid him an 80-dirham fine—about eight bucks—only to be told we now had to go clear the paperwork at the police station, back near the plaza. The brother-in-law, now fronting for us, led the way into the dimly lit police station. A surly guy in khaki just finishing his couscous wrote out the paperwork. Without the benefit of carbon paper it took half an hour to make a duplicate. For his efforts, he wanted 40 dirhams more.

By now we had to push the Toyota just to get it started. From the police station it was back to the junkyard, where a new indifferent officer wanted another 20 dirhams to release the car. So far the whole incident had cost me about $14. If it was a scam, it was not a very profitable one.

Throughout the duration of the search Abdul kept insisting "not my mistake"—a way to ensure he got paid for his earlier labors, I assumed. His only excuse was one I admittedly understood. "Yes, it is illegal," he admitted, even though there were dozens of cars parked around us when we arrived. "But for weeks they look the other way. Today, Allah knows why, they decide to tow." A sweep, in New York City parlance.

When we split, amicably, from him and his relatives, I gave him 300 dirhams ($30), a pair of sunglasses, and a T-shirt with a big gym shoe on it. He gave me his address (he wanted an English-French dictionary) and kisses on both cheeks. He didn't bother to ask for our address, since he admitted he'd probably never leave Morocco. Visas are too hard to obtain and he had no interest in seeing what he called "black" Africa. He suggested maybe we'd see him when we passed back through Marrakech. "Insha'allah," he waved good-bye. "God willing."

• • •

Late the next afternoon, after a morning spent idling by the cool blue pool of the Tichka, we drove back to the Place Djemaa el Fna. As soon as we stepped from the jeep I almost wished we'd brought Abdul, as instantly every imaginable kind of hustler approached, begging—not for coins, but employment. On the three-block walk from the gaudy La Mamounia hotel to the plaza, two guides literally start brawling over us. One of them grabbed Brigitte by the neck in an attempt to persuade us to hire him. I had to give the bolder of the two a shove in order to get him to bug off. "Aggressive little buggers," swore Brigitte, the understatement of the day.

In the square, several more fanatics approached and we shirked them off, ducking into the Agora Restaurant. Its terrace overlooked the plaza and we took a front row seat to watch the scene below. The pink-and-orange light of a late-day sun merged with the smoke from a hundred small fires, softening the panorama that sprawled twenty feet below. Hundreds of buyers, sellers, traders, con men, and thieves conduct business as usual across the cement marketplace.

Since its founding in the eleventh century Marrakech has been an important center of trade and business. Home to more than 1.5 million, Marrakech may be most interesting because of its Berber rather than Arab roots. The other imperial cities were built by Arab sultans; Marrakech developed as the metropolis of Atlas tribes—the Maghrebi from the plains, Saharan nomads and former slaves from Africa, traders from as far away as the Sudan, Senegal, and Timbuktu. All these strands still shape the city's souks and its very way of life.

Nowhere in North Africa is there another scene like the one that mesmerizes us. By day a marketplace, at night it's pure carnival. Circles of onlookers surround child boxers, sad-looking trained monkeys, clowns, veiled women selling woven straw baskets, lice pickers next to haircutters, dentists, witch doctors, letter writers. A cacophonous soundtrack is created by dozens of musicians playing everything from skin-covered, two-string guitars to ouds and violins, oboe-like *ghaitahs,* and trance-healers who pound out hour-long hypnotic rhythms with iron hammers, banging tall drums with curved sticks. The plaza's name literally means "assembly of the dead"—from the days when the heads of rebels and criminals were put on display here. As recently as 1912 slave auctions were held in the square. This night, half of Led Zeppelin—Jimmy Page and Robert Plant—are trailed through the crowd by a music video crew. Dominating the scene is the twelfth-century Koutobia mosque, its two-hundred-fifty-foot minaret towering over the city, like a sentinel, a gate to the Sahara. Five times a day a white flag is raised up its height, announcing prayer time, followed by the slowly rising note of a muezzin calling the prayer, joined by another until it becomes a great ascending chorus of clear tenor voices.

Lured by the minor distraction provided by the Zeppelin boys, we find our way into the center of the plaza. Rimmed by carts laden with or-anges, brought in this summer season from the coast, the center is domi-nated by long tables in neat rows covered with white paper. Vendors hawk everything from grilled sausage to goathead soup. As darkness settles, strings of electric light bulbs and gas torches provide a dim light for the sidewalk pharmacists who have spread their wares on blankets on the ground: Massage oil made from the *argan* tree; slivers of musk and amber; spanish fly; dozens of spices; a stone that stops bleeding; roots and leaves to cure rheumatism, toothache, bleeding gums, gas, diarrhea, and infertil-ity; secret combinations to make you thin or fat; ground bones to reduce enemies to impotence; earthenware saucers of cochineal for rouge; pow-dered kohl as mascara; henna; and sticks of bark used as toothpicks. Even dried pieces of lizard and stork, fragments of beaks, talons, gazelle horns, kef, and opium.

Successfully picking our way through the throng we climb stairs lead-ing to another terrace, atop the Café la France. Under a night sky haunt-ingly lit by torchlight, we watch none too bemused as a pair of tow trucks slowly, efficiently work the cars parked on the periphery of the square. They take them away, one after another, most likely to the same dusty lot we'd visited the night before. We ask a local standing next to us if the towing is unusual. "Nope," he says, "every night the same."

• • •

We drive away from Marrakech at dusk the following day, headed north toward Fez. For ten kilometers we fight our way along the roadside crowded with boys on mopeds and old men in turbans astride camels. Veiled women in olive, blue, rose and black kaftans are a subdued contrast against the sunbaked earth of the salmon-colored walls.

The drive from Marrakech to Fez takes ten hours and leads through a hodgepodge of towns with oddball names—Khenifra, Afrou, Infrane, Beni Mellal, and Kasba Tadle. The two-lane blacktop is remarkably good considering there were no modern roads in Morocco until the first decade of this century. You would never drive so fast—one hundred kilometers an hour—on any two-lane road in Kenya, day or night, for fear of hitting potholes the size of cows, or cows themselves. But King Hassan sees that the infrastructure is maintained in order to keep tourists happy, something the corrupt leaders in most other African countries lost sight of long ago, since they're too busy looting government accounts.

Men and women squat along the roadside; the men in long white gowns and turbans, the women in veils. The fields are surprisingly lush, blanketed with violets and buttercups, separated by rows of olive trees. In Beni Mellal we stop to see a hilltop kasbah (a minifortress, made of red, sun-baked mud) and drink from a fresh-running waterfall. In Khenifra we buy bags of olives, fresh bread, and Cokes in the central market. It is day's end and the butchers sit atop the marble counters, the floor around them littered with cow feet.

At the pretty hill town of Afrou we drive off-road through a cedar forest, to a vista offering incredible views over the desert valley floor. The ground is blanketed by blue-mauve flowers and golden grasses, and the skies a mixture of browns and blues, green and pinks, impossible to capture successfully on film. Ifrane is a modern ski resort, its hillsides filled with chalets and home to one of the king's many palaces. His biggest success to-date may be overseeing a strong economy while simultaneously keeping religious fundamentalists at bay. Debt is down and inflation subsiding, a new middle class has emerged, and a large privatization program has brought in foreign investment. But the main selling point is stability. King Hassan has been in power since 1961 and, with a gesture or two toward democracy, enjoys the political legitimacy of a dynasty that goes back three centuries. So far he's been able to avert serious Islamic opposition. But his most ardent opponents are fundamentalists who have already seized Iran and are threatening to grab control in Egypt and Algeria.

Algeria, another former French colony, is Hassan's worst nightmare. His next-door neighbor is locked in a virtual civil war (sixty thousand killed in four years) as fundamentalists try to wrest power, leading to brutal intimidation. In the past decade hundreds of leading figures, including intellectuals, politicians, and journalists have been killed. By comparison, despite a record of human rights abuses, Morocco stands as a bastion of stability for European governments anxious about a huge exodus to Europe from North Africa.

But for how long? Morocco's young are increasingly turning to political Islam for simple reasons: 70 percent of the population is under thirty, and unofficial unemployment figures stand between 30 and 40 percent. The sprawling slums of Casablanca and other cities are fertile recruiting ground. Whole departments in universities have been taken over by Islamists. Female students are told not to appear on some campuses unveiled and "un-Islamic" lecturers are boycotted.

So far, the Islamist message is muted, largely thanks to Hassan, who has fought off fundamentalists by being swift and occasionally cruel. While we were in Morocco a trio of Algerian fundamentalists held up a tourist hotel in Marrakech, killing two. Caught immediately, they were sentenced and locked up, probably forever. To help discourage others, within twenty-four hours after the holdup Hassan cut off all access to Algeria, affecting not only the bad guys, but commerce between the two countries, too.

You don't want to give the guy trouble. Maybe one thousand political opponents of the king have disappeared over the years. According to Gilles Perrault, a French journalist who has written books about the subject, trials in Morocco may follow modern protocol, but the sentence is often determined in the royal palace, and if the verdict does not satisfy the king,

the accused can simply vanish. The "royal whim," it's called. There are stories of men kept for sixteen years without seeing daylight. Hassan's response to Amnesty International's criticism of his record on human rights?
"Every head of state has his secret garden." In 1972 General Mohammed
Oukfir, one of Hassan's closest advisers, unsuccessfully attempted to blow
the royal Boeing out of the sky, with the king on it. The general was found
dead that night, shot in the back of the head. "Suicide," announced the
king, who then proceeded to lock up the general's family for the next
twenty-five years, at one point keeping them blindfolded in a small room
for a year. His rationale? "I know what would have happened to my own
children if General Oukfir had succeeded in taking my place."

• • •

We arrive at the border of Fès in the dark and are immediately picked up
by a scurrilous guy on a motorbike, another guide offering his service.
Though we have no clue how to find our hotel, the infamous Palais Jamaï,
I refuse his offers. He is relentless, following us for miles as we take wrong
turns, idling behind us as we ask traffic cops for directions. He pulls next
to my window at a traffic light, blue eyes shining against brown skin, and
I lose my temper. "Look asshole, don't you understand 'No'?"

"Yes, I understand."

"Well, for the last time, no."

"Okay, I understand," he says, then continues. "But you will need
help in the market tomorrow, no?"

"Yes," I admit, "but we'll have somebody besides you." He shrugs his
shoulders as we drive off, guns his motorbike, and follows us all the way
to the hotel . . . just in case we change our minds.

• • •

Fès is the oldest medieval city of the Arab world, suspended in time somewhere between the Middle Ages and the twentieth century. More than half
of the city's population of five-hundred thousand live in the wild old town;
electricity and tourists are their only connection to modernity.

Our balcony at the Palais Jamaï—a monster of a pink hotel, built in
the early 1900s by a pair of disreputable brothers catering largely to a
foreign crowd—overlooks the oyster-colored old town. In the center is

another of the king's palaces, broad and impenetrable. More than two hundred quarters or neighborhoods make up the city, each with its own medina, bakery, fountain, and religious school.

The soug itself is a nearly undefinable labyrinth of cubes and prisms, crowded together, one atop another. Corridors open onto squares, markets and fountains, all densely packed within a maze of passages, arcatures, overhanging upper stories, and blind alleys. Doors open inward onto central courtyards or gardens; from the street, social standing is concealed. Even the guide we eventually hire admits to getting lost, and he was born here. "Depressing, isn't it?" he pauses.

We plucked this guy from a cabal of human sharks that swarmed around the parking area in front of the hotel. A kind of ring-leader/pimp— the one with the biggest belly, the whitest djellaba—tries to maintain the peace among his whores, but they can't help but quarrel among themselves, seemingly all day long. I mingle among them for half an hour and in that time a dozen arguments verging on fisticuffs break out, involving, stomach-butting, finger-pointing, and red-faced screaming. Usually over something as mundane as who approached a customer first.

What you buy when you "hire" one of these un-medallioned guys is a personal shopping guide. Except you quickly learn that you have little control over where you shop. The worst thing about them is how they manipulate you from rug shop to antique store to pottery barn—all inevitably owned by friends, who will later kick back some dirhams for bringing you in. While Islam preaches despisal of material wealth, I've never seen a country where so many people have their hands out, expecting to be tipped for the smallest gestures—from opening a door, watching your parked car, showing you to the rug store, giving you directions, and on and on.

We hook up with Mohammed (the first son in every Islamic family is named Mohammed unless the father already bears that name; same with Fatima, for girls) and I found him usually siding with shopkeepers as we haggled. "Make me your most shocking prices," intoned one of his buddies, another Mohammed, as we bartered for a silver lamp. "Come on," chimed in our Mohammed, "it's worth it."

He was a nice enough guy and seemed a bit stymied by his job, which required dressing up in a striped djellaba every morning, leaving his blue jeans and white loafers at home. He kept his valuables in the hood of his cloak—Ray-Bans™, lip gloss, wallet, keys. In one pocket were small coins for beggars, in the other a thick roll of dirhams. Beneath the fold of his gown, a long dagger. "It's an okay job," he offered over mint tea. "But I'd rather be a salesman. " What the hell did he think he did all day? "Promise them anything, but lead them to a rug store," should be the official guide motto.

After two full days of wandering the souk he kindly invited us to his mother's home for dinner. A sheep was slaughtered in the living room and with the help of the other men, skinned and gutted. His mother and sisters sorted out the entrails, cut up the liver, and cooked on a charcoal grill set on the kitchen floor, filling the house with smoke. "Is it much different in New York?" they wondered.

• • •

A winding road takes us from Fès to Moulay Idriss, a pretty drive through meadows interspersed with olive trees and prickly pear cactus heavy with yellow fruit. Along the road boys sell pomegranates, soup, live chickens, colorful hats, and beautiful Berber blankets.

The small town dates from the late eighth century, and is considered second in holiness in the Islamic world only to Mecca. It is named for the great-grandson of the prophet Mohammed and the founder of the first Arab dynasty in Morocco. His tomb, open to Muslims only, lies at the heart of the town, which climbs a steep hill denuded of its once-prolific eucalyptus forests. The forests were cut down to accommodate the pilgrimages of late August and September when tens of thousands who can't afford to travel to Mecca come and camp here instead, to pay homage. For two months the slopes are covered in tents and the town is completely overtaken by dancers, acrobats, and storytellers as well as an endless procession of the faithful.

We stop in the center of town and ask a local constable to point out a "guide officiel." Bastille, a spry, bone-thin sixty-eight-year-old in a white skullcap and gray djellaba claps his hands "hello." He leads us to a family-run bakery (townspeople make their own bread and bring it to him to bake), shows us centuries-old wooden doors marked by the painted hand-print of "Fatimah" (for good luck), and into the markets, where baskets overflow with apricots, artichokes, beans, peaches, lambs' heads, and cows' feet, boiled eggs, and bulls' testicles.

We then climb to a vantage overlooking the mosque. We can see into the mausoleum decorated with a mass of colorful stained glass windows. The black and white marble pillars of the courtyard are plain, ribbed, or carved with floral motifs. The tomb rests on a catafalque, draped in gold, silver, and silk, a gift from Hassan II in 1978.

Chain-smoking Winstons, Bastille attempts to give us pagans an education (it greatly helps in Morocco if you speak some French, since most of the population does). The town was named after a holy man who fled to Morocco from Damascus during a massive Muslim civil war, around 787. Welcomed at the nearby Roman outpost of Volubulis as an imam—both spiritual and political leader—within three years he'd created a sizable kingdom and managed to set up the infrastructure of an Arab court. In short order he built the city of Meknes and began work on Fez (which would be finished by his son). But when word of his success leaked back to the East, his old Sunni enemies had him poisoned, thinking his influence would disappear. Wrong. He was so popular that his example instilled in the local populace a new belief in Islam, even winning over many of the previously pagan Berbers. Perhaps his most lasting contribution was that today Morocco's leader is viewed as Imam, "commander of the faithful," in every aspect of their lives.

Bastille is the most moderate Moroccan we've met, so we ask about women's place in Islamic culture. On several occasions we've witnessed distinct separateness and in some cases outright disdain for women. Brigitte's been nearly chased out of several cafés when she's gone to ask directions; most women on the streets are wrapped in veils and long kaftans. This guy is savvy enough to bend to our western leaning and say that yes, women have a place in society and he likes to see them out and about. But he also reminds that the Koran claims men are superior and wiser than women; that's why you see no women in the cafés where Moroccan men seem to spend much of their day. (Perhaps the still-prevailing attitude is best summed up in Paul Bowles's *Spider House:* "In Fez, it was often said, half jokingly, that if the Moroccans has been really civilized men, they would have devised cages in which to keep their women.")

And how does he feel about peace among religions? A born statesman, Bastille replies about the relationship between Muslims, Jews and Christians, "Everything is always zig-zagging."

• • •

After cruising through Volubulis, Casablanca, and Rabat, our round-trip tour of the imperial cities is accomplished and, for the time being, we are free—guide-free that is. After a brief pit stop in Marrakech we head south, into the desert, exchanging the Arab culture for the more nomadic life. By the second night in the south I'm regretting that we came to Morocco in August, the heat of summer: It is 2 a.m. and I'm sleeping on the roof of a small hotel in Ourzazate. It is still more than one hundred degrees, way too hot inside to sleep. But getting to this place was definitely worth it.

Leaving Marrakech we passed beneath a beautiful eucalyptus overhang that lasted several miles, shading the narrow asphalt as well as the walled houses that line the roadside. Climbing the winding roads of the mountains, over the highest pass in Morocco's Atlas, the air cleared and the color of the native dirt turned from tan to brown to ochre to deep red. The High Atlas is North Africa's greatest mountain range, the historical and physical barrier between the northern plains and the limits of the Sahara. Limestone plateaus are covered with lava and spare forests of cork, oak, and cedar. The area of ample rainfall, bountiful agriculture, and placid village life to the north was called Bled Al-Makhzan, the land of imperial governance. To the south, a rocky, sandy, and sun-baked expanse stretched into the Sahara. This was Bled Al-Siba, the land of disorder. We can just make out the domed peak of M'goun (13,350 feet). In the near distance are deep valleys, almost bottomless canyons, craggy peaks, and mountaintops eroded by wind and rain.

It is so windy atop the passes that it blows hats off heads and empties cars with doors casually left ajar. Boys run into the road bearing cracked quartz shining bright emerald, coral, and lapis in the sun, yelling "cinq dirhams, cinq dirhams"—about fifty cents. We stop, lured by the unearthly iridescence of the rocks, only to find they'd been spray painted the glowing, unreal colors. At another roadside attraction we are offered Berber necklaces and smooth globes and eggs of marble. We end up trading sunglasses and French headache powders for a ball of marble as big as a grapefruit.

On the way down the backside we begin to see remnants of hundred-year-old kasbahs, the minifortresses built by the Berber powers. For clarity's sake, a kasbah is a fortified castle, while a *ksar* or *ksour* is a fortified town. Both are made of mud mixed with fibers from palm trunks, called *pise*. Modeled after the Romans, the massive towers of the kasbahs were intended to shelter and protect people and animals. A narrow door opens onto the first floor, where livestock is kept. A staircase or ladder leads to second-floor granary and third-floor living quarters. Almost all have high small windows and incised geometric carvings on crenellated towers. Designed to look inward, to courtyards and communal space, they are grand, and defensive, domestic, and warlike at the same time. Heavy rainstorms—unusual but occasional in the northern Sahara—have a tendency to reduce them to muck.

Three hours south of Marrakech we pull off-road, engage four-wheel-drive, and head for the kasbah known as Telouet, one of the most extraordinary sights of the Atlas. It also offers a glimpse into the melodrama of Moroccan politics. Unfortunately it is fast crumbling into the dark red earth due to wind, occasional rain, and neglect. Its interior garden and star-shaped pool are overgrown with weeds and almond trees, much of its ceiling is caved, allowing pigeon and stork droppings to streak the interior walls. Yet Telouet offers a glimpse into the not-so-distant wild life led by the powers-that-were in this harsh land.

This pass and the mountains to the east were the stomping ground of the amazing Glaoui brothers, the greatest and most ambitious of all the Berber tribal leaders. Their kasbah headquarters, a vast complex of buildings, is just forty-four kilometers off the main road between Marrakech and Ouarzazate. The luxuriously appointed kasbah was abandoned when the property of "the last of the Atlas chieftains" was confiscated at independence, in 1956. Since its resident was a good friend of the French the new government threw him out and let his kasbah rot, out of spite.

The story of the Glouai brothers—Madani (1866–1918) and T'Hami (1879–1956)—rise to power (best documented in *Lords of the Atlas,* by Galvin Maxwell) is wild. In the mid-nineteenth century their family were simply local clan leaders, controlling an important Atlas pass—a long-established trade route from Marrakech to the Draa and Dadès valleys—but lacking influence outside of it. One fateful night in 1893 changed all that when, during a terrible winter storm, Morocco's sultan, Moulay Hassan, on returning from an ill-fated burning raid of the Tafilalt region, found himself at the mercy of the brothers for food, shelter and safe passage. With shrewd political judgment, they rode out to meet the sultan, feting him with every detail of protocol and, miraculously, producing enough food to feed his entire three-thousand-strong force.

Their efforts were well rewarded. By the time Moulay Hassan began his return to Marrakech he had granted them rights to all the lands between the High Atlas and the Sahara, and left behind at Telouet vast amounts of the royal armory, including the first cannon seen in the Atlas.

By 1901, the brothers had eliminated all their opposition in the region and when the French arrived in Morocco in 1912 the Glaouis were able to dictate the form of government for virtually the entire south of the country. They pledged loyalty to the French, helped thwart attempted national rebellions, and got themselves appointed "pashas" of Marrakech, with their family becoming bosses in all the main Atlas and desert cities. The French went along, arming them to rule, as Gavin Maxwell writes, "as despots and perpetuating the corruption and oppression that the Europeans had nominally come to purge."

In Marrakech, T'hami was the last of the great southern tribal leaders, an active and shrewd supporter of colonial rise and a personal friend of Winston Churchill. Cruel and magnificent in equal measures, he was also one of the most spectacular party-givers around. At wild banquets held at his Marrrakech palace "nothing was impossible," according to Maxwell. Hash and opium were freely available for the Europeans and Americans to experiment with, and "to his guests T'hami gave, literally, whatever they wanted, whether it be a diamond ring, a present of money in gold, or a Berber boy or girl from the High Atlas."

Telouet is actually two big castles. The first, built by Madani and his father in the mid-nineteenth century, is today in ruins, reduced to little more than a foundation. The second, T'Hami's creation, is accessed by massive double doors and a rubble-strewn courtyard. We bump up a narrow hard-sand road and park literally at T'Hami's front door.

A uniformed cop and a caretaker greet us. For 30 dirhams—$3—they offer a tour. For an extra 20 dirhams, the bored caretaker whispers, he'll show us "behind the closed doors." Inside are even more mazes and locked doors and connecting passageways. The main halls and reception rooms are still in good shape, with delicate iron grills on the windows and fine carved ceilings. The reception room gives a sense of the style, quality, and luxury of the place. The bedroom is long and tiled in blue and white. Standing in the middle of it I can't help but imagine what it must have been like for the big fat pasha to have his way with all those Fatimas on these very tiles, a century before.

As we prowl around "behind closed doors," the so-called "guardian of the kasbah" nonchalantly pries loose tiles off floors and walls, wondering if we would be interested in buying a small piece of history.

• • •

From Telouet we take a narrow sand track, headed forty-five kilometers south through mountain valleys to Ait Benhaddou. A good, two-day walk without car, this mule track clinging to the valley side takes us up and down through some of the most beautiful and isolated countryside in the High Atlas. Once the main road over the mountains, it requires fording at several points. Posed at the lip of a one-thousand-foot drop, tires barely grabbing the soft rock-and-sand, we debate the necessity of wearing seatbelts near such precipices: The question is, would you rather be crushed inside the car or risk being killed by being thrown free? I wear mine out of abject fear of having my globe smack the windshield.

While the predominant color is sand, I never expected to find such greenery in the middle of the desert. The valley is littered with small communes, all making abundant use of the narrow but life-enhancing river. Terra-cotta mud-pie homes are built into steep cliffsides, overlooking sophisticated green, terraced gardens sustained by irrigation from the trickle.

Palm trees line the river, along with cabbages, corn, pomegranates, and figs, as well as pink and red roses.

At Anemiter, one of the largest and best-preserved fortified Berber villages in Morocco, we see bone-thin women in dresses of bright yellows, blues, and reds, carrying heavy loads on their backs, or nudging burros loaded with greens. Tintin and Mickey Mouse are painted on exterior walls of the schoolhouse. Kids run after our car when we slow, clambering at windows, climbing onto the spare tire, running dangerously just in front of the rolling wheels, begging for "un dirham, un stylo, un bonbon."

During a long day of driving we see just three other cars—a Mercedes station wagon and two Land Rovers filled with tourists. Late in the day we meet a trio of motocross bikes carting Italian riders. For real adventure, they report, they suggest the wilder off-roads east of Tizi n'Tichka. They are coming north from Zagora, where we are headed, and report it had been one hundred forty degrees during the day and dropped to only one hundred ten at night.

"We slept on a roof, naked," says one of the drivers, his face and hair caked with sand and mud. "It was just too, too hot to sleep inside, or to wear any clothing at all. It was okay—we saw the most incredible skies of stars any of us had ever seen. But I'm looking forward to bed." They brought their bikes by ferry from Italy, and have been on the road for a month. From their leathers wafts a barnyarad aroma. "What I want," says his girlfriend, eying the rivulet of a stream in the valley below, "is a bath."

The last town before we rejoin the asphalt is Ait Benhaddou, a fortified village classified by UNESCO as one of the world's cultural treasures, older than Fez. It is dominated by a tall, fortified granary, still in use, and thick walls and angled towers of pise, from which the villagers survey their crops and the surrounding area. Densely packed, multistory dwellings create an utterly urban atmosphere, yet their inhabitants still live a nomadic existence. Dependent on the temperatures, they migrate from room to room, from rooftops where they sleep at night to ground-level chambers where they escape the midday heat. Doors of the houses are decorated with Berber paintings in blue, red, and yellow. Over the past few centuries the town has survived flooding, siege, and drought. Restoration is under way on some buildings, but moving very slowly. The town is inhabited by just five families. When we drive through, we see no one.

• • •

Ouarzazate—the gateway to the Sahara—was created as a garrison and administrative center by the French and today it is a comfortable, if slightly boring, rest stop. During the 1980s it was a bit of a boomtown, advertised as a staging point for saharan adventure. David Lean shot *Lawrence of Arabia* at Ait Benhaddou; Bertolucci used Ourazazate as a base when making *The Sheltering Sky*. Orson Welles shot *Sodom and Gomorrah* nearby; for *Jesus of Nazareth* the whole lower part of the village was rebuilt. Importantly, it is the junction of the Dadès and Draa river valleys, which lead into the Sahara. It is in Ourzazate that I sleep almost comfortably atop the roof of the hotel Riad Salam.

The southern oases were long a mainstay of the precolonial economy. Long belts of date palm oases, scattered with fabulous mud architectures of kasbahs and fortified villages, these are the old caravan routes that reached across the Sahara to Timbuktu, Niger, and Sudan, carrying gold, slaves, and salt to Marrakech and Fez. But by the nineteenth century the advance of the Sahara and the uncertain upkeep of the water channels had reduced life here to bare subsistence even in the most fertile strips. When the Algerian border was closed shortly after independence in 1956, these towns were finished. The people who remain support themselves by date harvests and tourism, surviving much of the year on what they can make selling henna, barley, citrus fruit, and roses. But lack of rain—and men, who have fled for jobs in the north—means life, like the desert itself, is hard.

The road to Zagora qualifies as one of the world's most beautiful drives. Heading south, the countryside is dun, the sky white, metallic, huge. Big chergui winds burn southeasterly across the wide, smooth road. The asphalt climbs, twists, and turns up into the mountains before breaking through the scarp at the pass of Tizi 'Tinififft, offering fine views back to the north, the Atlas mountains framing the horizon. At several points we pull off the road, brake the car, and walk into the desert, to get a sense of the heat, the stillness, the isolation. We descend into the Draa valley at Agdz, where the road is dirt and blood red, the shops painted white or blue.

Zagora is the last town on the road, situated at the most productive stretch of the Draa. In ancient times the Draa was a permanent river, the longest in Morocco. Today it rises near Ourzazate and travels just one hundred fifty-six miles before disappearing into the sand.

We find a room in Zagora and take a big walk into the desert at sunset, through the palms and oasis cultivation. Scorpions and skinks scurry out of our way; desert sparrows sing. We'd been warned to be on the lookout for the horned viper, which likes to hide just below the surface of the sand and kill its prey with a fast-acting poisonous venom. A road sign at the end of the sand path reads "Timbuktu—fifty-two *jours*." That would be by camel?

We climb partway up a rocky hill to watch the sun set, to look out across the palms, across vast sand dunes. This landscape, finally, is what had drawn me to Morocco, an imagery stuck in my head for twenty years.

In the near distance we spy a Berber tent set up on the edge of the harsh desert and walk toward it. Made of sheep-wool rugs, a family of four is inside, and though we speak no common tongue, they invite us in using hand signals. Though the nomadic life has largely disappeared, these folks continue to trek back and forth between desert and city, trading the old-fashioned way.

We pass beneath an awning made of narrow strips of woven wool and hair sewn together, slung over a ridgepole supported by two uprights. It looks like a circus tent, but can be put up or taken down quickly, as the weather or danger necessitates. A trio of big, dusty camels are staked in the sand nearby.

Inside, the main area is reserved for men and guests, closed off by fiber mats decorated with colored wool. Mats and cushions almost cover the sand floor. There is a storage area for corn, barley, and wood, and a women's area with a bed, bench, and loom. Their hospitality is generous, offerings of mint tea and sweet almond cookies, and it's unfortunate we can't have much of a conversation. When we tire of trying to communicate with our hands, we just sit quietly inside the open flap of the tent, and watch the sun drop. We gaze at the wide, red horizon, sneaking peeks at our hosts. They do the same. Shy smiles are shared. The air is heavy, laden with the smell of mint and the late-day heat acts like a sedative. There is no sound, but for the wisp of a gentle wind sweeping across the dunes. It might be the most memorable sunset of my life. But the best thing about this transcendent scene? No guides. We got to this best place of all in the most rewarding fashion. By ourselves.

WILD MAN IN AFRICA

Peter Beard has been both applauded and chastised during the thirty plus years he's lived in Kenya. But perhaps his greatest accomplishment, which no one can contest, was following the dream that took him to Africa as a teenager. While every one of us imagines setting sail, escaping to the wilds, of leading a life filled with adventure, few manage. Beard made his dreams real. As a result he has lived a life matched only in fiction.

The product of a wealthy, patrician New York family, Beard first visited Africa in 1955 when he was seventeen. He was looking simply for adventure, desperate to immerse himself in a place so different from the streets of Manhattan and the summer houses of Long Island. He was drawn initially, after reading Isak Dinesen's *Out of Africa,* to the life of a great white hunter. He sought out and met the last remaining characters Dinesen made famous—Bror Blixen, Philip Percival, "Cape to Cairo" Grogan, even Dinesen herself. He hunted on some of the last great safaris to leave from Nairobi's Norfolk Hotel, in the footsteps of Teddy Roosevelt. He lived for months in the bush with just a native tracker as a companion. He hunted big game, for food and pleasure, and in the name of science. He followed on foot herds of beasts for days on end, camera in hand, learning about the animals, and himself. Granted unique permissions by park administrators and wardens, he roamed the savannas and forests of Kenya like few had before. When hunting was outlawed, Beard picked up his camera and captured some of the last images of Africa as it had been at the turn of the nineteenth century. A self-acknowledged remittance chum,

Beard has never loved life as much as he did through the 1960s and into the early 1970s.

Since 1962 he has made Hog Ranch—a forty-five-acre camp on the outskirts of Nairobi—his home. Around its campfire, in its studio, or atop one of the half dozen treehouses scattered around the property he has hatched his photography and acclaimed books. *The End of the Game,* its first draft written while he was still a student at Yale, stands as a classic documentation—in words and pictures—of the fast-evolving relationship between rapacious man and the diminishing wilds. *Eyelids of Morning: The Mingled Destinies of Crocodiles and Men* and *Longing for Darkness: Kamante's Tales from Out of Africa* are books only Beard could have assembled, both eclectic and prescient, part history, part scrapbook, crammed with existential anxiety and doomsday forecasts. No matter the medium—words, pictures, or films—his take on Africa serves as both an intriguing introduction for the layman, as well as a record of just how fast his adopted home has changed since he arrived.

Everyone who has crossed his path has a different take on Beard. One friend calls him "an American born into wealth and privilege, a charter member of the jet set, he could easily pass as a romantic figure right out of Solomon's mines. He has the looks, the bearing, and the natural assurance and flamboyance of the Hollywood's Great White Hunter. " Next-door neighbor and photographer/biologist Ian Douglas-Hamilton insists he's a "scavenger"; Kenyan Dr. Harvey Croze dismisses him as a lousy ecologist. *Newsweek* once dubbed him, "Tarzan with a brain." Over the decades he has been diversely labeled a naturalist, fashion photographer, prophet of doom, stoic, diarist, garbage collector, felon, bum, racist, anthropologist, social chameleon, raconteur, celebrity, schizophrenic, court jester, despiser of mankind, and eighties existentialist. All and more are true.

Nothing irks Beard more than when he's dubbed "a jet-set socialite." Yet he's done little to evade the tag. Since he was old enough to drive he has courted, been linked with, even married to some of the world's most famous models, actresses, daughters (and wives) of billionaires, *Playboy* centerfolds, and royalty. Most people recognize his name for marrying America's sweetheart Cheryl Tiegs, and many of his friends are household names. One day at his stateside house in Montauk, during the course of a couple of hours he fielded phone calls from Lee Radziwill's biographer (Jackie O's sister was a longtime sweetheart), Terry Southern (with whom he wrote a screenplay), and Lauren Hutton (one of Hog Ranch's most frequent visitors).

The years of wild life have taken a physical toll. Today, at fifty-five, he bears the weathered look of an aging movie actor or beach bum. While he appears younger than he is, he's starting to wear down from years of bush life and hard living. His stomach is bad and most mornings begin with a slug of Maalox. He prefers "soft" food because his teeth are literally worn away from incessant nighttime grinding (he claims he can't afford to see a dentist). He often cups a hand behind his right ear to hear and can no longer read without glasses. An unaccountable, incurable skin disease he calls "African crud" rashes his ankles. Most photographs he takes are with a point-and-shoot automatic.

What has saved Beard from ignominy and perhaps even an early death is his passion for his adopted home. Though regarded by some as a loose cannon, he can be a forceful spokesman on the fate of Africa, the future of its people, and the end of the game. He hangs on in Africa because—like his hero Isak Dinesen before him—he regards it as the last great place from which to watch evolution.

On a 1954 trip to England with his family, sixteen-year-old Beard read Karen Blixen's *Out of Africa,* which she wrote under the name Isak Dinesen. He credits this singular book with triggering his lifelong obsession with both the authoress and the place she loved. With what he describes as "an incredible amount of luck and a lot of pushiness" he would eventually meet Blixen, at her home in Denmark. To this day he speaks of her reverentially. "*Out of Africa* was the first meaningful book I'd read and clearly the best," he once wrote. "All the dark mysteries of nature finally found a voice in one of the few outsiders who had the intelligence to go to Africa to listen rather than to tell. She was lucky—of course she made her luck—to be in one of the greatest places on earth and at possibly the greatest time."

Beard first visited Africa in 1955, accompanied by Quentin Keynes, grandson of Charles Darwin. They saw Madagascar and South Africa, the grand parks at Umfolozi and Hluhluwe, and made short forays into Tanzania and Kenya. "Everything I knew about the place came from books," he says. As a boy he had filled his rooms at home and college with antlers, horns, and the stuffed heads of various animals. "I thought of Africa as a place where there was still plenty of room, where you could actually live life rather than have your life run by a world where you wake up in the morning to a traffic jam, rush to catch a bus, struggle to get to the office."

His timing was fortuitous. He arrived in Kenya when the nation was entering an era of incredible shake-up, politically and environmentally. He was fortunate to meet and befriend the last generation of settlers before they died. He quickly assimilated himself into the group of young white Kenyans—politicians, scientists, entrepreneurs, hunters—who would emerge as the country's leaders in the years to come.

When Beard first moved to Nairobi he took a room at the New Stanley Hotel, where the action was. He would come down in the morning, get a small table at the Thorn Tree, buy the papers, and before long several tables would be pulled together and fifteen to twenty people would be drinking coffee, eating, and sharing their most recent escapades. Some of them are still among Beard's best friends in Africa: Tony and Betty Archer; Bill Woodley and his wife, Ruth Hales; John Sutton; Glen Cottar; John Fletcher; Murray Watson; Mike Prettyjohn. From those long brunches he latched on to the best safaris of his life.

In 1961 Ruth Hales worked for the safari company Ker and Downey, which had a kiosk at the hotel. Knowing that Beard was looking for a guide to the bush, she introduced him to Douglas Tatham Collins, one of the most colorful hunters in Kenya and a former district commissioner of Somaliland. An incurable romantic and confirmed bachelor, he first helped Beard purchase a fourthhand Land Rover and a cheap 9.3 mm gun. Pooling their resources—Beard brought the Land Rover loaded with food, Collins the native trappers, gun bearers, and cook—they set off for the first of many tours of the Greater Shag, Kenya's northernmost desert and bush country.

In Collins's company Beard saw virtually every hectare of wild Kenya. From the open plains under Mt. Kilimanjaro to Tsavo West and then northward, through Makindu to the desert of the Northern Frontier District. They spent months away from Nairobi. Along the way Beard sought out the last living remnants of the pioneering days. He interviewed, photographed, and learned from these men whose reputations had been secured in the writings of Blixen and others. He listened intently to their tales from the past and forecasts for the future. He had come to Kenya in many ways a blank slate and on these first journeys his mind was indelibly marked.

Every day brought new encounters with a plethora of beasts, including black rhinos, lions, cheetahs, hippos, buffalo, and massive herds of elephants, reticulated giraffes, gazelles, dik-diks, and warthogs. He suffered through the hot desert life of the NFD, discovered the mystery of the African night, and heard strange legends about snakes that could run as fast as men and elephants with tusks so large that they had to walk backward.

Along the way they hunted for sport and food. In fact, hunting was one of the primary reasons the young Beard was so excited about Kenya; he admired the lives of the great hunters and was anxious to experience something akin to what they had. He had learned to shoot as a boy in Alabama and Long Island, and was an excellent marksman. His first kill in Africa was a hippo at Donya Sabuk. Handed a .375 he took careful aim using a tree as a rest. "It wasn't a hard shot, but it had to be done right, within about two inches of the ear," he recalls. "Up came the head of the cow with its distended eyes. A rifle crack ruptured the silence; a thud and a monstrous sinking. Not a bird or anything stirred. The kill had been too quick for me to know exactly how I felt; it was strangely exciting. The result was two tons of meat, which was carved up for workers on a nearby estate." Following kills were more dangerous and exhilarating. (One rainy evening he shot a leopard with a .375 broken in half and at the last minute tied together with a rope. The leopard jumped five feet in the air and then fell to the ground dead; the rifle shot knocked Beard to the ground and bloodied his eye.)

These were not big-money safaris. When they ran out of food or grew tired of trying to eat zebra (often cooked in a can of sand and gasoline when no wood existed and no thorns burned), they survived on spaghetti, passion fruit, biscuits, and fig newtons. Hungry and in search of dinner, one Sunday Beard made a long, hasty shot at an impala, wounding it. In the hot pursuit that followed he tripped in a warthog's hole, breaking his left ankle in two places. "The impala died nearby, and I crawled up to watch these two hungry Turkana boys pulling it apart and gobbling up the kidneys raw. They broke the bones to suck out marrow, the sound of which was beyond description."

When he and Collins split up after three months, Collins continued onto Somalia. Beard headed for Laikipia, two hundred miles north of Nairobi, to learn the intricacies of "game control." He took a job on the ranch of Gilbert Colvile, who had begun with eight Boran cows in the 1940s and twenty years later had amassed a herd of ten thousand. Unfortunately cows and wildlife could not coexist in the same fields due to tick-born diseases transmitted by the nondomesticated beasts. The only alternative for farmers anxious to squeeze profit from the now fenced-in land, was to eliminate the competitive game. As well as being challenging hunting, this was to serve as a first and firsthand introduction for young Beard in the effect on wildlife when humans move in.

The work was hard, stalks long, the shooting fast and usually from quite a distance. Unlike trophy hunting, in which the target lies in a single vital area, in control work, after the first steady, calculated shot everything is on the run. The shooters' main targets were zebras, buffalo, and cattle-killing lions, and they shot plenty of each. A day's hunting began with a painstaking, tedious stalk until a skittish herd was within range. They made certain that each gun could bring down two or three animals. Back at camp skins were pegged down for salting, and dried ones from the previous day were stacked. Dinner was around seven o'clock and sleep came soon after dark.

It was arduous, dangerous, enlightening work. (Though Beard calls it "work," like virtually all his experiences in the bush he was never paid, per his request.) He remembers one day in particular, running after buffalo full out, carrying heavy guns.

> Bryan Coleman, a professional hunter, carried a fourteen-pound .577, which could stop a buffalo by sheer impact. I had a slightly

disintegrating Husquarua 9.3 millimeter I had bought from an elephant-control officer in the New Stanley's Long Bar. It might seem that running through the narrow, 'wait-a-bit' thorn-pulling tunnels would be the most exhausting part of the ordeal, but it was not. There was an intense exhilaration as we plunged on faster and faster, snapping branches and pulling through vines, soaked with sweat, thinking of nothing but how that bull would look, how long the dogs could hold it at bay, how far apart the horns would be, how big and how mean it would be.

Ahead of me Bryan fired two shots. Unbelieving, we froze and all at once a blackness burst through the branches. I turned and let off two shots from the hip and then felt an explosion from behind. Another buffalo, wounded and down on its front knees, was circling with its hind legs before collapsing in a heap. Bryan lay between us a few feet away in the dirt, dazed. I hadn't seen him because he was run over by the first black, wounded form. As he rolled over, yet another buffalo appeared, a cow with her head down, and he got off a perfect heart shot as she turned.

Man versus nature. It was a theme that would become Beard's primary focus. He wrote at the time:

In the fight of men and domestic animals against nature and her complex balances there is no compromise. In areas where there is a winner, the winner is absolute. In an environment ruled by nature's balances, man cannot play around without expecting unsavory repercussions. For instance, on the Fletcher estate not far from Colvile's, a successful anti-vermin fence had so protected the reproduction of Thomson's gazelles that seven thousand of them had to be shot. And when they built up again in a year or two, someone had to buy another seven thousand rounds of ammunition.

At first Beard had hunted for pleasure, for sport. In the mid-sixties he hooked up with several of the numerous scientific outfits studying wildlife in Africa and from them learned the work of a slaughtering hunter, shooting hundreds of crocodiles, hippos, and elephants. The purpose of such hunting was to gather enough scientific evidence, after dissection, to better understand the animals' mating, reproductive, nutrition, and aging processes. Game was plentiful, cropping made sense and was usually paid for by governments anxious to learn how to better manage the wildlife they hoped could one day pay for itself. Carrying his camera with him everywhere, he documented cullings of hippopotamus and elephant populations in Uganda, Tanzania, and the Congo, all suffering from overgrazing and overcrowding. It was fascinating if occasionally dangerous work, and it introduced him to a wealth of wildlife professionals.

The Kenyan national parks, organized in 1946, were run by a small, army-trained band of wildlife adventurers. Beard befriended them all—Mervyn Cowie, David Sheldrick, Peter Jenkins, Bill Woodley, Ian Parker. He purchased property from Cowie; walked every step of the Abedares with Woodley; lived for months with Sheldrick and his wife, Daphne; attended drunken bashes with Jenkins, Parker, and the others after long days and weeks in the bush. They welcomed Beard for his outsider's humor, bush sense, and photographic achievements. Bill Woodley is both Beard's mentor and best friend in Kenya; he remembers his young protégé in near mythic terms. "Peter could run faster, walk further, shoot straighter than anybody. If hunting had lasted, he'd have been a great hunter. But he loved the bush . . . with or without a gun."

But Beard's fascination with big game went beyond that of the average hunter. One day in Uganda he was working with a pair of scientist/hunters, Ian Parker and Lionel Hartley. They were tracking and shooting elephants, under the employ of the Nuffield Unit of Tropical Ecology. Late in the afternoon, armed with rifle and camera, Beard found himself separated from the others. He could hear Parker and Hartley shooting on the other side of the hill when an angry bull came charging over the hill, directly at him. He stood his ground, for while the elephant appeared intent on skewering him, Beard curiously welcomed the experience of being charged. Meanwhile Parker and Hartley had come to the top of the hill, but were one hundred yards away. They both knew that a shot to scare or wound the big animal would be extremely difficult, yet Hartley shot once anyway. Miraculously, he dropped the angry elephant and it skidded to a halt, dead, ten feet from Beard. But his response was irritation rather than thankfulness, apparently unshaken by the charge, but infuriated by the shooting. "I wasn't ready to run yet," he explained to Hartley, "it just wasn't time yet." While the photographer admitted it may have been as close as he ever came to death in the bush, it was also perhaps the most exhilarating moment. Today his pair of hunting friends still shake their heads in amazement over Beard's attitude and confidence.

Perhaps his most thrilling months were spent in the company of a grizzled, eccentric rhino trapper named Ken Randall, a South African whom Beard still calls "the craziest man I ever met."

Randall made a living on government contracts, catching rhinos in the hunting blocks and releasing the adults in Tsavo National Park. Beard remembers those chases—which entailed bouncing around on the running board of a Ford Bedford through the baobab and commiphora forests at forty miles per hour while attempting to lasso two-ton beasts—as "my first and best job in Kenya."

The rhinos—black and five feet tall at the shoulder—were difficult to spot from the ground in the dense scrubland, which meant running into game was often sheer luck. Randall refused the assistance of airplanes, so ropers and spotters balanced precariously on the roofs of the lead truck, followed by an ambush vehicle carrying a crew of ropers, diggers, pullers, and general helpers. Day after day the crew bumped along from dawn to dusk. When the chase commenced, the chief priority of the spotters was watching for burned-out baobob stumps—vast black pits, sometimes twenty feet across—into which the entire catching truck could disappear. Uncaring, slightly mad, the begoggled Randall would floor it over blind gullies, termite hills, boulders, rocks, acacia stumps, and thirty-foot trees. The windows of the truck had long ago been broken out, its cab was filled with tree branches, dirt, and leaves.

Once captured, the rhinos were trucked eighty miles into Tsavo, where they were disinfected, dewormed, deticked, and kept in log pens, made from great tree trunks dug deep into the ground and wired together with sturdy cross beams. (On more than one occasion Beard paid natives out of his own pocket to construct the pens.) At first, each beast would hurl itself against his commiphora prison, shaking the pen and frightening the captors. The irony was that once released into their new home, nothing stopped the rhinos from running right back to their old stomping grounds in the hunting block. "This was conservation at its crazy best," he wrote.

In the mid-sixties Beard and biologist Alistair Graham spent parts of several years living on the shores of Kenya's Lake Rudolf, hunting, dissecting, and documenting the lives of crocodiles. Graham had been hired by the Kenya government to study the Nile crocodile, a previously ignored and little-probed creature. Their job was to assess the biological status of the lake's crocodile population in order to help the game department shape a policy toward an animal traditionally despised as a dangerous pest. Though contracted by the government, there was no money to pay for the survey, so Wildlife Services would have to finance its study out of what they could get for the skins of the five hundred crocs to be killed for investigation. Beard signed on as Graham's partner. "His devil may-care manner was a tonic for the rest of us, though he clearly confirmed the Turkana's suspicion that all white men were completely crazy," wrote Graham at the time.

The pair of white men and a half dozen Turkana helpers set up camps on either side of the lake, at Ferguson's Gulf, Moite, and Alia Bay. At the time the region was menaced by *shifta*—roving outlaws hostile to Kenya and sympathetic to the neighboring Somali Republic. Because of the risk of banditry the scientific team kept as mobile as possible while on the east side, storing gear when not in use on the west side at Kalokol. This meant crossing the lake every month, for skins had to be turned into cash regularly in order to keep the study going. Continuity was essential, so for a solid twelve months in 1965–1966 Beard and Graham rarely left the lake. Beard's main assignment, other than photographing carcasses, was hunting, day and night. His limitless energy and enthusiasm were indispensable catalysts to a sometimes flagging project; often he managed to turn mishaps into laughter.

Throughout their year together Alistair was constantly amazed by Beard. "When Peter sees a dangerous situation, he has to get involved. What he likes most about Africa is to do your own thing there, a way of life you create with no plan. To Peter, something is creative only if it happens by surprise. He can't—won't—accept the normal responsibilities of society."

Horrendous conditions nearly made the crocodile study impossible. Lake Rudolf—once part of the Nile—is deceptively treacherous; winds average twenty to thirty miles per hour across it and whip up on a whim to fifty or sixty. "It's just like an ocean," says Beard. "We often saw crocs being tossed about in ten-foot waves." On the first day of what was to be more than a year on the lake, their boat sank. During the course of their study its replacement, Alistair's nineteen-foot converted lifeboat known as *The Curse,* was swamped four times and eventually sank.

For shelter they designed blow-through canvas sheeting rigged on steel frames; tents would have been too heavy, too wind resistant, and unbearably hot inside. These open shelters offered the only shade, so they served as dissection room, bedroom, and storeroom. Sand was in everything and flies were a major annoyance. By day the black volcanic shore was furnace hot, interrupted randomly by violent whirlwinds that tore through the camp like miniature tornadoes, scattering anything not weighted down with stones.

Their diet was mostly catfish and tilapia, supplemented by Ritz crackers, Hellmann™'s mayonnaise, bread-and-butter pickles, condensed milk, and a few treasured tins of grapefruit. Soup was concocted from grand-sounding packets like Egg-drop, Mushroom, and Chicken Noodle, but the vile alkaline water polluted everything. Black volcanic sand was in every mouthful of catfish, perch, turtle, zebra. "The cook's forte consisted of dropping slabs of catfish, some fat and plenty of sand into a pan and heating it for an indeterminate period," remembers Beard. "The result was then dumped, wordlessly, before us. There was, to be sure, nothing to say." The natives existed primarily on crocodile meat. (Beard: "I have eaten nearly every kind of wild animal meat and found all of it good with the single exception of croc. It is an oily, pungent flavor however cooked, cut-up or disguised.") Occasionally they were treated to Nile turtle or croc eggs. Their teeth turned brown from drinking the alkaline lake water, which Beard claimed tasted "like melted jelly-fish." Hyenas and lions stole and ate several fresh croc carcasses even though they'd been anchored well offshore. Scorpions crawled into sandals, damp-skinned toads were found in every jar and metal box, poisonous night-traveling carpet vipers hung from tent frames. They could not have picked a more difficult and dangerous location for a scientific survey.

Alia Bay was where Beard and Graham engaged in some of their best crocodile hunting. Using .270 silver-tipped bullets, they learned much about crocodiles simply by pursuing them. Their goal was to shoot a minimum biometric sample of five hundred during their stay, or forty to fifty crocodiles each month. (At the time it was estimated there were thirty thousand crocs in the lake, plenty to cull from.)

It proved an arduous task. They needed a random sampling of ages and therefore shot any adult available. The bigger, older, and smarter the better, but "monster pebbleworms"—as Beard and Graham referred to those more than thirteen feet long—were rare. Most ranged from six to ten feet.

Hunting day and night was a necessity.

We had hoped to hunt from a boat, but the wind ruled that out," [wrote Graham.] Then we found that because the lake was shallow a long way out, most of the crocs were out of range of a hunter walking along the water's edge. So we had to go in after them. Our technique was for one of us to walk in front with a torch, followed closely by a rifleman. Behind him came one of the men to tow our kills along. This was necessary because if we left them on shore they were quickly stolen by the lions or hyenas that followed us when we were hunting at night. The torch bearer would cast around for crocs, whose eyes shone red in torchlight. Finding a suitable one, we would try to approach without alarming the wary animal, which more often than not would silently submerge and disappear. Once down, a croc can last up to an hour without breathing. Although the light dazzled the crocs, many things worked against us to warn them of danger. It was essential to keep downwind, for their sense of smell is extremely good.

Their hearing is keen, too, and this was our greatest problem, for the ground underfoot was seldom easy to traverse soundlessly. Mostly it was a vile ooze studded with sharp chunks of lava and rocks. Every now and then someone would plunge into a soft patch, for it was a constant struggle to keep upright. Many were the crocs lost at the last moment as somebody subsided noisily into the lake. Scattered about were hippo footprints, deep holes in which the lava chunks clutched at you like gin traps. A shoe torn off deep beneath the mud was almost impossible to retrieve without alarming a croc floating a few feet away.

Close calls were almost a daily occurrence. Alistair shot one big croc, walked up to it, and was surprised when it began thrashing about, snapping its jaws viciously. Stumbling, he felt it whip around and its jaws close on his leg. He let out a muffled howl and managed to wrench his leg clear with no damage but deep gashes. On another night Alistair was bitten by a spitting cobra. Luckily it was only a scratch; he jumped aside at the last second and the fangs only grazed him. Two teeth marks about a centimeter apart were the only evidence of the strike; from each tiny wound trickled small tracks of blood.

Beard remembers the twenty-minute journey back to camp as chilly and uncertain. "We all expected him to keel over, dead," he says.

On yet another night a twelve-footer came like a torpedo from more than thirty yards offshore straight at the flashlight, which Beard was holding. Graham was so surprised that his two or three shots failed, then the gun jammed. "Scared stiff I held the flashlight out to the side and ran around in tight circles," says Beard, "waiting for a finishing shot. Alistair hurled his rifle to the ground, took out his trusty Colt .45 and at point blank range, fired again and again. The scaly leviathan was on auto-pilot and it took several loads to weigh it down with lead."

Another night one of their native hunters was grabbed from behind by a ten-foot croc on Central Island. He managed to get away after a grizzly tug of war that sent him to hospital in Nairobi with massive injuries. Animals weren't the only beasts they had to watch out for. Merille, Rendile, and Boran bandits passed by their campsites many nights, looked them over, and kept walking. They were lucky. In Loingalani, near the southern tip of the lake, Somali bandits with automatic weapons raided the only fishing lodge on the lake. A Catholic priest was killed, the lodge's manager shot in the back of the head, and an Italian driver speared and skinned.

The crocodile survey ended in typically Beardian fashion, with the sinking of *The Curse* on September 17, 1966. Three crocs short of five hundred, Alistair dropped Beard and a knock-kneed skinner nicknamed the Wildman on Shingle Island. They were to spend one last cold, windblown night hidden in trenches scooped out of the sand, waiting to shoot anything that came ashore early the next morning.

When Alistair returned in *The Curse* the next morning to pick up the hunters and the last crocs, the wind was blowing twenty to twenty-five miles an hour, covering the lake with whitecaps. Celebrating the conclusion of a year's hunt, they decided to make one last trip rather than two and loaded the boat with all three crocs, gear, and men. Two miles from the mainland the winds worsened and green waves began pouring over the narrow stern of the wooden boat. They quickly jettisoned the crocs, but it was already too late. In seconds the boat filled with water, and sank. The trio found themselves adrift in rough seas. Worse yet, the Wildman, who could speak neither English nor Swahili, could not swim a stroke. "His eyes were wide and rolled back, searching Heavenward," remembers Beard.

Alistair quickly disconnected the gas tank and emptied it of fuel so that it would float. Pushing it toward Wildman, they spent the next frantic minutes trying to teach him to swim, by madly kicking his feet while clutching the tank. The wind was now blowing about thirty miles an hour, and the air a foot above the choppy sea was full of spray. Swimming in what they hoped was the right direction, the Wildman and Alistair, who was desperately trying to hang onto his glasses, headed back for Shingle Island. Beard stayed behind: His diary was in the sunken boat and it contained the only records of the year-long crocodile hunt. He found it after four dives into the metal cockpit of the boat, which lay twenty feet under.

"For the first time one of my diaries contained something irreplaceable: all of Alistair's croc data, markings, measurements, and tail-scale sequences for age-criteria studies. This made it vital to save," remembers Beard.

His swim to Shingle Island was a blur. Clutching his diary he swam against the current and waves. The island, a sand bank the length of a football field lying very low in the storm, was barely visible above the chop. He tried not to think about the thirty thousand crocodiles that hungered in the lake. Eventually on shore ahead of him he spotted his two friends, apparently hugging, slapping, rubbing, and shaking each other. When he stepped ashore he understood their frantic behavior. The high octane aviation fuel dumped into the sea had badly burned their skin; the wind on shore immediately brought the resulting pain to their attention. Assessing their options—stuck on the island with no one within a hundred miles to miss nor rescue them—Beard decided he could make the two-mile swim to the mainland. With the red fuel tank as his float, he set off at 2 P.M. and he paddled and kicked for hours to reach shore.

The next day, his skin sore and scabbing from gas burns, he rigged a larger float. He tied the fuel tank and an empty jerrican together, then flattened another jerrican to serve as a sail. After affixing emergency rations of Skippy peanut butter and honey, he set off for Shingle Island. If he misjudged the position of the tiny island, he risked being blown past it into forty miles of open lake. After another several-hour-long swim, he found the island. Then he and Graham kicked the makeshift craft back to the mainland. The next day Alistair would retrieve his plane, borrow a boat from Ferguson's Gulf, and go after the Wildman. The survey was indisputably over. By taking just one chance too many they had brought it to an abrupt halt three crocs short of their goal of five hundred. To top it off they had lost their boat, engine, guns, and all other equipment.

• • •

Today Kenya's fast-swelling population is touching Beard in a personal way. As the country nears implosion Hog Ranch is threatened by the imploding Nairobi populace. Together with neighbors Beard has paid for a ten-foot-tall chain-link fence to wrap a communal one hundred fifty acres, in an effort to protect what is left of the Mbgathi Forest from fast-encroaching development. But that is merely a Band-Aid™. Roads are being surveyed and wells tested all around Hog Ranch. It is a matter of time before the expanding metropolis devours his once-private domain. "If things get really bad, we're on to the Congo, the Riviera of Africa," he says only half in jest.

One evening, sitting on the porch of Hog Ranch's kitchen, I ask Beard if he ever thinks about leaving Kenya and not returning. Thoreau, after all, left Walden after just two years and never went back. Karen Blixen was in Kenya for seventeen years, then retreated when the going became too difficult. Beard has been here for more than thirty years. I wonder out loud if perhaps he has stayed in his paradise too long. Around every corner he has found the end of something and it has soured him. "I disagree," he says, when I suggest my theory. "I still think it is a great place, affording the greatest evolutionary perspective, the last chance to have your feet on the ground where we began. I think the thing to do is just sit back and enjoy it and know that it is the greatest show on earth. It might be the last show, but it's the biggest, the most exhilarating, phantasmagoric, riveting, devastating, great.

"Mostly I feel like the wildebeest out there in a rainstorm . . . You just put your head down and wait."

THE END OF THE WORLD

In 1535 Spanish conquistador Diego de Almagro was ordered by his queen to find the best route to Chile. He supposed there would not be much to discover in the great northern desert, so he moved his troops over the Andes, into the central part of the country. Five hundred Spaniards and more than fifteen thousand Indians, including some Incas from Peru, accompanied him. The Incas told the Spaniards the little they knew about the tribes of Chile and explained the Indian name for this new land, translated simply as "the End of the World."

There is a sense of the new and a little bit of business as usual in Chile these days. This, for example: The day I arrived in Santiago, robbers fled a downtown bank on foot, burst into a nearby home, and took the three inside hostage. Quick to the scene were the Ninja Turtles—Santiago's highly visible, bullet-proof-jacket-wearing, motorcycle-riding elite police force. They didn't even consider negotiating; instead the Turtles barged into the house, guns blazing, killing the bad guys—as well as the hostages. The message was simple: hostage taking doesn't wash in Chile. These Ninja Turtles don't negotiate.

• • •

The next afternoon I sat in the bar at the Hotel Carrera, with two friends from the States. They were off for a week of whitewater rafting on the famed Río Bió Bió. Looking out the window over the Constitucional Plaza, signs of success, and capitalism abounded: men and women in business suits, stores selling a wide variety of imported goods, restaurants and bars doing brisk afternoon business. All this thriving capitalism in a postdictatorship democracy was hard for us *Norte Americanos* to adjust to. Across from us sat a trio of uniformed men, whom we watched out of the corner of our eyes, convinced they were similarly watching us. Walking around Santiago we half expected to bump into Jack Lemmon or Sissy Spacek still engaged in their desperate search for their "missing" son and husband.

But this was the nineties. Pinochet is out, democracy is in. Yet the horrific statistics of his reign are invariably stamped on visitor's memories: 2,279 people killed, another 50,000 tortured. For sixteen years constitutional rights were suspended; Chileans could be arrested for up to twenty days without charge. The fortunate were shot by firing squads. The unlucky were beaten, mutilated, half drowned, or electrocuted before their bodies were ripped by bullets. Most were urban workers and peasants, but some were intellectuals, small businessmen, or politicians. It is these truths that for more than two decades discouraged casual visits to the twenty-six-hundred mile long strip of land squeezed between the Andes and the Pacific.

The Pinochet era ended in 1989 when a plebiscite (called for by Pinochet's own revision of the constitution) ousted him. Despite all his wrongs, 43 percent voted to keep him president.

• • •

Santa Lucia Hill is one of the loveliest parks in the Americas, regarded as the birthplace and bulwark of Santiago. It was here that Don Pedro de Valdivia founded the city and from here Don Casimiro Marco del Pont later defended it from attacks by Independence-seeking Chileños. Mapuche Indians had earlier dedicated it to the God of Pain and Christians erected on its summit the very first hermitage. First president Bernardo O'Higgins initially had the idea of using the hill as a cultural attraction when he tried to build an observatory and a parthenon atop it. But decades passed before historian, politician, writer, and patriot Don Benjamin Vicuna Mackenna made O'Higgins's dream come true. From 1872 to 1874 he directed the work by convicts, which transformed the hill from a pair of twin fortresses to the unique park it is today.

After climbing hundreds of steps to the top—and passing dozens of hugging, necking, preening teens, and adults—the reward is a three-hundred-sixty-degree view of the city and the mountains that rim it. From this vantage the view of the city of six million is peaceful, docile. (Only the smog of a million cars interrupts the romance.) It is a peace produced by economic and political stability that can be felt from the marbled lobby of the Hotel Carrera to the blue-collar barrios that ring the city.

In fact an economic miracle is under way in Chile. The GNP is booming, there is no debt crisis, and foreign investment is pouring in at an annual rate of $1 billion. Salaries are increasing, unemployment on a downward spiral. Chile has become a model for the third world, the best economy in South America. Santiago remains one of the most under-discovered capitals in the world, starring an old-world romance crossed with new-world, big city convenience.

It is painful for many to admit that a lot of Chile's extraordinarily successful economic reforms were carried out under a brutally repressive dictatorship. During Pinochet's reign state companies were sold off and businessman encouraged to consider the global market. In the northern desert, farmers are using Israeli drip-irrigation techniques to produce bumper harvests of grapes; high in the Andes a consortium of Australian, British, and Japanese investors has opened the world's largest, privately owned, copper mine. Renewable pine forests in southern Chile are exporting almost $1 billion annually in lumber, wood chips, and pulp. The salmon industry rivals that in Norway. One industry Pinochet's reign discouraged is booming. Tourism has become a billion-dollar-a-year industry, as hordes discover a majestic wilderness for years considered off limits.

From high atop Santa Lucia the Andes shield a land of rare beauty and extremes, of volcanos and ice, desert and sea. "Chile was invented by a poet," wrote Nobel Laureate Pablo Neruda. His homeland has become the new playground for adventuresome Europeans and North Americans. Warm, cheap, fun, and incredibly underexplored, Chile is on the verge of becoming the hippest hangout on the globe.

• • •

The flight south from Santiago to the last city in the Americas, Punta Arenas, takes five hours. I arrived in the early evening and after walking several miles along the rocky beach that lines the Straits of Magellan, stopping every few minutes to peer across the wind-whipped sea to the hump of land that is Tierra del Fuego, I stopped into a steakhouse, El Estribe. The steaks were cooked over an open fire, accompanied by *papas fritas* and a salad of artichoke hearts, white asparagus, big black olives, chased by an abundance of vino *tinto*. I was the lone customer late on a Sunday, and the proprietor snoozed at the next table while a Chuck Norris escapade blasted away on a television hung above the bar.

When Punta Arenas was founded in 1848 it was not considered suitable for "human subsistence," due to the wet, cold, and windy conditions. Originally the only people who lived this far south were prisoners. The first immigrants were tough escapees from Switzerland, the United Kingdom, Spain, and Yugoslavia, who made livings hunting sea wolves, mining coal, milling wood, and mining alluvial gold. The town grew based on its isolated position at the bottom of the western hemisphere; until the opening of the Panama Canal, Punta Arenas was the only way ships could move from the Pacific to the Atlantic. Maritime and meat freezing plants were big economies, then petroleum exploitation began in the 1950s.

Today Punta Arenas is a quaint, isolated, almost-modern village of one hundred twenty thousand, built on a sloping hill overlooking the Straits of Magellan. It could have been plucked straight out of *American Graffiti*, except for its fading remembrances of dictators past, that is, white-gloved policemen, in waist-length coats and *bandoleras* patrol the streets. A jack-jawed Bible thumper screeches from the public park every day. Ratlike dogs roam the mostly dirt streets and sleep in the tall grass in the medians. While five years ago fashions were stuck in the fifties, today it's as if a tidal wave of leather and denim had been blown ashore. Saturday nights, harmless youth line the main street. Come Sunday morning the same strip is filled with strolling mothers, fathers, and children.

It is windy here year-round, so windy that few natives walk with a straight back. Most days, even during the eight-week summer, are beset by turbulent, gusty sea breezes, discouraging skirts, toupees, and reading newspapers on the park bench. Most of the year it is cold—in the six months they call winter, the ground is covered by snow, and the harbor iced over. In the summer the sun is out eighteen hours a day; in winter just eight.

The major controversy in town is the widening ozone hole. SPF 30 sunblock is prominently displayed in every other store window. Farmers report that during the past three years, a small but growing number of sheep grazing at high altitudes have developed temporary blindness—same with rabbits. As a result some mothers forbid their children to play outdoors between ten and three o'clock; sales of dark glasses are growing.

It is a town, unremarkable in many ways, where the video store owner drives a Mercedes and you can book a hotel room in Antarctica.

Tourism is the driving economy, in large part due to the fact that every cruise ship headed for Antarctica stops at its sole dock for a day or two, discharging thousands of parka-wearing, video-camera-bearing guests. Hotels and restaurants are opening before they're even completed. The wallpaper in one hotel I stayed in peeled off the walls as I slept, not because it was old and decrepit but because it had just been slapped up, with cheap paste.

• • •

In the restaurant at the Club Hipico, plastic covers have been placed over the green-and-white checkered table cloths. The worn plank floor is patched with tin, and red-faced Chilean men line up at the plywood bar for tumblers of home-brew whiskey, poured by the glassful from a gallon jug. The establishment is a family affair, run by mom, daughter, and granddaughter. Mom is fifty and sports a black eye and toothless grin. Her hair is dyed auburn.

Red, white, and blue streamers hang from the ceiling, streaking a faded painting of Jesus and a calendar featuring an Australian bathing beauty. The green paint on the walls is thin and cracked, the screen door scarred from years of slamming behind winners and losers alike. In one corner sits an old man, his beret pulled low, wearing a sport coat over a V-neck sweater. His hair is greased back and he sucks down *pisco,* a grappa-like liqueur, mixed with Sprite, one after another. Just beyond the window the afternoon's fillies parade. The track is dingy and rundown, but the whole town is out for the weekly Sunday races.

I bet 1,000 pesos on number six, *Douquier*, in the first race. He wins and pays 10,000 pesos. I buy shots of *aquardiente* for the old man who gave me the tip, and his friends.

• • •

The day after the races I sit in a steaming kitchen in Puerto Natales, three hours up the coast from Punta Arenas, negotiating with Eddie. I am trying to get to Chile's biggest national park, Torres del Paine, and Eddie drives people there in powerful, but worn-out, Chevy Suburbans.

A Chilean of Danish descent, he sits in front of a roaring natural gas stove, the late-night kitchen sweating like a sauna. Two Bibles, leather covers worn, pages bent and tattered, sit open on table. An assistant washes dishes and his wife shuttles between the kitchen and an upstairs bedroom where their two children sleep.

Eddie's grandfather sailed here in 1910, via New York. The economy in eastern Europe was bad, so he got out. Mined slate in the fall and spring and grew cabbage in the short summer, first in Argentina then the eastern edge of Chile. His first son was a horse trainer, who died early of pneumonia from too many winters slogging across deep snow. Eddie had recently given up farming for tourism.

Upstairs three bedrooms are rented to Germans, French, and Canadians. An American river guide sleeps on the floor of his storefront office. He charges 1,500 pesos, about $4.50, for bed and breakfast. If you sleep on the floor, 1,000 pesos.

The town is not much to look at. The paint on houses had been long-faded by harsh conditions of this port town. The windswept glacier that bounds the Ultima Esperanza, that reaches two hundred miles inland, means cold six months of the year. Tiny dogs haunt the streets, not much bigger than the average American rat and twice as ugly. Yet the streets are packed with Euros, a few Asians, and a few Americans lured by the majestic surroundings and the rugged majesty of Patagonia that surrounds Puerto Natales and stretches for hundreds of miles each direction.

• • •

The next morning is gray and drizzling when I join six newly made friends and head for Torres del Paine. To the south, owing to erosion by ice and sea for thousands of years, the coast is broken up into countless fjords, peninsulas, channels, islands, and coves. As we drive north fields of sea grass spread out along both sides, the eastern slopes of the Andes turn more gently into extensive plains and pampas. This part of southern Patagonia was discovered by Hernando de Magallanes in the spring of 1520; one hundred years later Darwin and his *Beagle* stopped along the coast for several months.

We stop for coffee at a bodega advertising a caged condor. The bird is out back and we pay five pesos each for a peek. Inside the proprietors have caught onto the tourist boom—they sell condor feathers, allegedly fallen from the big guy they keep out back. But it doesn't take too vivid an imagination to wonder how many of the endangered birds they'll shoot to maintain an inventory as demand grows. I wander across the highway and look out over the fields dotted with cows. The azure sky is filling with autocumulus. A half-eaten sheep, killed by coyotes, lies just inside the fence rail.

• • •

Galloping across the pampas aboard a chestnut mare six hands tall, through big flakes of falling snow, dodging dead, ghostlike branches of low-slung oaks, pounding across streams four feet deep, up and down gulleys, racing to reach the first refugio before dark, across saw grass pampas, scaring parakeets out of trees, and causing riots among herds of guanacos. We are led by a trio of silent *arrieros*—Chilean cowboys—wearing yellow rain slickers and black berets. As we ride, the snow falls faster and wetter.

As we near the empty *refugio*—small plank buildings the park maintains for visitors and charges nothing to stay in—I race one of the cowboys, Geraldo. Twenty-eight-years old, he is five foot eight inches, wears a brown sweater, blue jeans, rubber boots, and a silver belt over a colorful woven band.

He lives in Puerto Natales and in the winter works cutting trees for a Japanese paper company. For five months he herds horses. He earns 50,000 pesos a month—about $140. His employer gives him food when he's on the trail, but he saves it and trades labor, like firebuilding, water fetching, and dishwashing in order to share his clients' meals. He takes the accumulated boxes of spaghetti and tins of tuna home to his wife and three kids.

He works thirty days, has four off, and hopes he can maintain this pace until he's sixty or sixty-five. It's a hard life, under brutal conditions. Chileans in Patagonia don't live particularly long lives.

We'd ridden a dozen miles through thickening weather, without catching sight of even one of the park's fifty majestic peaks; it's too cloudy. There is a window of good weather in southern Chile, especially in the mountainous region of Torres del Paine. It is usually from mid-January to mid-February and the best days are cold and sunny, boasting spectacularly blue skies and views.

The ride is the beginning of a ten-day exploration of an underseen mecca, Chile's biggest national park. The craggy peaks—hidden from us by thick clouds—are like no others in the world, granite sculptures rising from the Cordillera like Gothic cathedrals. Even the colors here are new to us. *Paine* (pronounced Pine-ay) is the Araucanian word for rose, precisely the color of the tip of the mountains. Algae and pulverized glacial rocks give the rivers and lakes intense shades of blue or glaucous green. Tiny red fuchias and blue monkhoods sparkle like gems in the calf-high saw grass.

• • •

We are exploring the park by novel means, on horseback and by raft. Most visitors to the 691,000-acre park see it by foot, hiking a well-traveled circuit around the mountains. We bartered for the horses and services of the arrerios with the wife of one of the park rangers; the raft was flown down from the States. My traveling companions are a pair of veteran North American river guides, a young bohemian from Seattle spending a year in South America, a Chilean guide-in-training from Santiago, an EPA bureaucrat, and an interior designer from Dallas named Houston.

After our first restless night on the *refugio* floor—seven crammed together in one room and one of us had to sleep lightly enough to tend the fire all night—we woke to cloudy skies. We are to ride to Lake Dickson, where only one of the arrerios has been, and that was sixteen years ago. It is a wild ride, highlighted by a side trip through a bog paralleling the Rio

Dickson. The big horses begin to sink one at a time into the muck. Rearing and snorting, they fight to plunge ahead, but instead sink to their bellies. The cowboys cuss at the sinking horses, but too late. Gingerly we lead them from the muck to higher ground, then continue just below the tree line.

By the time we find Lake Dickson and begin to inflate the fourteen-foot rubber paddleboat, it is snowing again. The temperature on shore is forty degrees; on the water it drops to thirty-five. We bundle up in wet-suits, rain gear, and life jackets. The backdrop of the iceberg-laden Lake Dickson is of craggy peaks rising behind blue-ice glacier.

This first descent of the Rio Dickson, that drains from the lake, is not special because of the rapids; they are relatively simple Class IIIs. This is unique because no one has ever brought a raft into the park. We'd heard from one park ranger that he and a friend had attempted to run the river in a Zodiac a couple years back. But his friend had been pitched out in one of the rapids, broke a leg, and they had to call for help.

Our yellow craft is definitely a novelty. As we float down the river a smattering of hikers shout down, amazed to see us. After two miles, past several rapids, and through stretches of calm, the clouds that have choked the gap since we arrived begin to lift. By the time we hit the lake broad patches of blue sky have been revealed. Stroke by stroke we are granted peeks at the toothish maw of the Dickson Glacier. But by the time we pull the raft ashore near the *refugio* from which we started the day, the clouds are closed around the mountains.

• • •

Our third night in the park and we still haven't seen its most spectacular peaks. Tonight's *refugio* is crowded with cookers: climbers from Germany, trekkers from Italy, lovers from Nova Scotia, and a handful of Chileans. There are a dozen just turned-out members of the Israeli Army; apparently there are cheap flights from Tel Aviv to Santiago.

The room is dark, lit by two candles. A wood-fired stove is laden with a variety of cook pots, emanating a broad wafting of hot food. A dozen people try to sleep in the second room; probably twenty tents are set up around the building. Throughout the night climbers continue to traipse into camp, head lamps bobbing in the distance, on this late summer day. They are headed to, or from, campsites at the foot of the towers the park is named after. The tallest was first scaled in 1958 by an Italian expedition and two years later by a team from Argentina. The park has become a mecca for the world's best climbers.

The mountains of Torres del Paine—fifty peaks more than eight thousand feet tall—are different from all others because of their incredible shapes. Created by the crashing of tectonic plates, floating, relatively coldly and stiffly, on the warmer and more mobile upper surface of the earth's mantle. Slipping and sliding against one another, forever moving, about a foot a year, they produce the great geological dramas of the planet. The peaks of Torres del Paine are a tremendous granite batholith pushed to the surface over one million years ago by great internal pressure and movement of large molten masses of rock. The towers—Cuerno Norte at twenty-four hundred meters, Cuerno Chico at twenty-two hundred, and Cuerno Principal at twenty-six hundred—rise at the very site of the collision of two of the world's largest plates, the South American plate and the Antarctic plate.

The park is also a Biosphere Reserve, one of a dozen global reference points for the study of man's impact on the environment. Wildlife is plentiful, the park is filled with guanacos, nandues (a type of ostrich), zorrinos, (gray foxes), wild hares, pumas, and mountain cats. Birds, too, caiquenes, condors, eagles, caranchas, black woodpeckers, red-breasted loicas, pink flamingos, black-necked swans, and brightly plumed ducks.

Oddly, there is essentially only one kind of tree here, the lenga (*Nothofagus pumilio*). Most have grown bent, nurtured by the constant winds.

A rainbow glints off the Tendal Glacier as the park's superintendent Guillerma Santana pours glasses of pisco and vino tinto. He has invited us over for a slide show, and to meet the president of Germany's branch of the World Wildlife Fund.

Last year was Torres del Paine's biggest season; twenty-one thousand visitors came. By way of comparison, Yellowstone draws that on an average day in July. There is only one hotel in the park, and it is open fewer than six months a year. Torres is the biggest funded park in Chile, but superintendent Santana tells us the government does not yet see it as a moneymaker. The government's focus remains on economic progress, often at the expense of Chile's wilderness. Santana figures the best thing for his park is not to attract too much attention.

He also worries that the park's popularity may outstrip the ability of the government to keep it up. Currently just ten rangers patrol its almost seven hundred thousand acres. As he talks the sun sets over Cuerno Hornes, the sky turning pink and blue, a half moon rising. The black tips of Cuerno Hornes—hard, sedimentary rock formed by the erosive power of ice, water, and wind—nearly sparkle.

Park management says the park is underoccupied, but Santana is satisfied with underoccupation. "My main priority is conservation and protection of the natural resources. Tourists and promoting them is not my priority," he says with a smile. He is provided with a small house and a salary of $4,800 a year. He claims he is one of the happiest bureaucrats in all of Chile. "This is my home," he says, glancing out the window.

• • •

With the skies cleared we decide to get as close to the towers as we can, by a combination of horseback and foot.

We set off behind Pepi, the park's most veteran ranger; he's been here sixteen years. Hook-nosed, with drooping eyelids and big hands, Pepi is forty but looks fifty. He is truly a modern gaucho, dressed in a wild-colored fleece jacket and pants. His horse, a tall white stud, is named Puma.

The horses take us uphill, tredding a narrow path across stone fields, up steep rises, along gravel landslides, over crevasses, paralleling a roaring mountain river and the Argentine border. A gale-force wind threatens to blow us out of our saddles. Our line of seven horses stretches out over a mile, discernible only by the reds, yellows, and blues of rain jackets and parkas. It is an exhilarating ride, bordering on ominous. Bending to get a drink from the fast-moving river, Pepi pauses. "This is the purest place on earth," he says.

The afternoon is spent hiking to the climbers' camp below the towers. It is built in thick woods just before the tree line ends. The park has built a foursome of climbing huts, turning the woods into a kind of hobbit village of wooden buildings, covered by plastic sheeting, with big stone fireplaces. Interior walls are covered with graffiti from bored climbers past. The climbers here today, mostly Italian and German, are big, burly, men of few words. They spend their days waiting for a thirty-six-hour window of clear weather. Due to the sheerness of the tower's walls and the formidable winds, the climbers must be ready on a moment's notice to sprint to their base and climb. Often they wait a month, even two, and some never even attempt the climb. While they wait they eat soup and pasta, drink herbal tea, and do thousands of sit-ups and push-ups each day to stay in shape.

After a thirty-minute stop we scramble over a boulder field, sweat dripping down the inside of polypro, toward the base of the towers. The reward when we reach the rim is an unbelievable panorama. A glacial lake, blue glaciers, snow, the trio of towers. It is five degrees—we started the day at eighty. Like most of our days in the park we have seen four seasons each day. We ask everyone we meet what is the best month to visit and invariably we are told a different month by each. Pepi's wife tells us that ten days ago her kids were swimming in rivers that are now icy. One thing everyone agrees is that winter is much more predictable: cold, clear, and windless.

That night along the Rio Paine, Pepi and his boys slaughter a lamb and roast it over a fire. The process takes five hours and when it is cooked we stand around the fire, picking meat off the bones. "Ribs are best," offers Pepi, "because they are closest to the heart."

• • •

Puerto Montt is the biggest town in Chile's Lake District, five hundred miles south of Santiago. A working seaport, it has in recent years become a mecca for both foreign and Chilean tourists. Vendors sell woolen goods and curios for blocks leading to the more than fifty small restaurants that line the sea. The buildings in town are sprawling and ramshackle, frame houses of varying heights and shapes and repair. Many look on the verge of falling down, their paint peeling and additions tacked on at every imaginable angle. It has rained for three straight days, so everything is wet and dank. Garbage washes down the gutters, including plastic bags as well as the guts of sheep, goats, cows, and fish tossed straight out kitchen windows. Perhaps the most impressive site in all of Chile sits on Puerto Montt's docks: Mountain-high piles of chipped eucalyptus and pine awaiting shipment to Japan, where it will be turned into chipboard and cardboard boxes.

This time of year, these small towns of the south—Puerto Montt, Los Angeles, Santa Barbara, Temuco—fill with itinerant boatmen and river guides, most from the States. Veterans of rivers from Nepal to Alaska, they gather here because of the half dozen American and Chilean companies that run the Bió Bió River. They live on the cheap waiting to hitch onto a next trip, passing along the names of their favorite *residencials,* restaurants, bars, and pot connections.

I am tripling in a room in a comfortable *residencial*—a family's home, they charge $4 a night—with Gary Bolton, an eighteen-year veteran of the Grand Canyon, and Barry Tessman from Marin County, whom I'd met on a plane flying out of Punta Arenas. We are each waiting out the torrential rains. I am to hook up with a team hoping to raft the previously unrafted Futaleufu River on the Argentine border, perhaps the toughest raftable river in the world. But it is raining in Futaleufu too, raising the already fast-running river to unrunnable levels.

We spend the wait learning a new game of pool. Late in the afternoon we climb thin, rubber-coated stairs covered with a dusting of sawdust and urine to a cavernous, second-floor pool hall. Hung above a string of cheap shoe stores, *ferreterias,* and papas fritas shops, it is a smoke-hazed retreat from the downpour.

Fifteen tables in various stages of repair are in constant use, mostly by the town's teenagers and hangabouts. Women are never allowed. The game we play is *color,* something like eight ball, except the balls begin spread around the table against the banks rather than massed for a break. The pockets are far smaller than on tables we are used to, so slop does not cut it.

In one corner of the room, behind a tacked-up section of plywood paneling, a raucous card game runs long into each night. Loud laughter and cursing is interrupted by a beer bottle being smashed against the wall or a drunken body falling to the floor. A doddering waiter services the room, delivering a nonstop caravan of cervezas and hot dogs. One old man buys us drinks one night. We have been the only gringos in the place all week and he wonders why we are here. When told it's for the wilderness, he laughs. "Typical. We're trying to get out of the bush, off the farms, and you're coming here to see just that."

After sitting in Puerto Montt for a week, the trip to the Futaleufu is postponed. The rains have raised the river to 30,000 cfs (cubic feet per second, a measurement of the speed of moving water); last year when a team of rafters ran sections of the river it was running at 10,000 cfs and was then barely raftable. The postponement actually gives me some relief; the river has never been successfully run, top to bottom, and we are approaching this trip with caution.

The last time a full descent was tried was 1985. A North Carolina kayaker we met was a safety boater on that ill-fated trip.

The river had not been properly scouted and never run. A cocky head boatmen had seen it by float plane and was convinced he— and four boats and fifteen passengers—could run it. They were fine on the upper stretches, where the big boats just powered through the tight gorges. But midway down the river, where the rapids get bigger, more technical, virtually unrunnable, the big boats were too unmaneuverable. They survived, barely, until they reached a rapid we'd dubbed Terminator. By then the passengers were scared shitless and the kayakers were worn from having to rescue swimmers. When they saw Terminator—which looks more like a lake than a river—the passengers got out and the boatmen ran it empty.

But two of the big boats collided mid-Terminator, forcing one down the middle, into the teeth of three huge, alternating holes. He hung on for a half hour, forty-five minutes, but was finally thrown. His boat was literally torn apart—boxes, frame, everything was stripped by the power of tumbling water. As we watched from the shore, the raft popped into sight every few minutes. We found what was left of it a week later in Lake Yelcho, thirty miles away.

• • •

It is past midnight when Ernesto, the only bartender in the small town of Futaleufu picks up the dice cup and begins to roll. For an hour he has been professing ignorance of the game or its rules. Asked to join in, he shrugged his shoulders, smiled, and took another swig from a cask of wine he kept beneath the bar. He watched while we rolled, beating out a Latin rhythm on the bar with his fingers.

Finally he consented to play and when he began to roll, the five dice tumbling powerfully from the worn leather cup, it was obvious he had thrown them before. Slamming the cup down on the scarred bar with a powerful flick of the wrist, he beat me for peso after peso. By the time he shuttered the bar, my pockets were empty, and Ernesto was still smiling. "Good luck," he laughed.

• • •

The rains finally stopped, at sunrise fifteen of us load into the back of a cattle truck, already piled high with rafts, kayaks, food, and gear. As we waddle out of the town of Futaleufu, forty three degrees south, thirteen hundred kilometers from Santiago, we make several stops to pick up laborers hitching to their jobs on the farms nearby.

This stretch of soft green hills bordering Chile and Argentina is one of the most virgin regions in the world. It was first colonized in 1912 by Chilean families from the island of Chiloe who crossed over from the Argentinian side as the mountainous geography of Chile made access difficult. It was officially founded in 1929 and has not changed much since, despite the annual appearance of a few dozen kayakers. The farms that line the ridges are big, many owned by families from the north; a sparse population of three thousand is spread out so the area appears desolate, majestic. A smattering of plank-board houses and farms fenced by thick stumps are spread apart by miles.

The Rio Futaleufu runs one hundred miles, from its source in the Los Alerces National Park in Argentina to the Chilean Lake Yelcho. The Tehuelche Indians translate Futaleufu as "great waters." As we drive along the pocked dirt road to the put-in, the river makes spot appearances. It is impressive even from a distance, a deep, clear azure. Its banks are lined by a temperate rain forest; where the river squeezes between high rock walls, marbleized granite rises a hundred feet. Its tributaries run down from glacier-laden hills; though the rain has stopped, the river is still running at eight thousand feet, the edge of raftability.

Only one hundred of the world's best kayakers have run the Fu. The numbers are small for a simple reason. "It is way too dangerous," according to the river's gringo veteran, Chris Spelius, who first walked its shores in 1985. No one has attempted a top-to-bottom raft descent since that ill-fated trip of 1985. We are going to try, accompanied by twice the normal number of guides and safety kayakers. Technology is on our side; eighteen-foot, self-bailing boats were not available in 1985. They should be able to withstand the monstrous rapids in the narrow gorge named Inferno—"Big enough to swallow a rail car," warns Spee— and yet be maneuverable enough to allow us to "sneak" around the even bigger rapids, like Terminator.

• • •

In the cab of the cattle truck the trip's leader gives directions to the put-in. Eric Hertz has come closer than anyone to rafting the Fu. Last year he and a trio of friends successfully ran the river in pieces—first the midsection, then the top, then the bottom. He is an outfitter from upstate New York and, like most other commercial operators who sell trips in Chile, he is constantly on the lookout for new rivers to run, new adventures with which to lure the thriving adventure travel market.

Before we launch our two-boat, five-kayak parade, safety kayaker Eric Neiss gives a little speech praising the mighty river and preparing us for the titillation to come. He calls the river "rowdy."

The first trio of rapids are forty-five minutes from our put-in, in the gorge called Inferno. Cliff walls rise one hundred feet from the river; its freight-train power sluices through a narrow gap studded with boulders as big as semitrucks. At this point it is impossible to walk out of the valley, the only way is by river. Three Class V rapids are lined back to back. Thankfully they are separated by pools of calm water. The kayakers go first; they will wait in the pools below each rapid to fish rafters tossed from the rafts out of the Fu. We watch their descent from shore and our jaws drop as the first two kayaks, twelve feet long, disappear completely from sight in the waves and holes that roar through the canyon. "Deceptive, eh?" mumbles Hertz, tugging on his helmet strap.

We are the first boat and approach the first rapid a bit too conservatively, in an attempt to hug the wall. Instead we are pushed sideways toward the middle of the river and a string of twelve-foot waves. As we drop into the first, about to be enveloped by a wall of water, the paddler in front of me, a veteran of twenty years of river running, flashes a quick look back and his gray eyes are filled with absolute terror. He can see what is coming, wave by wave, and instinctively drops to his knees and quits paddling as one after another pounds over the rubber bow of the boat, pushing the one-ton boat nearly on end. The morning is spent bashing through one tough rapid after another, inevitably stopping after each to pick up a paddler or two launched from the rafts.

We pull out at Zeda, a Z-shaped tumult through sculpted rock granite too tough, too unpredictable for the big rafts to attempt. From the cliffs above we watched the kayakers attempt to thread a line through the Z, with varying degrees of success, though eventually all make it through. When the pair of big rafts are sent through empty they end up banged into a violent corner, water bubbling around them like uncorked champagne.

The boats are wrestled away from the face of the wall by our lead kayaker, Chris Spelius. If any gringo can claim rights to the Fu, it is Spee. Around southern Chile his reputation precedes him. "Do you know Super Gringo?" the lady at the ticket counter in Puerto Montt had asked when she heard we wanted to fly to Futaleufu.

A former Olympic whitewater kayaker, Spelius is now forty. He has spent his life in search of great rivers and has kayaked on six continents. Once he found the Fu his searching ended. The Fu, he says, is the greatest whitewater river in the world. He first heard of it in the early 1980s; when he visited in 1985 the town had no electricity and no plane reached it. Until the past couple of seasons he has had the river essentially to himself.

Handsome, blond, and brawny, he looks too massive to squeeze into the cockpit of a kayak. He had shown up this morning in a hot-pink paddling jacket, with pink and yellow sunblock applied like warpaint on his cheeks and nose. Colorful feathers hang from his sun-bleached hair. When he first visited the Fu he walked both shorelines before kayaking it. When he finally put his boat in the water above the Inferno gorge, he carried only food and a sleeping bag. Over the years he has ingratiated himself with the locals, in part by encouraging the kayakers he introduces to the river to bring supplies for the local school. A year ago he bought ten acres of river-front property. On it he is building a camp for the kayakers he hosts from around the world. His property sits at the confluence of Rio Azul and the Fu, and fronts the only sandy beach on the river. For now it has a toilet, a shower, and tent sites for ten. Someday Spee hopes to build a house high atop the nearby hill, overlooking the river and the craggy peaks beyond, Tres Monques (Three Monks).

Most who have kayaked the Fu, have done so with Spee's direction. Now he says he's happy rafters will be joining them each season. "I love to watch them flip," he laughs. As we load the big boats to continue downriver, Spee surfs into the big waves, showing off, twirling his wooden paddle above his head as the blue spray of the Fu sparkles in the sun around him.

• • •

After two days on the river we are all agreed on one thing: The Fu is barely raftable. If there was a waterfall anywhere along it, it could never be at-tempted. Ironically, too, if any section of it ran five miles to the east, through Argentina, tougher import and customs laws in that country would make it inaccessible.

Just past Zeda we scout a monstrous rapid dubbed Throne. Hanging from thin trees high above the river we hear the torrent before we can see it; a rock as big as a house (the Throne) splits the river. Fifteen-foot waves crash up the big rock, forcing torrents of water wide to the left and through a narrow chute to the right. The concern is that the power of the river would force our boats to the right, inevitably flipping them and sending all paddlers on a bad swim. We opt to push the boats through empty again.

From that point on we run every one of the rapids below, dozens of them, with names like Más or Menos, Big Stuffer (where one of the one-ton rafts was pushed upright, tossing out three paddlers) and Casa de

Piedra (which took two hours to scout). When we get to Terminator, the riverwide rapid that had eaten a bigger raft in 1985, we plot a course that sneaks along the rocks on its left side. If we had strayed into the middle, we'd have been chewed up and spit out. It is followed immediately by the Himalayas, the biggest waves on the river. There is no river like this in the world; it is runnable only because, by a fluke of nature, each rapid is followed by a sanctuary of calm water. If it was rapid upon rapid, it could not be rafted—because if a paddler fell out he would be carried on a miles-long swim through boulder-strewn waters. Gary Bolton, who has run rivers around the world, called the Fu, "the most beautiful, most difficult river in the world. "

Standing above Terminator, a Chilean guide who has attempted the river before, unsuccessfully, is equally respectful. "Sometimes the rapids keep coming and coming, as if the river was throwing them at us to discourage us, to get us out of here."

• • •

Past Casa de Piedra (House of Stone) the river is calm all the way to Lake Yelcho. After clearing this last rapid we lie back, floating casually downriver. A white-beaked condor, wings spread wide, soars high above. The hills are studded with burned-out skeletons of lenga trees, like white crosses in a cemetery. The tops of the mountain glaciers are ash covered, the result of the recent eruption of a nearby volcano. We pull the boats ashore in a meadow filled with cows and pigs. In the middle of the rocky field sits a blue-and-orange measuring gauge. Chile's powerful power company, Endesa, is monitoring the flow of the Futaleufu, with its eyes on someday damming it to produce hydroelectricity.

We spend five fast days on the Fu and feel fortunate to have seen it, and survived. But having made the first descent, I wonder about the motivation that prompts us to "take on" nature in such fashion.

Some people come to such rivers with the mind-set of "beating" the river, emerging "victorious" at river's end. But nature cannot be beaten. All the Lexitron, GoreTex, Lycra™, and polypropylene in the world can't protect man against the whims of nature. The only way we survive the Fu is by giving into it, by following a very thin line, propelled along by breaking waves, skirting holes the size of rail cars, cheating the most dangerous rapids. We survive the Fu. But beat it, conquer it, win? Never.

This is not a yahoo's river, nor one for the stereotypical river boatman, the classically handsome, bad-joke-telling, skirt-chasing guide who encourages paddle-slapping after each rapid. The Futaleufu is more a thinking man's adventure. We spend as much time contemplating the wonders of the shoreline as we do studying the magnificence of the river.

It is unlikely that swarms of rafters will ruin this place—it is too hard to reach, too formidable once found. The Endesa signs are far more ominous than the rapids.

THE COLCA PLUNGE

Arequipa, Peru, dazzles in the midday sunshine. The conical peak of the volcano El Misti, 5,822 meters high, rises above the city. To its left is the higher, more ragged Chachani (6,075 meters) and to the right the lower peak of Picchu Picchu. Isolated in a fertile valley tucked between desert and mountain, crowned by turquoise sky, Arequipa was a key stop on the cargo route linking the abundant silver mines of Bolivia to the coast. It is called the White City because it was built from the white rock that spewed from El Misti. It is also infamous for being the hometown of two of Peru's most notorious citizens: Novelist and failed presidential candidate Mario Vargas Llosa and lawyer-cum-terrorist leader Abimael Guzmán.

We are on the road to the Quecha village of Huambo, a journey of nearly nine hours. We crest forty-five hundred meters before dropping down toward the lip of the Colca Canyon, where we are headed. The dirt road that leads us winds through dusty plains, up hills, over two tall passes, and through chaparral. We glimpse traces of early settlers—partial stone walls, remnants of stone huts. It is completely arid and we wonder how anyone could have scratched a living out of this baked sand. We camp on a soccer field in the six-hundred-year-old town, next to a walled cemetery. I find a comfortable spot against the wall and am kept alert by a haven of thrushes rustling inside a thorn bush, the clip-clop of horses on dusty soil, the giggle of children as they peek around corners.

• • •

Like many South American countries long held captive by dictators or terrorists, Peru's myriad wildernesses have been kept somewhat secret. But it boasts a variety of very special places: Like the planet's driest desert, its highest navigable lake (Titicaca); the longest left break (at Puerto Chicama); the Amazon; Machu Picchu, the largest adobe city in the world; great climbing; and fishing comparable to New Zealand. In the world there are thirty-three different ecosystems—twenty-eight exist in Peru. It is unequaled in South America for its archeological wealth. Twice the size of Texas, it is home to more than twice the number of bird species in the entire North American continent. Peru also boasts the world's deepest canyon, which is what we've come to see, by raft and kayak.

The Andes mountains here are the most beautiful and accessible on the continent and the Cordillera Blanca its most famed range. Huascaran, at 6,768 meters above sea level is Peru's highest mountain and the highest mountain anywhere in the tropical world. Most of Peru's Andes lie between 3,000 and 4,000 meters and support half the country's population. It is a rugged and difficult landscape with jagged ranges separated by extremely deep and vertiginous canyons. There are few roads, thus few travelers. Admittedly, the country has some baggage. Like the occasional bomb. A few months before, in Lima, terrorists blew up a Kentucky Fried Chicken, simultaneously decapitating the statue of JFK in nearby Kennedy Park. In December, fifteen more bombs exploded in Lima, killing five, wounding fifty. Seven banks were robbed (Bottom Line: The terrorists are running out of money.) and Lima's electricity was knocked out on Christmas Day and New Year's Eve.

Guerrilla violence has cost Peru more than $23 billion and twenty-five lives over the past thirteen years. At the end of the eighties, tourism had dropped to 15 percent of what it once was, forcing hotels and other businesses to close. But relative peace has been secured since the 1992 capture of Guzmán, leader of the Shining Path. He is now serving life imprisonment and a kind of calm has transcended—today you are four times as likely to die in a traffic accident in Lima as in a terrorist attack. One result is that tourists are beginning to return to Peru.

Our hike down to the Río Colca—6,000 feet, from 10,600 to

4,600—departs from the dusty town square of Huambo. Burros loaded with personal bags, food, rafts, and kayaks lead us down a narrow dirt path through surprisingly green pastures. They are surrounded by stone walls to keep out roaming burros and goats and dogs and fed by an elaborate irrigation system that brings water down from twenty thousand feet by stone and cement viaducts.

In the near distance we can see striated hills, crisscrossed with scree slopes of sandy black gravel. Once we leave the terraced fields the path becomes increasingly littered with sharp rocks threatening to puncture rubber soles. Just sixteen degrees off the equator the sun is wilting. We drink water taken from the canals, heavily dosed with iodine. The funkiest-looking cacti I've ever seen—half dead from a distinct lack of fluids—line the path. The deeper we get, the windier it gets, threatening to blow the uncareful down steep slopes. Slip and by the time you reach the bottom you've bled to death from rolling over sharp rocks and cacti.

When the river finally appears in the distance, a murky brown ribbon running between a crack in the canyon wall, we can also make out a small village. Canco comprises just six families, living off the corn, wheat, and cane they grow. Even from up high we can tell the river is running high. Its chocolate-milk color is not a good sign either, implying recent rains. Though the river is not known for high volume, if it is much higher than the 400 cfs we expect, the big, technical rapids downriver will be hard or impossible to run.

When we reach the river it is quickly ascertained it is running at 1,000 cfs. The higher water fosters concern among the more experienced members of our crew. A long guide meeting begins. There are few options: We can wait here a couple of days and hope it drops; we can hike back to Huambo; we can set out and pray it doesn't get any higher. None is particularly attractive. All are set against the backdrop that once we set off into the canyon, for forty miles there is no way out but downriver.

I sit in the shade of a ten-thousand-foot-tall cliff and write, listening to the quiet rush of the muddy river and watching a trio of Peruvian fisherman cast their nets. Standing waist deep in the river, every ten minutes a net is swept downstream by the river's swift, unpredictable power.

Across the river to my right is a tall scree slope of black-and-tan gravel. I'm surprised it hasn't slid and filled in the river. To my left tall tan hills seared by V-shaped striations are stacked higher and higher until I can no longer see their peaks. Around the bend are active volcanoes, Coropuna (6,425 meters) and Ampato (6,310 meters) and the Chili Range, featuring the 5,597-meters-high Mismi. Giant saguaros and brush cling desperately to the sides of the canyon and strange flora flourish in the spots free from lava and rich in volcanic ash. Huge rocks balance precariously over the river, like enchanted castles.

The 236-mile-long river begins at 4,500 meters and drops to the Pacific. Its headwaters are formed by a fan of tributaries that spread in an arc for more than sixty kilometers over the mountain range. A pair of streams flowing from the Soracancha, Irachoqui (4,600 meters) and Antajahua (4,780 meters), initiates the river.

For experienced river runners the Colca is regarded as a very inaccessible and technical river, marked by sharp, undercut rocks. You do not want to fall out of the boat. What makes the river truly special are the imposing walls. At points the river narrows to ten feet wide, with a vertical wall rising four thousand meters on one side, three thousand on the other.

This night the sun sets at 6:30 and most of us are asleep by seven. The melodramatic last words of the night are uttered by Duillio Vellutino, a young Peruvian kayaker who has been on the Colca more than anyone. "You haven't seen anything yet," he says, pointing downriver. "The Colca lives down there."

When we wake, the river is still muddy and high and fast. At 800 cfs it is twice what it was a week before. The boatmen put on confident faces, but I know they are nervous. Once we leave this first camp the only way out is down. Climbing out of the canyon, over ten-thousand-foot mountains of crumbling stone, then walking across god knows how many miles of desert would take tremendous endurance. Few of us are anxious to be so tested.

We take off, four boats and three kayaks, at ten o'clock. Already there is a strong wind in our face. By noon it will be so strong we will be forced to quit. This establishes our pattern for the week-long trip—on the river by 6:30, in part to beat the wind and also to escape the insidious, invasive, mind-fusing bugs.

• • •

The first rapids are short, laden with rocks hidden just beneath the surface, obstacles not even the best river readers can predict. They grab at the boats, stall them, tossing paddlers forward and boats off course and into trouble. These are particularly tough conditions, requiring tight, specific maneuvers—which are repeatedly foiled by unseen, underwater boulders and "river snakes."

The day began with a hike to Pope John Paul II Falls, a torrential spill of roaring brown muck. Here the river is split by a monstrous rock, three stories tall. The left side of the river cuts hard around the center rock, then disappears under a rock ledge emerging in a powerful jet and joining its other half now pouring over a sixty-foot drop. Where they meet is a tumult of pounding, spraying, brown backwash. The sound is like a crashing freight train. Duillio climbs down to the edge, sits cross-legged, and offers a silent prayer. I suppose he is asking for a safe journey. This is a trick no doubt picked up from the Polish team who were the first to run the river, in 1981, and named the spot. I follow his example, sending my own best wishes to "Apu," the god the local Indians regard as supreme being and creator of water.

Our second day on the river would be our longest. At day's end, trip leader Mark Kocina pronounced it the greatest rafting day in Colca history. I prefer to call it Joe's Day, in honor of the eternally sunny Joe Dengler, whose day it certainly was not.

His adventures began—following a warm-up tumble over a string of Class IIIs and IVs—with a very, very technical Class V. (Class VIs are waterfalls.) Two big drops through a narrow channel, featuring two big holes and capped by an overwhelming hard left turn that threatened to slice—or decapitate—bodies on the left, or right, of the boat depending how the boat emerged from the last hole—forward, backward, or tea-kettled (upside down). If the boat went upside down, swimmers would be tossed into a swirling miasma of undercuts and life-sucking holes.

Joe—at twenty-seven, the youngest of the four guides, and the most eager—"volunteered" his boat to make a test run. The four-man, self-bailing boat nearly sank as it turned around and submerged out of control before being pushed violently out of the channel.

Mark—never one to be upstaged—went next, suffering similar if different results. All paddlers stayed in the boat, but barely. After watching the near calamities of the first two, the other boats decided it wasn't worth the potential swim and were carried over the flats and dumped back in the river below the rapid.

Joe's day took a turn for the worse around the next bend. We came upon him and his three paddlers stuck in an unenviable position—standing on the pinnacle of a small rock, midriver, their one-thousand-pound rubber boat having completely disappeared beneath the surface, wrapped around the rock they were standing on. Only a glimmer of yellow just below the surface told us they hadn't lost the boat completely. Apparently they had tried to run left of the barely exposed rock, been pushed right by the powerful river, and were now in a tough spot.

Dispatching his mates, actually pushing them gently into the rapids below from which they could easily swim ashore, Joe stayed tiptoe on the rock as throw lines were tied together and a human chain assembled onshore. With one end attached to a D-ring on the boat's bow, the onshore pullers strained on the rope. As they leaned back, pulling against the push of the river, the tip of the boat came slowly, slowly to the surface and the same power that imprisoned it pushed the boat free. Joe hopped on, bronco style, slightly embarrassed by the miscue and happy that the only damage appeared to be a repairable tear in the bottom of the rubber boat.

Unfortunately, in the very next Class IV rapid, the back of his boat hit a rock and flipped Captain Joe backward from his position on the rear pontoon. He was underwater for just a second before popping up, one hand grasping for and grabbing hold of the black safety rope ringing the raft. In the next second he'd pulled himself with one arm back into the boat and was upright, paddle in hand, wiping muddy water from his eyes, ready for the next rapid.

As if that wasn't enough punishment to his guide-pride for one day, late in the afternoon as we sat onshore his empty boat worked its way free from the shore and ghosted downriver. As it drifted past we laughed harder than we had all day. Joe sprinted for the nearest kayak and headed off in pursuit.

Over the fire that night the joke was that the next morning Joe was going to show up at his boat to discover that his crew had jumped ship, reassigning themselves to other boats.

"It was not my day," admitted Joe.

There is controversy over whether or not this is the world's deepest canyon. Most guide books avoid the controversy by calling it one of the world's deepest canyons. Its closest rival may be the Brahmaputra.

What is irrefutable is that the canyon cuts 10,607 feet into the earth's crust, twice as deep as the Grand Canyon. In many ways it is an ongoing geological experiment begun ten thousand years before with the eruption of a volcano near present-day Arequipa, an explosion that threw into the air a million tons of rock, dust, and lava, and subsequently covered the riverbed. Slowly, the river, undaunted, began to break up the thick rock layer and push toward the Pacific. The base of rocks is more than five hundred million years old. Outcroppings are covered by thin layers of calcereous and sandy material. On both sides of the steep slopes are beautiful subvertical stratifications—sandstone, limestone, slates, and quartzite alternating in the almost vertical scarps. Everything is covered with thick volcanic layers.

The valley was a surprisingly productive farming area even before the Incas claimed it. During the Incan Empire the Colca Valley was vital, laced with a sophisticated network of irrigation channels. We can still make out remnants of steep stairways cut into the bare rock walls. When the Spanish reached the valley they found terraced fields and thriving herds of llamas and alpacas. When the canyon became part of the route linking the silver mines of Bolivia to the coast, the farmers were snatched from their homes and forced to work in the mines. When the railroad reached Arequipa, the Colca Valley was forgotten.

Until the 1970s. That's when the Colca was opened up, due to a massive irrigation project intended to service the barren Majes Valley on the far side of the mountains. The Majes is one of the driest deserts in the world; the project brought it water. That necessitated constructing huge dams across the Apurimac (the source of the Amazon River) and Colca Rivers and building more than one hundred kilometers of tunnels, four hundred kilometers of roads, and forty kilometers of canals. The $700 million power plant generates 650,000 kw of electrical energy and waters sixty thousand hectares.

One benefit of the Majes project is thanks to the roads archeologists are just starting to dig into a vast number of ruins previously inaccessible. They suspect that the local Collaguas reached a level of sophistication comparable to the Incas.

The incredible geology continues to floor us. It is four in the afternoon and we're camped beneath a football-field-sized overhang across from Condor Falls. On the wall across the river are the colors tan, green, gray, brown, and black. Textures run from smooth overhangs worn down from wind and water to jagged sharp outcroppings, to tall spires to intermittent scree slopes. Interrupting are the stains of sulphuric drippings of springs hidden deep inside the walls. The five-hundred-foot-tall bridal veil falls—dubbed Condor Falls for the nests at its pinnacle—is one of the canyon's most dramatic sights, tumbling down in three distinct sweeps.

The tumble starts seemingly as mist, flowing through a W-shaped slot, filtered by tall grasses. It sprays fifty feet across before rejoining in a single stream. Halfway down the wall it spurts again, misting over a flat of black rock and then pouring over a stairstep of smooth black, moss-covered rock. Its final drop is through a narrow slot onto stacked slabs of rock and over a boulder bed, and into the Colca. Blown by the steady breeze the last drop creates a perfect shower for six, which we take full, naked advantage of.

As we shower a shout of "Condor" goes up and we jump out and stare at the sky. We've sighted four already (as well as lots of osprey, and starlings), but each is an event; this one has a wingspan of more than ten feet.

The condor is known as "Lord and Master" of the Colca. The structure of the canyon creates perfect soaring thermals and has been named a national sanctuary for their conservation and protection. We watch from far below as they drift, flying without moving their wings, circling then disappearing over the next ridge. From here we can barely make out the nest constructed atop the steep, inaccessible rock but that's what keeps the big bird near. On day four we're drifting between rapids, studying the tall walls set right on top of us, when Duillio says, "Look, look how grow the river." He's pointing to a crevasse in the mud-colored walls, where—fifty feet up—is crammed a thick stack of uneven bamboo sticks and odds and ends of driftwood. When the Colca runs high and fast, starting in January, this river rises fifty to one hundred feet.

Today is most spectacular for the variety of shapes the rock takes. "A general havoc," is how Mark defines the geology we're seeing if not always understanding. Chocolate swirls, twists and turns, organ pipe, sawtooth, Devil's spins, Dinosaur spines, all split by slopes of scree as tall as ski hills, a geologist's wet dream. I never knew there were so many shades of brown.

Giant cracks are everywhere, created by the splitting, tearing, renting, stretching of the earth. It looks like the whole place could one day split wide open, swallowing itself, the entire canyon altered by a single shudder, a heavy downpour. I would not want to be around this place during a heavy rain or during an earthquake.

We've been on the river four days now and each day remark that what the Poles did in 1981—the first descent, with little knowledge of what lay around each turn, carrying too much gear, no maps, and rough-hewn river skills—was as brave as John Wesley Powell's first descent of the Colorado River.

At any point they could have rounded a bend and found themselves squeezed into a box canyon, with up the only way out. Soaring canyon walls and forbidding desert would have made escape impossible. Or they could have gone through a series of big rapids too big to slow down for and then been launched over a one-hundred-foot waterfall. Who knew?

The half dozen descents since have benefited from the maps made by the Poles. That hardly means the trip is a cinch, nor is it for everyone. Water could rise, big rapids could cut boat or man, undercuts could suck either down under, injured could not escape. Camps are small, bugs are fierce, light loads mean light food.

Today's rapids were fast, bumpy brown tongues lapping over steep drops, winding through gardens of big boulders. Midday we passed through a thin chasm that reduces the river to about eight feet wide—or about the width of the boats. We squeeze through by aiming straight for the slot, then lifting paddles out of the water and throwing all our weight toward the center. Beth Rypin's boat literally gets stuck between the opposing walls; she likes her boats hard and her heavily pumped Princess was just a couple inches too fat to fit without some wrestling.

Camp is under the shade of a thorny tamarack tree and the bugs are at their worst. Thankfully, they too go to sleep when the sun goes down.

During the night an ominous rock slide on the far side of the river wakes the whole camp. Everyone bolts up. It lasts a minute, a long time in an otherwise silent night. Sparks light up the dark as a crescendo of rocks slide into the river. Those sleeping nearest the water move higher.

The intrusion was perhaps made more ominous because in a few hours we were to meet the biggest rapid of the trip. Known as Reparez (named by the Poles for Peruvian geologist Gonzalo de Reparez, who mapped much of the canyon), we'd been mentally preparing for it all trip.

Just above Reparez we pull the boats out of the water and scout. After an hour of pondering, here's the course we chose: After squeezing through a narrow slot, which dropped four feet, we needed to paddle hard to an eddy in order to line up for the next slot/drop. From there we would paddle hard to river left, push the boat over a short, unrunnable drop, and then back paddle like madmen—just to reach a point from which we could properly address Reparez.

Mark's boat doesn't back paddle fast enough and slams into the biggest rock, throwing everyone out of boat. Tyna comes up gasping for air; Rod bumps up under the boat several times before emerging. Next up, Beth's boat doesn't quite make the upstream ferry and gets hung up on a big underwater rock. For fifteen minutes they rock madly, attempting to dislodge it. Finally, with the help of an onshore throw rope and tug, they're off and safely through the meat of the rapid.

Our four-man crew is next and, thankfully, we go through without incident. When Captain Steve Jones shouts "Go, go, go," we paddle furiously upstream, positioning the boat to be swept through the tight channel. We drop hard left, then hard right, between big rocks before exiting over a third steep, ten-foot drop.

Reparez is followed by a night at a camp we call Suicide. The decision to sleep there was perhaps the most foolish/dangerous move of the trip. As we made camp, clouds were gathering, rain was threatening. The walls around us were all steep; the river just below was a horrendous, un-runnable mishmash of house-size rocks. If the rain had come, if the river had risen or flash flooded, we'd have been finished. Up would have been the only way out and few of us—in bare feet and shorts—would have had been able to climb to safety.

Thankfully the rains stayed away and the next morning, our last on the river, dawned bright and blue. After a smoothly organized, two-and-a-half-hour portage through Poles Canyon we ran the last big rapid on the river (which *National Geographic* had dubbed "death-defying," but which we found highly doable). It necessitated tipping the loaded rafts onto one side in order to squeeze them through a narrow slot, then poising atop a rock before plunging into the rapid. Once in we threw all our weight to the left, then to the right, then left again, then put paddles out over the bow to pull the boat over the six-foot drop. We did it with just three men in the boat, one of whom weighed one hundred pounds dripping wet.

The rest of the day to the takeout was spent "reading and running," bumping over long trains of shallow boulder gardens. Fun, but jarring. When we cleared the last canyon wall, grassy plains spread out before us in tableau, like a soft water color. There were some whoops of joy, but most were quiet, tired, reverential.

The next morning it felt odd to wake beneath open skies. For a week the view above had been limited to a sliver of blue, just a slash above the tall canyon walls. The ability to roll your head from side-to-side and see blue sky for one hundred eighty degrees—as well as the dusty panorama of the mountains we'd left behind—seemed both luxuriant and unreal. We'd grown used to the confines. The closeness of the canyon had enveloped us, held us, and then kissed us out safely at the bottom. We felt fortunate for many reasons, but mostly just to have seen and felt this most inaccessible place.

The day after we left the Colca Canyon a helicopter buzzed high overhead. Later we heard it carried Peru's president, Alberto Fujimoro, on his first fly-over of the region. Afterward he told a newspaper that he'd seen rafts on the river and hoped he could encourage more tourism in the canyon and the south of Peru.

THIRTEEN THINGS CUBANS
LOVE ABOUT CUBA

The night sky over Havana—as seen from the rooftop of the Hotel Ambos Mundos—lights up like the Fourth of July, thanks to a midsummer night's storm. The red-tile roof of the former governor's house, the white dome of the capitol, and El Morro, the fortress the Spanish built to protect their provincial city, are silhouetted with each crack of lightning.

I watch the storm alone except for the wait staff of two, in white jackets and black tie, smoking cigarettes, waiting for their shift to end. Their flicked cigarette ashes over the balcony threaten to blow into the open window of the room just below where Hemingway lived for ten years and wrote *For Whom the Bell Tolls*.

Halfway around the world the night skies are being lit up by B-52 bombings and scud missiles; Jorge and Pablo are curious about the United States, post 9/11. I respond as best I can—"It's a new world, isn't it?"—but then push my own question on them: What is that Cubans like most about Cuba?

Given the continuing standoff and embargo that separates the United States and Cuba, things here could be better: The average monthly wage is less than $10. Cuba's once-vaunted health care and public service systems are breaking down. Food is short. Bellmen at tourist hotels earn far more than doctors. It would be easy to surmise that Cubans are unhappy with their place. Instead, while many are angry about the status quo, most look past it day by day, if for no other reason than they must, in order to survive.

Jorge is the first to answer my question, with a smile, looking out over rain-soaked Havana. "What do Cubans like about Cuba? I'll tell you, my friend, the biggest secret in Cuba is that we are most proud of simply surviving what we call 'the struggle'."

MUSIC

Even the morning sounds of Havana have a rhythm. Outside my window a street sweeper jangles a chain against his thigh as he works. A window washer down the block whistles a salsa beat. And out the window of a tiny apartment comes the tinkle of a prerecorded piano, the ensemble making for a perfect if accidental sunrise orchestra.

It is not a cliché, no stereotype: Music is everywhere in Cuba.

Venture just a couple blocks south of the heavily-touristed barrio of Havana Viejo (Old Havana) and the noontime streets are packed with students in white shirts and maroon kerchiefs (Fidel's Young Pioneers) and construction workers laboring on the interminable renovations. Taxi drivers sing a cappella, waiting for their next fare. Old men astride motos with sidecars smoke cigars and snap their fingers to music drifting down from an open window above.

At La Dichosa, on the corner of Obsipo and Compustela, the band is called simply Quinteto. A narrow metal grate allows streetside voyeurs and fans to watch the music without entering. The fivesome are four men in their late thirties, plus a long-legged, pencil-thin female flautist. The front man wears an untucked red polo shirt over jeans and a pot belly, a yellow ball cap, and giant smile. She—Paula—is in a white Macumba T-shirt and white lace miniskirt, attracting generous stares from passing men.

School kids press against the grate. A tiny black girl with colorful ribbons in her hair dances joyously with an all-blonde classmate, spinning and hooking to "Chan, Chan" (a tune made famous to gringos worldwide thanks to the success of *Buena Vista Social Club.*) Old women, young girls, office guys, all shaking hips, smiling, eyes atwinkle on a crowded city street corner midday on a Tuesday.

The band's leader, with the red shirt, is named Enrique. I buy him a beer and talk music. "Look, we all know it is a very poor country. I am a college professor who must play music for a living because the money is better. Music is the one thing that makes us all—all—happy. It is cheap to produce, reaches many people and puts a smile on their face.

"Did you see those kids dancing outside the door, the school kids in uniforms? That is our future, man. Do they look miserable? No, of course not, they're kids. They are not desperate. Not yet. They couldn't be happier. Why? The music. I promise you, it's the thing that holds this country together."

Quinteto is just one of dozens of such bands plying the bars and restaurants of Havana, from noon until long into the night. Across the street from the Ambos Mundos, six nights a week, it's the BVSC's figurative cousin, Son al Son.

The band's lead singer is eighty-three; the average age of the ten-piece orchestra is over seventy. Its director, the youngest at fifty-five. Their manager, a tall, clean-domed black man named Pablo, says they would love to play Carnegie Hall one day. But for now they're happy to have a six-night-a-week gig and most-often packed houses.

Over the band, Pablo shouts into my ear. "We don't have so many things to export to the world, you know. We feel our music is one of our most important—most valuable—exports. Something the world looks to Cuba for."

SAFETY

On a hot summer day I take a taxi from downtown Havana twenty minutes to the pristine beach town of Megano, to visit friends. Whenever I see these most beautiful beaches I imagine what they might be like—will be like?—if/when Americans can fly here in an hour or so, from Miami—or Toledo, Baltimore, Denver. Will that be a better thing? I'm not sure.

My driver has a classic Cubano experience. A mechanical engineer, he quit his factory job ten years ago to drive a taxi "because there's more opportunity."

"I would love to go back to work at the metal-making plant, but the salary is too low—$10 a month." He is thirty-eight years old, born and raised in Havana. "Do you know Cuba's biggest import today? More than sugarcane or cigars? Doctors. I mean, why train to be an engineer when you see engineers driving taxis because the pay is better."

Figuring that he sees a lot of Havana, in all contexts, I ask what it is he likes most about Cuba. "Safety. That is the best thing about Havana," he says, "You can go anywhere, almost, in the city at any time of night, and feel safe, no problem."

In Megano I get a similar response. My friend Paul—a Canadian married to a Russian, but living full-time outside Havana—talks about the remaining "innocence" of the country, especially in the countryside. Beyond Havana "it is truly a paradise," he says. From his patio we can see the aquamarine sea pounding onto a long, unadulterated sand beach.

Up the street from his house is a dormitory compound where Cuba's "special police" are trained. Specifically, their charge is to protect the tourist trade—now Cuba's biggest economy—by watching the street corners and trying to slow sales in illegal cigars, prostitutes, dollars. As proof of their importance, these black-bereted cops are paid $45 a month—four and a half times the average state wage and more than state-paid doctors.

Paul agrees that safety is a sure thing here.

"I live near a hospital and I see nurses and woman workers cutting through heavily overgrown fields late at night, at five in the morning, without any concern about personal safety. It's just something you don't think about here. You simply feel safe."

WOMEN . . . IN LYCRA

"Do you see that?" my walking companion asks out loud. I'm on the Malecón, the sea surf pounding over the breakwater and a young *jintero*—hustler—has picked me up, on the pretense of practicing his English. He's pointing to a trio of women walking several steps ahead of us. Each is clad in their own version of Saran Wrap-like Lycra—the favored material of women across the island nation—in myriad colors and patterns. "That is what I like most about Cuba," he laughs. "No question, without second, first and foremost. A beautiful woman wrapped in super tight clothes. What, my friend, could be better? By the way, would you like to meet one of those girls? That can be arranged."

RACIAL DIVERSITY

Quick—try to describe what a Cuban looks like. You might come up with swarthy, dark-skinned, black, white, brown, graying, thick, thin, tall, and slender, like butter or molasses or honey. But there is no correct response. Cuba is truly a melting pot—50 percent of all marriages are now biracial—much different from the States, where our diverse populations still tend to stick mostly to their own kind.

I'm in a different Havana nightspot—it's easy to find a new one, every night—listening to yet another great Cuban septet wailing. Looking around the room I see men and women of every age, many races, completely commingled. At the street level there is much more acceptance here of skin color. (Admittedly there is a glass ceiling in the government, which people of color tend to bump up against.)

Jorge is tall, his head razor-shaved and blacker than midnight. He is handsome and wearing wire-rimmed glasses and a perfectly pressed navy shirt, sensible since his day job is in a laundry. Nightfall finds him hustling for tourist tips simply by sitting with them, speaking in near-perfect English, about Cuba.

I buy him a beer and a man approaches, fair-skinned, with a pencil-thin mustache and perfectly pointed sideburns. The pair embraces, strongly, smiling.

Introducing me, Jorge says, "He looks like some kind of hit man out of a bad movie, doesn't he? But he's not. He's my first cousin."

"People are always asking me—Hey, how'd you get a Puerto Rican cousin? I say, man, he's not PR, he's as Cubano as you get. When I look around Havana, man, I simply don't see color."

HITCHHIKING

Renting a car in Cuba is as simple as checking into a hotel. Passport, $200 deposit, and I have the keys to a perfectly fine Toyota. Within minutes I'm into the tunnel that leads out of Havana, headed toward A-1, the country's main west-east highway, and the coastal town of Trinidad.

Except that one thing Castro's Third Way has not provided for are road signs. For fifteen minutes I'm going round and round and round a roundabout, guessing badly each time as to which spoke to choose.

Pulling to the side, I ask the counsel of a seventy-three-year-old man standing with his hands in his pockets. He's just out of the hospital and with nothing better to do offers to show me a shortcut to the highway. The twenty-five-kilometer back road leaves him far from home, but for a $10 tip he couldn't be happier. Smiling, he says he's got all week to get back home.

My next big surprise is the hundreds of hitchhikers crowding every exit along the six-lane highway. They put out their thumb—or hold out peso bills—for simple and obvious reasons: Owning a car and buying fuel are much too expensive enterprises for the average Cuban. Out of a sense of curiosity—and guilt (what I'm paying for my rental car for three days is the equivalent of two year's earnings for most of these folks) I pack them in to my little four-door.

A trio of army men in green uniforms who can't even afford the bus/trucks that are the sole public transport working the highway. They are curious about America's new war. A twentysomething girl with wild black curls, black miniskirt, and pink hi-top sneakers on her way to see her boyfriend. She admits her get-up doesn't hurt her getting rides over the competition. A conservative trio of working women—bank attendant, nurse, teacher—who squeeze into my tight front seat since the back is filled with uniformed school kids. A girl with a distinct limp and sparkles on her just-made-up skin. An older woman whose orange hair perfectly matches her orange handbag and somehow doesn't crack a smile though nearly sitting on my lap for thirty minutes. To a one, they say hitchhiking is generally good for socializing except, of course, when it's raining.

All seem happy for the lift until the last fellow I pick up, just before pulling off the highway and heading down the narrow road that leads through Cienfuegos toward Trinidad. He is tall, easily six foot three, sweating from a long day in the fields, wearing an unsheathed machete on his belt, carrying an empty gallon jar for water. He's on his way home is all I can get out of him.

COWBOYS . . . & MORE MUSIC

Just shy of Trinidad, surrounded now by tall green fields of cane and dark, humid skies, I pull off A-1 and quickly plunge deep into Cuba's cowboy culture.

The geography has changed, from the green flatlands leading out of Havana to low, tree-covered hills laden with farms—beans, wheat, tobacco, sugarcane—and spiked by palm trees. Drying grains are spread along the roadside. Cowboys on horses ride out of the fields astride strong black horses. They wear straw and leather chaps over their jeans. Shirts are open, machetes flapping against their thighs. Saddlebags filled with greens from the fields. Some are picking up kids from the school bus; others stop at neighbors' doors for an end-of-day chat.

I pass a bicyclist with a passenger riding on the back fender. He carries a guitar, which he strums as his friend pedals. I'd seen the same thing earlier in the day, substituting a boom box for the guitar. Music is literally everywhere.

I pull into a service station. A fading Lada station wagon has its back lid open, baring a sound system more powerful than a Paris disco, pumping out . . . what else . . . Cuban disco music. It's so loud I'm concerned the station's underground tanks are at risk of exploding. A black girl in red Lycra shorts wiggles her hips next to the car, the look in her eyes daring anyone who passes to suggest she turn it down.

One thing about music here: It's not only Cuban music they like. During my first hour in Trinidad I make note of ministereos playing from behind most closed doors music ranging from Diana Ross and Barry White to Nirvana and Michael Jackson. (Reminding me of a hustler I'd met in Havana who told me the saddest days of his life were when Tupac and the Notorious BIG were killed in the American hip-hop gang wars.)

TRINIDAD

Early morning, on the steps of the Casa de la Music, a woman sweeps the thick cobblestone steps, shaking her hips in the early morning heat, in rhythm with the practice session going on under a nearby veranda.

Trinidad's buildings, painted in every shade of ocher, blue, green, and pink, glow against the verdant backdrop of the Sierra del Escambray. It is an elegant city, which grew extremely prosperous in the nineteenth-century sugar boom but was then hit hard by competition from the sugar beet. Today its well-preserved fine palaces and family mansions illustrate a gentle economic decline that lasted more than a century, monuments to the town's past glory.

Isabelle works as a guide at the Museo Romántico, perhaps the most insightful of all the museums in town—and there are more museums per capita in Trinidad than anywhere else in Cuba. Wearing a perfectly ironed green suit and cooling herself with a hand fan she walks me through the three-story house overlooking the main plaza.

Originally known as the Palacio Brunet, it is the most eloquent expression of Trinidad's golden era. From the twenty-three-foot-tall first-floor gallery to the kitchen outlined in delft tiles and the luxurious drawing room with its marble floors, cedar ceiling, neoclassical paintings, and crystal chandeliers, it is evidence of a rich, rich life. The mansion was abandoned as a family home in the nineteenth century when the count in charge put his energy into building an elaborate theater (for an actress he quite admired) and left the home to fall to ruin in the early twentieth century.

Isabelle and I stop at the open windows on the third floor and gaze over the same vista—we can see all the way to the white sand beaches—that initially drew the sugar growers to this place.

She sums up what Cubans like about Trinidad: "It reminds us that good times—truly good times—can exist here. It's just a matter of timing. It is bad timing that we are living during the low ebb of a cycle. We all, in our hearts, hope that cycle will turn up again, soon."

CIGARS

On virtually every street corner in Trinidad—as in Havana, Cienfuegos, Vinales, Santiago—I am offered a chance to buy black-market cigars. Though illegal since the government controls all pricing and sales of the country's lucrative tobacco industry, some of the cigars offered by street corner vendors are legit. Workers in the cigar factories, for example, are allowed to take two, three, four cigars a day home with them. Many sell them rather than smoke them. Other street wares being proffered are nothing more than rolled banana leaves. Caveat emptor!

During my visits to Cuba I have passed up a thousand such whispered come-ons and do so again when the wizened old man on one street whispers, "Cigaro? Cigaro?" It's not until I pass him by that he nearly shouts—"Oy, gringo, I have the best cigars for you!"—that I can't help but turn around. His smile, and directness, is hard to pass by.

Looking up and down the street for the vice cops, he pulls me quickly off the street and inside his narrow home. His thirty-year-old son watches a midday game show on television, waving hello without turning his head. It is so humid I break into a sweat as soon as I stop moving, seeking freshness under the whirring ceiling fan.

From atop the electric meter he pulls a round bundle of twenty-five hand-rolled, unlabeled cigars. He claims they are Romeo y Julietas, which are made in a factory just down the street. Moist and undoubtedly fresh, before I can yes or no he bites the tip off one and lights up, offering it to me with a wave of his hand. It may be the best cigar I've ever tasted; wrapping the bundle in old pages of *Granma* he asks for $4. When I give him $5 and explain the change is for him, he is ecstatic. Reaching again to the top of the meter he pulls down a bundle of petite cigars. "For the ladies?" he poses.

Opening the door to the street he again looks up and down the street before whispering, "Adios, gringo, buen viaje!"

THE BEACH

Five miles from the car-less, cobblestone streets of Trinidad are two side-by-side beaches. Playa Ancun—long, sandy—boasts a big, industrial hotel catering to European tourists. But if you hang a right before arriving there you end up in Playa la Boca, where the locals hang out. Craggy, black, volcanic rock forms a twisting shoreline replete with nooks and crannies, perfect for sitting and watching the surf crash, or used as diving boards into the deeper pockets. It's easy to forget when you're in the middle of Cuba's big cities that you are on one of the biggest—most varied, potentially most beautiful—beach-lined islands in the Caribbean.

As the sun falls, the beach begins to fill with locals. They come for the same reasons I would if this were my hometown—to meet, relax, have a beer, play volleyball in the shallows, walk their dogs, linger with their kids as the sun sets.

I take a seat in a low plastic chair under a *palapa* and work my feet deep into the sand. To the south are rolling green hills, in the sky to the west massive, growing cumulus. Small white waves are breaking on the rocks across the small bay; a lone fisherman toils in a small rowboat. An old man approaches, selling paper cones of sugar and coconut cakes.

I make small talk with a trio of military guys who've come to the nearby bar to negotiate for cheap bottles of rum. A laugh-filled argument breaks out over the best thing about the beach.

"It's to be close to the nature," poses the first.

"Yes, that is true," contends the second, "but I think the best thing is to dive into the sea, to wash away the day, to get rid of your troubles, even if it lasts only a few minutes."

"You are both *loco*," insists the third, turning his head toward the beach. "It is for the *chicas*. And don't try and tell me another word."

A CLOSE SHAVE

I arrive at the house/workplace of Orestes at lunchtime and find him counting his week's earnings, a big pile of peso notes piled on the table in front of him. He had been recommended as the best barber in Trinidad—perhaps in all of Cuba—by my *National Geographic* friend, photographer David Allen Harvey. It took questioning a few neighbors to pin down his house—there is no barber's pole out front—and when I knock he opens the door in his T-shirt.

His workroom sits behind an orange curtain off the living room of his elegant colonial home. His father was a custom's agent, until the revolution, when that job became unnecessary. Orestes was eighteen when "the bearded one" took power; Trinidad was an interesting place from which to watch the country change, he explains. It was the last counterrevolutionary part of Cuba, the spot from which the Americans based their last-ditch efforts to help keep Castro from gaining power.

I throw down a cup of sugary coffee and climb into Orestes' aged, U.S.-made barber's chair. His strong hands apply menthol rub to open up the pores, followed by a thick layer of foam shaving cream. He presses and pulls and flattens my skin to skillfully scrape a two-day growth down past the nub. I can feel the long, smooth scrapes of his ultrasharp blade up my neck. I lie back, hands neatly folded, eyes closed as long scissors skillfully reach into my nostrils and ears. Finished, he towels me off, and applies another layer of stinging menthol. When I put my hands to my face it's like touching the proverbial baby's bottom.

"I haven't been this clean since . . . well . . . maybe never," I propose.

"You should do this at least once every two weeks," he says.

"How often do Cubans get a shave?"

"Whenever they can."

Before I leave he throws open the heavy wooden shutters allowing afternoon light into his workplace and asks me to take his photo.

COMMUNITY

Each September 28 the national Committee for the Defense of the Revolution throws a nationwide party. One big, giant block party, celebrated on every corner of the country. The idea originated with Castro, in the year after the successful overthrow of Batista in 1959, as a once-a-year way to remind neighbors to be, well, neighborly.

I happen to be on the cobblestone streets of Trinidad as the party takes shape, but the exact same thing is happening on every street across the country. Block parties—fiestas de la cuadre. Beginning at 5 p.m. open wood fires are built beneath giant blackened steel pots filled with chicken or beef stew, more than enough to feed the entire block. Townwide there's been a day-long run on bottles of Havana Club rum. Similarly a line a block long stretches out of the bakery where traditional, heavily frosted cakes are made. Moms and kids fashion stars cut from aluminum beer cans and string them along with multicolored balloons and miniature Cuban flags across the street.

Everything is targeted for 10:30 p.m., when the stews are judged ready and the dancing begins. Kids are allowed to stay up and even the oldest folks in town bring their rockers out onto the street for the night (though most are admittedly asleep by the time the fun begins.)

I find myself, an obvious outsider, moving from party to party, tasting stews, rums, punches, and cake—enough cake to sink a rowboat and enough rum to allow me to argue, gently, with the old Communists who've hung effigies of Misters Clinton and Bush outside their doors. The rum allows me to dance, too, with literally a hundred different women (most of them my mother's age), all to the delight of the by-now quite drunken men.

CLASSIC CARS

To reach Vinales—the lush, green capital of farm country west of Havana—I opt for the most popular ride in Cuba, a 1951, two-toned green Chevrolet with horsehair-tufted red-vinyl interior.

I woke to a monstrous fall rainstorm—this is a month before the heart of hurricane season—and floods inundating Havana's streets. It is a tempting day to stay in bed and listen to the rain. But when I meet my driver—nicknamed Chino, for his slanted eyes—his enthusiasm is like a dose of strong caffeine. "The rain will go away soon, my friend," he said. "And the sky will be blue over Vinales."

Out on the road the still-flooding rain proves a minor challenge for his car since it leaks just a bit, through the floor, the trunk, the slightly cracked and taped windows. Whenever Chino nonchalantly "tests" the rain-soaked brakes of his lumbering old car by punching them to the floor he nearly sends us into a three-hundred-sixty-degree spin.

Before arriving in Cuba the first time, I thought these classic old American cars were a cliché, something found only in Havana, kept around to please tourist's cameras. In fact, they are everywhere, in every town, in various stages of repair, some hidden in falling shacks, most driven proudly around town. The most valuable job in all of Cuba may be the repairmen who keep the big beasts on the road.

Chino drives car #18, and works for the government-owned Gran Car Company, which keeps forty of these classics on the road. During his chauffeuring days Chino has escorted visiting business honchos in

Mercedes and Citroëns, but prefers the classics, in part because they attract a more varied clientele. Today he's simply happy to be driving again. For seven years during the nineties, with the end of the Cold War and the disappearance of most Russian investment in Cuba, Chino had a variety of menial jobs—on a farm, in a bicycle factory—until he got a call from Gran Car.

Twenty miles from the turnoff to Vinales, the rains stop. "Los amigos," Chino shouts above the cassette of Cuban rock music, "Mira! El ciel es azul!" Look, the sky is blue!

What we discover under the now-blue sky is a phantasmagoric landscape, just ninety-three miles from Havana. Giant knolls—*mogotes*—tower over a serene vista of red soil patterned by the greens and browns of *bohios* and tobacco and corn. It is just one of the valleys in the Sierra de los Organos, so named by the sailors who glimpsed, from a distance, the organ-pipes of its hummocks. The strange mogotes form a vast karst terrain, the result of millions of years of erosion by underground streams.

Built on land devoted to cattle breeding since 1607, Vinales was founded in the nineteenth century as a result of the rapid expansion of tobacco farming. Today it is the heart of Cuba's cigar country.

THE RURAL LIFE & FAMILY

Well-connected friends had told me to seek out one Armando Fuentes when I arrived in Vinales. The largest landowner in the valley he was billed as a most generous, knowledgeable, and welcoming host. That at sixty-two he resembles Paul Newman made him hard to miss in this small agricultural town.

On a perfect blue-sky day we hire horses and wind our way through small farm fields, following a variety of muddy red-dirt trails that lead among the mogotes. We pass simple campesino homes; plank construction atop cement slabs, with corrugated metal roofs. We are surrounded by green and even the simplest home has a luxurious flower garden filled with impatiens and passion fruit. The fields are aplenty with avocados, sour tangerines, guava, yams, sweet potatoes, *caro,* and the king of all crops— tobacco. People are out, on Sunday afternoon, together, working, but at a leisurely pace, cleaning gardens with a machete, baking bread, sawing planks for a new house, grinding coffee for an afternoon pick-me-up.

After two hours in the saddle we arrive at the top of the hill, at the simple mud-walled house where Armando lives during the high season. Two of his boys have just arrived with a bull-drawn cart loaded with supplies—burlap sacks of corn, sections of corrugated metal, sacks of tobacco leaf, and bottles of rum.

His family settled this land in 1902 and even after the revolution—when the government took much of the country's private land—Armando was allowed to keep his. Smiling and red-cheeked, he is short, wearing a straw hat and an unbuttoned blue shirt, worn jeans, and beige rubber boots. His wife, Isabelle, the mother of his two sons, died four years ago. They'd been married forty years and before taking us on a walking tour of his land he brings out from inside the house a framed photo of his wife, which he hugs close to his chest.

Sitting on the porch—two gringos and eight Cubanos—Armando opens two bottles of rum, which are passed around as his farmhands roll cigars from a single leaf. Everything spread in front of us is owned by Armando. Though by far the wealthiest man in the valley, he doesn't gloat, nor want to talk about his mostly comfortable life. Instead, he turns the subject to family, which he regards his favorite thing about Cuba.

"Yesterday, today, tomorrow, that is what makes Cuba special," he says. "The fact that we are most happy surrounded by our family."

"I don't know if you have sensed it, but we are all one big family here. Take me. I have everything I want. A beautiful countryside all around. Good friends of all races. I have a beautiful family. What else does one man need?"

INSIDE GUATEMALA

Carlos and I are driving over a rough dirt road toward Sayaxche, a small village on the shores of the Rio de la Pasion, deep inside Guatemala's rain forest. It is early morning and we watch in silence the sunrise over the savannas littered with palm trees and the one-hundred-fifty- to two-hundred-foot-tall *ceibals,* the country's national tree. My companion—and guide—wears a gray-red-white striped shirt, quasi-matching pants, and Adidas. A rough tattoo (Isabella) is scratched onto one forearm. Educated in Belize, Carlos has lived and worked in Honduras, Salvador and Mexico. For the past five years he's worked as an expert guide to the astonishing ruins the Mayas inexplicably abandoned some one thousand years before.

At Sayaxche, wooden longboats, painted in fading blues, yellows, or-anges, and greens, troll the river. Sunday is shopping day and families come from three hours upriver by boat to shop for grain, rice, and vegetables. Women in clean dresses and rubber sandals carry empty bags up the gravel road that leads into town, past the brightly painted advertisements deco-rating the walls, promoting Crush, UniOil, and Texaco. Their men, in pol-ished cowboy boots and hats, head for the bars. I sit on the river's bank as Carlos negotiates for a boat. Small boys—barefoot, or wearing knee-high rubber boots—proffer colored ice from round, dirty Styrofoam coolers.

A thin old man in a straw hat steps next to me, cups his hands, and sips straight from the muddy river. Off a boat comes a fisherman, his striped shirt barely covering his belly, carrying a pair of sea turtles, one in his hand, one slung over his shoulder. Our craft—*The Marisol*—is twenty feet long, partially covered by a torn plastic tarp and powered by a fifteen-horsepower Mercury. We pull away from shore as the sky begins to cloud. As we push downriver we spot an occasional dugout pulled to the riverbank. Some are empty, others host a lone fisherman.

On shore people wash clothes and hang them to dry. Herds of small buffalo stand in clumps beneath willow trees. A flock of parrots whistles from tall ceibals; turacos dart back and forth across open meadows. There are alleged to be alligators in the river, but we don't see a one. The water is still and green, quiet but for the hum of the outboard. After a two-hour motor we pull ashore at an unmarked spot and head up a mosquito-heavy trail for the ruins known throughout Central America as "the Mayan Art Gallery."

It is a tough, short uphill climb to the major plaza. Orange caterpillars and red frogs crawl and dart across the path; columns of leaf-cutter ants carve their own trail, lugging leaves thrice their size—the equivalent of a human shouldering a grand piano. A solitary monkey watches from above, then soars, Tarzan-like, from vine to vine. A small national park, Ceibal boasts a circular temple, one-of-a-kind on the Ruta Maya that extended from Mexico to Honduras. First settled around 800 BC, the town of Ceibal grew to ten thousand by AD 830. It was one of seven ancient cities that formed an interlocking society around Lake Petexbatun and Rio de la Pasion, once a major Maya trade route for the shipment of quetzal feathers, chert tools, jaguar skins, jade cobbles, and fine pottery. Today the ruin's stelae—tall, story-telling tablets planted straight up in the ground—are among the finest and best preserved of all Maya sculptures. Ceibal was known for its ceramic makers and much of the ruin is still unexcavated. After an hour inspecting the park it begins to rain and we take refuge under a thatched roof hut in a clearing. The heavy, daily rain lasts just twenty minutes and is accompanied by loud thunder claps as it moves upriver. Back in the boat we pass extra-long dugouts loaded with the Sunday shoppers heading home. Unexpectedly we also pass a trio of brightly painted dugouts pulled to the shore and being loaded with freshly split wood. I am reminded of a story I'd heard just before arriving in Guatemala.

A year ago a high-ranking Guatemalan government environmentalist, three policeman, and a newspaper reporter stumbled upon an illegal logging camp and a dozen boats loaded with logs. The reporter photographed everything. That night the outsiders were greeted by a group of loggers and uniformed soldiers, who stripped them, beat them, took them to a military base, and beat them some more. This is the dilemma facing Guatemala today: On one hand it is pristine, historic, and safe; yet you can't get past the feeling that lurking just around the corner may lie uncertainty, corruption, and possibly a good beating.

• • •

Inevitably, visits to the Ohio-sized country begin in Guatemala City, where it is easy to feel like you never left New York City. Noontime crowds fill the Taco Bell on Avenida la Reforma and wolf down Taco Suaves and Nacho Supremes. The commercial strip—6th Avenue—resembles NYC's 14th Street: Everything—from fine china and steak knives to Whoppers and pizza slices—is "on sale." The narrow streets are thick with diesel exhaust and dust and people. The city is growing (already over two million, it is Central America's biggest) and tourism is booming; A half dozen new banks and another half dozen hotels are in midcompletion.

The National Plaza and Cathedral occupy the center of town; a shiny big Westin anchors the high-end district; burgeoning slums surround. Back in my room I turn on television to find forty stations. Yet for any similarities to the States, Guatemala is still definitely third world: Every door, from banks to shoe stores, is watched by machine-gun-armed private policeman. It is what lies beyond the limits of the sprawling city that draws tens of thousands of tourists each year. Guatemala is a compact, diverse landscape that ranges from active volcanoes to lowland jungles, rain forests to crystalline lakes. Renowned as the "Land of Eternal Spring," temperatures year-round average seventy-five degrees. In a day it is easy to climb from sea level to twelve thousand feet. There are more than three hundred species of birds; six hundred different kinds of orchids. But the true charm and beauty of Guatemala is its culture, evident from the steep hillsides planted with coffee to the ruins at Tikal. Indians—descendants of the Mayas—still represent the majority of the population; the rest are a blend of Indian and Spanish (Ladinos) and a very small number of blacks.

In Guatemala City I have breakfast with the editor of the weekly magazine *Critica*. He explains there are three segments of people living in Guatemala: A very few rich, some in the middle, and mostly poor. But the economy is improving and he offers an example from his own household. Five years ago he paid his maid $20 a month, today she makes $40. In fact, the average daily wage is $2.28—or less than $70 a month. After Haiti and Bolivia, Guatemala has the lowest "physical quality of life" in the hemisphere. The majority (67 percent) live in extreme poverty, 45 percent are illiterate, 66 percent lack access to health care.

The small country has a bloody reputation; after a spate of increased violence in the early 1980s tourists stayed away in droves. Guatemala's bloody reputation was well earned: Since 1950 more than four hundred peasant villages have been destroyed by the military; an estimated one hundred fifty thousand people killed, the vast majority of them Mayas. A greater number fled to Mexico or the United States. Even more abandoned their villages, language, and traditional costumes and moved to the city, to blend in. The targets have included tens of thousands: trade unionists, leftist political activists, students, teachers, peasant and human rights activists, and many suspected of being only sympathetic. Only in the past half dozen years has tourism come back. The election to president in 1990 of Jorge Serrano, with his claims to want to negotiate a conclusion to the bloody civil war, restored the country's inexpensive, majestic appeal. While Serrano's first years were marked by a reduction in violence, the office of the Human Rights Ombudsman continued to record "extra-judicial" killings of human-rights activists—mostly Indians in small towns.

Today the guerrilla forces, such as they are, number fewer than one thousand. Most are in hiding, deep in the jungles of the Peten. (Some are rumored to have fled to Mexico and are lending their fighting experience to the Zapistas in Chiapas.)

Trouble broke out most recently in Guatemala City last May when negotiations between the government and its foes broke down and President

Serrano dissolved the congress and supreme court in a coup d'état. Apparently the military did not support the coup, because within a month Serrano was in exile in Salvador and Ramiro de Leon Carpio, the former Human Rights Ombudsman, had been elected the new president. Apparently the more things change here, the more they stay the same. Yet it was a mix of dissatisfaction and hope that I heard from the Guatemalans I spoke with. On the bus from the airport, for example, I overheard a tour guide admit without provocation that "If it weren't for corruption, we would be in very good shape."

Later he insisted he was hopeful it would change, soon. "Just like the rain and winds that come in the afternoon to wash and blow away the smog, we could use a good storm to clean things out." As Maya expert Robert Wright reminds, there is an old Guatemalan saying: *Hay descontento general, pero no hay generales descontentos.* There's general discontent, but there are no discontent generals.

• • •

To really see the country you've got to hit the road. Rent a car, get on a bus, bring your bicycle, but somehow get on the Pan American Highway. From Guatemala City you climb quickly to six thousand feet and are immersed in cloud forest. From November to April there is little rain, but skies become hazy from the slash-and-burn fires in the countryside. The best sightseeing months may be from May to October, when frequent showers clean the air and turn the hillsides lush and green. The steep hillsides are planted with coffee, still reaped by hand, a holdover of the Mayas. The surrounding fields are laden with bananas, sugar, cotton, and cardamom. Flowers are one of the countries biggest exports; oil, recently found along the Mexican border, is expected to be another. Most of the rural population works in agriculture, some make tile and ceramics. Jade is prevalent, in a myriad of shades. Tourism recently displaced sugar as the country's second-leading commodity—after coffee.

With a friend, a veteran Guatemalan traveler, we head for Antigua. Once the country's capital city, it is today its mystical, magical heart. The drive takes just forty-five minutes. In Antigua the sing-song of Spanish floats from the centuries-old courtyards. Jacaranda and eucalyptus trees, figs, African tulips, and bougainvillea rise and crawl above the adobe walls, which are art pieces themselves, tinted in faded pastels of pink, blue, green, and white. The scent of wood smoke is everywhere. Looking up, the town is ringed by volcanoes—one still active—set against skies that are an eternal mixture of blue and clouds, rain and sun.

Antigua is a colonial city grown to be one of the most beautiful in Latin America. Originally known as Santiago de los Caballeros, it became the third capital of the New World, after Mexico City and Lima. In 1700 it had a population of seventy thousand, sixty cobbled streets, six thousand houses, eighteen convents, thirty-two churches. It weathered more than a dozen major earthquakes, not to mention volcanic eruptions and floods after its building in 1543, but was finally felled in 1773, when it was evacuated because of a particularly severe earthquake, and the capital was moved to Guatemala City. Parts of Antigua have never been rebuilt, making for part of its charm.

Its population of thirty thousand is part old world, part Soho. Ruins mix with hip retail shops, Indians sell their wares on street corners, expatriates live in $500,000 haciendas behind bougainvillea-lined walls. Its square is ringed by classic Spanish American baroque churches. The people are a blend of gringos-on-holiday, Mayas, and Latino businessmen. (Antigua is also home to more than thirty Spanish-language schools. Four hours of private tutoring a day costs about $50 a week and one guess is that twelve thousand a year come here to learn Spanish.) We shop at the town's two big markets and stay at the Casa Santo Domingo, a luxury hotel built among the ruins of a sixteenth-century monastery. The rooms are subtle and opulent, but a monkish ambience is definitely felt in the hallways, lit by candlelight, fountains filled with fresh bougainvillea petals. Early the next morning, driving out of Antigua we pass schoolkids on bikes and urban-gauchos on horseback. We stop at a corner vendor's and buy oranges peeled and sliced in half and layered with chili, pepper, and brown salt. Eaten like an apple, they are—despite all the incredible steaks and black bean soup I'd been eating since arriving—my first real Guatemalan taste adventure.

• • •

The rutted road that drops down into Chichicastenango is like a bobsled run, only dusty and corrugated. The town, founded by the Spanish in the early 1500s, is a riot of tiny cobblestoned streets. Stepping out of the car the overpowering aroma is of incense burned on the steps of the stately Church of Santo Tomás.

Chichicastenango boasts Guatemala's biggest open market, rivaled in all of Latin America by only those in Oaxaca, Mexico, and Otavalo, Ecuador. For more than seven hundred years this location has been the center of trading between Indians, then Indians and the Spanish. If you were to come direct, it is ninety miles (two and a half hours) west of Guatemala City. Markets are on Thursdays and Sundays and the town begins to fill up—with vendors and shoppers—the afternoon before.

For such a tiny place, there are two very good hotels, the Santo Tomás and Mayan Inn. Each boasts colorfully clad room-boys, marimba bands, and colorful parrots in central gardens. We opt for the Mayan Inn—where there are no locks on the big wooden doors and the focus of each of the twenty-four rooms is the fireplace, to be stoked by your very own, native-clad "Right Hand Man," who upon check-in provides you with his card introducing him as such.

The market is held under the watchful eminence of the big church. Built atop the archeological remains of a Mayan temple in 1540, Santo Tomás is a splendid example of colonial architecture that has survived numerous earthquakes. In the early morning hours on market day the steps of the church are deserted. Gap-toothed men in dirty white shirts swing baskets of incense, back and forth, back and forth, filling the air with an element—an aroma, an aura—that so far cannot be captured by gringos with zoom lenses or video cameras. In the market, everything is for sale at a hundred interlocking stands and storefronts. There are more than three hundred variations of style and color woven into its one-of-a-kind textiles, made into jackets, pants, purses, vests, coin purses, and balls. There are wooden masks, leather goods, jewelry, pottery, carved wooden stelaes, skeletons, angels, and folk art, including painted chairs and exaggerated wooden animals, along with more practical flowers, fruit, and vegetables. It is a shopper's paradise, starring an almost overabundance of stuff. By invitation we are led down back alleys, through courtyards, and into back-room after backroom filled with inventories of everything from the gaudily painted wooden animals to overdyed vests. These literal cottage factories churn out the valuable "antiquuities" so sought after by shoppers. That they are so manufactured does not diminish their value; each piece is handmade, one of a kind. But my traveling partner, a veteran of the market, claims she sees new "products" each visit, dependent probably on the demands, or suggestions of some foreign buyer. This trip the hot new items are wooden angels and black-and-white painted wooden skeletons

• • •

On the road leading to Lake Atitlan we see two firsts: Tree branches flung into the middle of the road instead of orange cones to indicate road work ahead, and police blockades. We'd been told to expect the latter, that they were looking primarily for drug runners heading from Salvador toward Mexico and the United States. A heavily armed policeman randomly waves our rental car to the side of the road. He wants to see passports, car registration, driver's license. After showing the documents to several of his peers and some conversation I couldn't quite make out, he waved us on. It was not an unpleasant stop—from the hill we looked over a verdant green valley and the hummocks of blue-tinted hills in the distance.

Though Lake Atitlan—which one guidebook dubs "the eighth wonder of the world"—sits at five thousand feet it does not come into full view until we'd descended a steep switchback. It was worth the wait. Flanked by a trio of volcanoes (San Pedro, Toliman, and Atitlan) and purple mountains, the shimmering eleven-mile-long, one-thousand-foot-deep lake never looks the same. Today it was whipped by afternoon winds—*xocomil,* "the wind that blows away sin." Nearby hills are patterned with coffee trees and red bougainvillea and surrounded by a dozen Indian villages. The best known, Panajachel, is nicknamed "Gringotenango" for its global reputation as a hippie haven.

In the morning we rent a boat, captained by a thin young man named Reyes, and head across the lake to Santiago Atitlan, a small village known for the coronas, or halos, the women wear on their heads. After docking we climb cobblestoned streets, to the sixteenth-century Franciscan church.

Men and women in the market wear traditional embroidered costumes and whisper to each other in Tzutuhil. Every small town in Guatemala seems to have an incessantly practicing marching band; this one is hidden behind the tall walls of a schoolyard.

After perusing the market, which is mostly fruits and vegetables and staples, we visit the imposing two-story church. Built during colonial days, the colors inside are distinctly native—clear and bright Caribbean blue, stark white with a dash of forest green. Clearly the saints are loved by this congregation. Each wooden replica has a special place on the wall and is completely dressed, down to bandannas tied around a neck or beautiful re-bozos draped over the shoulders. Even the wooden horse is festooned with a colorful halter. There are several altars, one appears fashioned from pure silver. Another features a Christ figure sharing secrets with a young Indian girl. We have come across the lake, though, hoping for a visit to Guatemala's anti-Christ, a much-beloved character known as Máximon. For a quetzal—about twenty cents—we follow a tiny boy (or is it a girl), named Robert (or is it Roberta?) up a twisting rough cobblestone path. No taller than my knee, he/she leads us through a residential stretch. We peek into courtyards where laundry is hung and corn is being husked to the hum of portable radios.

Finally we arrive at a small stone building. Inside is an altar (actually a wooden table) in front of which sits Máximon, dressed in western clothes, black hat, a cigar poked in his wooden mouth. His torso is swathed in a dozen brightly colored scarves. The room is small and grows quickly crowded. We are the only gringos. A half dozen traders, their loose *ciriettas* (bags) packed with goods, stop in and take turns kneeling in front of Maximon, offering gifts of coins, cigars, liquor. A drunk occupies one corner; a guitarist plucks off-key but rhythmic background music. We take the candles bought for this very purpose—blue for love, white for strength, orange for family—and light them in front of him. An *incendiario* full of incense is passed from individual to individual (to ward off bad spirits). When accepted it is waved under each armpit then in front of you, then passed along. I'm not sure what any of this means, but the ceremony is quite moving.

Scorned by traditional Catholics, Máximon's precise origin is unknown. He's also referred to as San Simon, Judas Iscariot, and Pedro de Alvarado, and is always seen as an enemy of the church. Some suggest he represents a Franciscan friar who chased after young Indians girls, explaining why he never has any legs. A pre-Columbian Mayan "saint," during Good Friday processions, in which giant floats feature Mary and a crucified Jesus, an alternative procession led by the pagan figure crosses its path. His followers believe that in this way Maximon "fertilizes" Christ and ensures a year of good crops. Traditionalists have over the centuries tried to discourage Maximon's followers, but they are persistent. In most towns groups of worshippers gather daily to make offerings, pray for the saint's blessings, and drink home-brewed sugarcane liquor. He's looked after by local *cofradía;* if you are shown the way, take along a pack of cigarettes, candles, a bottle of Quezalteca for the ever-thirsty saint—and his attendants.

After an hour inside the cool building we walk outside. The sun is shining bright, the sky graced with billowy clouds. Down the hill gleams the lake. The midday streets are quiet but for the distant honk of the marching band, practicing

• • •

The most vivid memory I brought back from my weeks roaming Guatemala was the several hours spent lost in the rain forest of the Peten.

The morning had gone smoothly, touring the Mayan ruins at Tikal with a small group and skilled guide. After climbing to the top of Temple IV, with its stunning view over the jungle, I made, in retrospect, a foolhardy offer to navigate myself back to the entrance along the perimeter of the 576-square-kilometer park. Within an hour I'd taken one too many rights and was deep into the jungle. I was far off the well-traveled paths, without a map. Above an angry family of howler monkeys squabbled loudly, compounding my ground-level confusion.

I retraced my steps two, three, four times, only to end up back where I began—lost. I climbed to the top of half-buried ruins trying to spot the peaks of the two-hundred-foot-tall temples that I knew rose above the rainforest less than a mile from where I was. But even they were masked by the dense jungle. As the paths narrowed they grew slippery with fine green moss, increasingly intersected by the exposed roots of one-hundred-fifty-foot-tall ceibal trees—the sacred tree of the Mayas. Though it was just after noon, it was very dark. Despite my perplexity there were benefits to being off course. I stopped often and listened, to the sounds of the jungle, to my heart beating. At one point I took a seat on a baobob root and looked straight up: Magnificent Spanish cedars, mahoganies, and *zapotes* towered above. Endless vines of lianas tied the whole mess together. The whirr of thousands of cicadas overpowered all other sounds. I'd read that more than two hundred eighty species of birds called this jungle home and I spotted a white heron, a hawk of some kind, and a tree full of parrots. Wild turkeys walked by and ignored me. Same for the spider monkey on the tree branch above. I also knew from my reading that just beyond the border of Tikal's heavily touristed paths roamed jaguar, puma, and ocelot. I decided to keep moving. The only sign of man I saw were half-buried slabs of limestone sticking out of the ground at odd angles. Covered with moss they were just some of the remnants of the two-thousand-year-old Mayan civilization that will never be unburied. These were sites—and sights—most tourists never experience . . . which made being lost worthwhile.

To the outside world and to many Guatemalans, Tikal is Guatemala. A cultural phenomenon that draws tens of thousands of cash-rich tourists, Tikal is compared by historians with all other Mayan sites: It had the largest ceremonial center, the tallest collection of pyramid-temples, the largest city area—fifty square miles—and a population estimated at fifty-five thousand. In sophistication it rivaled any world capital of the time and held perhaps the greatest collection of artists, artisans, and architects ever assembled in the Mayan world.

The Maya—who populated a trading route stretching from the Carribbean to the Pacific, from the Yucatan to Honduras—developed a unique society boasting a complex social, political, and scientific structure. Their research into mathematics and astronomy was far ahead of their peers across the Atlantic. They developed the concept of "zero," provided the foundation of the 365-day-a-year calendar, predicted solar and lunar eclipses, traced the paths of planets, built aqueducts and roads, built huge pyramids and temples. Tikal flourished during the third and fourth centuries, though its earliest structures were built around 2000 BC. Temple IV—from which I peered out over the rain forest just before getting lost—rises two hundred twelve feet above the ground and was until the nineteenth century the tallest structure in the western hemisphere.

For reasons even experts still only guess at, Tikal was abandoned around AD 900. Its overgrown ruins were rediscovered in 1848, but a century more passed before University of Pennsylvania archeologists excavated and reconstructed its heart. Today, ninety-five thousand visitors a year come to Tikal; only a small percentage climb to the top of Temple IV, because it is accessible only by a steep route of wooden and metal ladders. But the reward is worth it—from its peak, except for the pinnacles of Temple I and Temple II jutting just above the tree line, you look out over rain forest all the way to Honduras.

The jungle is the Peten, one of twenty-two Guatemalan states. The region once supported two million people; today it is home to three hundred thousand struggling to get by. With Mayan rain forest agricultural techniques long forgotten, those that remain take from the land whatever they can—at their current rate, farmers and loggers will finish off all of the Peten's forests in the next thirty years. The decimation is especially amazing considering that until 1970 the Peten was virtually inaccessible by road. In spite of the rapid decline, or maybe because of it, an active environmental movement has sprung up in the past decade. In 1990 the Protected Areas Act set aside large areas of the country for national parks and reserves, the largest being the Peten's Maya Biosphere Reserve, which covers nearly 15 percent of Guatemala and is the largest forest reserve in the Americas.

My visits over two days to Tikal (and Ceibal) were based out of the Camino Real-Tikal, an elegant bungalow hotel set above Lake Peten-Itza, forty-five minutes from the park. To my surprise and delight I found myself the night after I was lost (and found, by myself, thank you) shooting pool there with the brand new governor of the Peten. Appointed just one month prior he is a small man in his sixties, dressed in a Cubano-style shirt and wearing thick black-framed glasses. He spoke little English, but we agree to play "ball y negra"—eight ball.

The new governor had been a teacher and a judge before being appointed head of the largest of Guatemala's states. He tells me that just a few days before, he'd met with the country's president concerning the future of the Peten as a tourist attraction. They agreed what his state needed was two hundred fifty kilometers of new roads, to make it more accessible. I wasn't sure I agreed with that assessment—new roads would also make the area more accessible to oil companies and loggers—but wasn't about to argue with the governor.

Later that night, after midnight, a knock was delivered on the door of the hotel's resident manager. Two jeeps, filled with a dozen, half-drunk soldiers, were requesting he reopen the just-closed bar so they could drink some more and shoot pool. He quietly acquiesced, rousting two of his employees to help. The soldiers played games and drank up all the hotel's cerveza before gunning their jeeps off at 2:30.

When the manager told me the story over breakfast the next morning, he said it was an okay trade-off, that if he ever needed help from the military they would be more likely to cooperate. The example he used was that if someone were to become seriously ill at his hotel, he could call in a military helicopter to fly them to Guatemala City, rather than wait for the daily scheduled flights out of nearby Flores. What the late-night visit proved to me was that the military is king in Guatemala. Presidents, they come and go. Generals stay on and on and on.

• • •

Ironically during the weeks I visited, the new president attempted to purge congress of those who disagreed with him. The night I flew out of Guatemala City fights broke out in the halls of the legislature. Garbage was thrown from the gallery and peasant protesters stormed the building, occupying its one hundred sixteen legislators' seats.

The president has some valid complaints. Guatemalan legislators are no saints, having been accused in recent years of activities ranging from car theft to influence peddling. The new president was having trouble wrangling them, thus the call for mass resignation. Taking advantage of the confusion, the defense minister announced he was seeking the president's authorization to move forcefully against the country's small guerrilla armies, even though there was no indication they were rising up, or that they even still exist. At the airport, I talked over espresso with a Guatemalan businessman heading for Houston. He was unworried by the current "disagreement" in the government. "You may not feel it in the air, but the country is truly filled with hope," he smiled. I wanted to believe him.

THE NINE LIES OF
HECTOR VILLASEÑOR

Aaah, Baja!

Come spring, the Grand Sur—the skinny adjunct to the Mexican mainland, that one-thousand-mile-long peninsula once thought to be an island, with a growing reputation for attracting ticky-tacky retirement villas and their denizens—happens to be *the* perfect escape from mud season in the Big Norte.

We three kayaking fisherman have arrived not-so-fast on the heels of the Cochimi Indians, the conquistadors who supplanted them, and the randy mix that followed: Jesuits, ranchers, fishermen, revolutionaries, mercenaries, outright criminals, and snowbirds, all seeking exactly the same commodity, namely Escape, Diversion, A Change of Course.

Most important for us, having driven the length of the desert peninsula, from the High Sierras to Baja's southernmost tip, is some long-promised, expected-to-be excellent springtime fishing. Come spring the Sea of Cortez should be rich with bonito, corvina, grouper, needlefish, pargo, rock bass, sierra, skipjack, marlin, dorado, roosterfish, sailfish, snook, tuna, and yellowtail, according to our expert fishing pal, the Herbinator, invited along specifically for the long months he's spent in recent years plying the gulf and its beaches.

Which is a long way of introducing Hector Villaseñor.

1. "I, HECTOR VILLASEÑOR, AM THE BEST FISHING GUIDE IN
   LA PAZ."

We were sauntering down the *malecon* of La Paz, just an hour after we'd
pulled our heavily loaded Toyota pickup off the two-lane highway, road-
lagged but happy to have the smell of sea salt in our nostrils. Just past dusk
on a warm March night, the parade of cruising low-riders and inevitable
sidewalk-restaurant four-tops laden with bulbous tourists from north of
the border says *New* Mexico.

We'd come south for a couple weeks of sea kayaking but were looking
to bookend our trip with a few days of serious offshore fishing. We'd brought
gear, but little previous knowledge of the place. All we needed was a handy
local with a sturdy *panga* (small boat) to show us some of the premiere sites.
We were happy to pay. The Herbinator was particularly intent on fishing
around the small Isla Cerralvo, five miles off the mainland, known to be surrounded by vast late-spring schools of dorado, marlin, and tuna.

Before we can brake for even our first cold cerveza, our search seems
to have concluded. Hector V. boldly imposes himself on us from the sidewalk in front of a travel agency, his literal first words being "I am THE best
fishing guide in town." He corrals us, pulling Herb by the shirtsleeve toward a sandwich board covered with glossy three-by-fives. It is transparent
that he is equal parts carnival barker, sportsman, and con man (not to
mention self-confessed ladies' man) but we are tired and willing. Straight
from central casting—swarthy, thin-waisted, broad-shouldered, wearing a
long-sleeved dress shirt, khaki shorts, and a U.S. Navy cap—he gets close
as he pitches, smelling of cigarettes, beer, and, well, con.

Herb takes the lead, bumming a cigarette and quizzing him about
what was biting. A hundred feet from the becalmed gulf, beneath a dark
night sky, Hector points to the collection of street-lit snapshots. Blurry
photos of himself posing with a wide variety of clients—fat brokers from
Chicago, bikinied wives from Boston, doctors from L.A. and New Jersey.
Each picture also boasts a sizable fish. Promises (lies?) spill out of Hector's
mouth: If we choose to accompany him for a day, we were sure, like hundreds before, to see schools of marlins, thousands of snappers, and literally
tons of dorado.

Tired and thirsty, we are anxious to find a guide, ready to set out at daybreak. Hector lucked out—he was standing there. Even before he invites us inside to close the deal, it was essentially sealed. Herb takes a seat across the scarred desk from Hector. Dull fluorescent lights shine on three of his cronies, feet planted firmly atop similarly scarred desks. The boss is bald, dark, mustachioed; he smiles in lieu of English and holds out a pack of cigarettes.

As his closing tool, Hector reaches into a desk drawer and comes out with a worn spiral notebook half filled with handwritten testimonials. He riffles through the pages before finding what he is after. Proudly pointing to a five-year-old anecdote scrawled in blue ink, he invites us to read the glowing words of praise from Bill and Elsa, from Halifax: "Despite a day of nothing but four- and five-foot waves, as uncomfortable a ride as we could have asked for, we did catch two big Dorado."

The ambiguousness of the recommendation should have been a strong clue.

Before we get back out the door onto the street we've pooled $100 for a deposit. Hector walks into the dark night with us, pulling the door shut behind him. As we head off in search of dinner, he saunters away, the opposite direction, whistling a happy tune, our hundred bucks in his pocket.

That should have been our second clue.

2. "I'LL PICK YOU UP AT 5:30. SHARP!"

The next morning, fifteen minutes before the appointed hour, we are up. Groggy, but up. Camera and fishing gear packed in big plastic crates, the morning dark, muggy. Herb paces, nervous, somehow intuiting that Hector will be late, desperate to mooch a cigarette. From the courtyard below he keeps us apprised, counting down. "He's got ten minutes . . . five minutes . . . Now he's fifteen minutes late . . . now the son-of-a-bitch is half an hour late . . . I knew it, he's not showing . . ."

Hector had made a big deal out of presenting each of us with his card. On it were all of his phone numbers—office, home, even cellular, an apparatus he'd dramatically pulled from his desk drawer to show off. "I'm sure it was Styrofoam," Barry quips. Now all three of us are pacing. From the motel office I try the three numbers. Each goes unanswered.

At seven o'clock, we give up. Cursing Hector, itemizing what we'd do when—if—we see him again, we walk into town for breakfast. There, on the restaurant's patio, I recognize Hector's chrome-domed boss, sitting with a handful of pals, sipping coffee. He looks sincerely surprised to see us and shouts out, "Where's Hector?"

"Good fucking question," mutters the Herbinator, who is the most distressed of us all, since it was he who had taken the lead in "negotiating" the deal.

Informed that Hector was a no-show, the bossman jumps into his curbside silver Chevy, dialing his cell phone even as he U-turns across the malecon. He reappears ten minutes later, squealing to a stop in front of the patio. Eyes just opened, a half-dressed Hector stumbles out of the passenger door, pulling on his shoes, zipping up.

Both are apologetic. "It's my fault," offers Hector weakly, motioning for a coffee. Turns out he'd spent the night—and our deposit?—in the back of a camper belonging to a middle-aged Canadian woman he'd met the afternoon before. His eyes were red, his clothes the same as when we'd met the night before. "Guess the old internal alarm clock isn't what it used to be," he flails.

3.   "I'LL DRIVE, DON'T WORRY. WE'LL TAKE MY CAR."

The boss gives us all a ride back to our motel, where his teenage son waits beside a rusting, shock-absorberless Mercury Marquis. Turns out Hector doesn't own a car. That or he'd lost it in a bet, it was never made quite clear. Wedging gear boxes into the dusty trunk, there was not enough room for our poles; they rode cross-angled across the seats up front, tips sticking out the rolled-down window.

It was a one-hour drive due east by dirt road to Punta Arenas de la Ventana, the point of land closest to Cerralvo and where Hector planned to meet the panga and skipper. The day is already hot and the landlocked scenery bleak—dusty, dry, rocky, absent of even the hardiest cactus. If it wasn't for the incredibly majestic sea that surrounds this narrow spine, no one would ever stop here longer than for a roadside piss.

Chewing on tabs of Pepto-Bismol plucked out of the dusty shag of the carpeted dashboard, Hector quizzes us on what kind of food we most like and, in an effort to cover his skinny ass, tries to regale us with tales of fraternity boys and executives whom he'd escorted on all-nighters of tequila-shooting and whore-mongering before heading out to sea. "After, they always tell me the same thing," muses Hector, scratching his skinny knee. "They say, 'Hector, that was the best day of my life.'"

4. "I'LL BRING LUNCH." (TRANSLATION: I'LL BRING BEER)

Just before Punta Arenas we stop at a dusty roadside *mercado,* we assume to acquire lunch. It is a Sunday morning, and other than the teenage girl behind the counter we've seen no one for miles. Hector pulls a twelve-pack of Tecate out of the cooler. "You guys want anything else?" he asks. We study the barren shelves and, finding little more than stale bread and crackers, pass, convinced another stop for supplies is around the bend.

Next stop is in town; we pull into a dusty yard where a woman sits in the shade beneath an acacia tree, sewing. Hector honks two, three times while we study the nearby detritus. Minutes later our skipper, Marcos, stumbles out of the house, pulling a torn flannel shirt around his shoulders. Throwing a couple paddles and a nearly empty gas can into the back of his pickup, he guns the engine and lurches out of the yard with Hector in close pursuit.

We do make another stop before the beach. Another *tienda,* this one equally barren of food, where Marcos acquires a thirty-ounce brown bottle of Tecate, wrapped mysteriously in newspaper. (Why the newspaper? For its insulating purposes? To disguise its contents from the clients?) Properly equipped, finally we were off for the high seas!

5. "I'LL BRING ALL THE GEAR, I'VE GOT EVERYTHING WE'LL NEED"
(TRANSLATION: I'LL BRING BEER)

The tide long gone, we push and pull the heavy and beat wooden panga fifty feet down into the sea. It goes without saying that if we'd arrived on time three hours before, the boat would have then rested on the very lip of the sea. Funny, neither Hector nor Marcos seem bothered by the lateness;

the impression they give is that this is a perfectly normal start to a day of fishing.

As Herb uncorks and unwraps his preciously cared-for rods and reels, Hector watches intently. The gear he'd brought for his paying clients rolled around on the bottom of the boat. The pair of rods are in a similar condition to the Marquis—rusted, missing parts, badly out of alignment.

Marcos, young and handsome—though painfully and obviously hungover—steers the small Merc and we head out into the sea spray. A cigarette in one hand, liter of now-warm beer between his legs, he peers over the bow through polarized lenses for signs of fish. Hector, meanwhile, makes himself comfortable, trying out one of Herb's rods, popping open a Tecate, spinning his life story. Born in Tequila ("I swear I have tequila in my blood," he brags) he admits he's never strayed too far from the southern tip of Baja, accumulating a wife, three girlfriends (at the moment), and seven children along the way. "That's why I must work so hard," he winks, "lots of people depending on me."

6. "MAMACITA, MAMACITA, TU ERES LA MUJER MAS LINDA EN DEL MUNDO."

Fish-talk is not at the top of Hector's list. Talking about women is. And he's full of savvy advice. As we bake under the sun (the panga had no canvas top) he details his finely-honed approach.

"If you want to meet a Mexican woman, if you know what I mean, if you want to really *meet* her, it's very simple. All you have to do is go up to one, anywhere, on the street, in a bar, in a market, and say, 'Mamacita, mamacita, you are the most beautiful woman I have ever seen.' That's all they need to hear, and boom, they're taking you home. It's worked for me all my life . . . I am always surprised at how easy it is. It's as natural for me as catching fish."

7. "I'LL BRING THE BAIT." (SEE PROMISES 4 & 5)

After trolling for an hour a half mile offshore, in rough, sun-baked seas, Hector and Marco consult. It looks like we'll need bait. Of course, these south-of-the-border Einsteins have neglected to bring any. Which means for the next half hour we roar from fishing boat to fishing boat scattered around the incongruously named Bahia de los Muertos (Bay of the Dead) trying to mooch a plastic bag of squid parts.

8. "OH YES, WE'LL FISH ALL THE DAY AROUND ISLA CERRALVO."
Because the winds are way up, it means running out to Isla Cerralvo, which we can see just a few miles across the whitecap-swept channel—our goal since leaving the Sierras—is out of the question. We can see similar-sized pangas being tossed about violently. We don't hesitate to point out to Hector that if we'd gotten the start we'd planned we'd have gotten out to Cerralvo before the winds picked up.

As a result, we spend the day puttering around in figure eights never more than a half mile off the beach. "This is not fishing," Herb mutters over and over, barely under his breath, "this is bullshit."

9. "I GUARANTEE WE WILL CATCH DORADO, TUNA, MARLIN, SO
MANY THEY'LL BE JUMPING OUT OF THE WATER."
For several hours we try every trick: We troll, drop weighted lines, toss out big chunks of squid, drop weighted lines baited with squid . . . Nothing, no luck. It is hot, but windy; the seas are blue, blue, blue, but rough. Marcos points out a few jumpers in the near distance.

After five hours we catch a solitary, fluorescent green, fifteen-pound dorado. On its face, that wouldn't be tragic—anything's better than noth-ing—if it hadn't been for all those "jumping into your boat" assurances of Hector.

"It's okay," he reassures. "We can stay out all day if you want. I don't have anywhere to go . . . "Our luck is sure to change."

• • •

On the drive back to La Paz, Barry and Herb pass out in the back of the dusty Marquis, worn down by the heat of the Mexican sun. Hector and I continue to bullshit in the front.

The last Tecate nestled in his crotch, he is long past making excuses for our fish-deprived day. The only thing he's concerned about now is that he just might not get paid, given his late arrival, and such. The bossman is not going to be happy with him. On top of that, he knows that the Canadian lady is waiting for him in her camper, expecting him to return armed with cold beer and fat steaks. He needs the eggs, so to speak, so tries to butter me up. "I get the idea you've been around the world," he tries. "Probably fished everywhere, too, eh? Guess you know it better than anyone, fishing is all a matter of luck . . . and timing. That was our problem today—not enough luck, not enough time."

Later that night we try to visit Hector's office, intent on adding our own testimonial to his spiral-bound book. We pass his place several times but the doors are never open, the lights dim. As Hector had inadvertently implied, it was all about timing . . . even revenge.

RAPID DESCENT

Eric Hertz motions me into his room at the Camelia Hotel in downtown Kunming, China. A towel is draped over the floor lamp, the blinds drawn though it is nearly noon. The room is dark and dank and smells of sweat and the tang of pesticide spray.

"I'm scared," he says, "truth is, I'm very scared. I wish this trip was over and we were already safely down the river." Tomorrow we set out for the headwaters of the ShuiloHe, a wild 75-mile long, never-rafted, little-seen tributary of the Yangtze. Paralleling the Tibet border and set amid the folds of numerous fifteen thousand- to twenty thousand-foot mountains, should we have trouble on the river, getting out will be extremely difficult. Rescue is out of the question. Hiking out is a possibility, but probably more difficult than running the rapids. Finding a road would require bushwhacking up and over several fifteen thousand–foot peaks. We've brought several hundred feet of climbing rope, assuming that if we are forced to climb out it will require scaling sheer rock faces. We're not even bothering to carry radios because we're too far away from any potential receiver.

Hertz looks like he slept in his clothes. He learned about rivers guiding for a dozen years on the Grand Canyon; this is hardly the first time he's organized descents on big rivers. I have joined him often, on the first top-to-bottom descent of Chile's Futaleufu, as well as the first commercial trips down Peru's Colca and Apurimac. Since 1990 his specialty has been putting together trips on some of the world's most-endangered rivers—usually threatened by hydropower dams—and inviting politicians, environmentalists, indigenous natives, and journalists along in order to draw attention to the natural resource. That he appears so nervous today, makes me nervous too.

What we know about the river is far outweighed by what we do not know. We've got only muddy, photocopied maps and no scouting report. We know the river drops two thousand feet in the first forty-five miles; we don't know if the bulk of that might come in a couple of two-hundred-foot waterfalls. Our Chinese teammate Zhang Jiyue is China's most-experienced whitewater rafter, a member of the first team to attempt a descent of the Yangtze. He has seen only the spot where we will put-in. Two of our guides, Joe Dengler and Beth Rypins, just kayaked the Yangtze, and saw where the Shuilo He drains. Their report: "It's very big."

Until just a few years ago this countryside was completely off limits to any visitor, Chinese or otherwise. Except for the few hundred Tibetans who live in small communities near the river, this is unexplored territory. The Shiulo He is one of only a few rivers in the world that has not already been explored. We're here partly because true "firsts" are almost a thing of the past. But as I leave Hertz to repack my bags, he announces "this is definitely the last first for me."

• • •

We reach the Shiulo He at noon, four days of hard driving after leaving Lijiang. From where we put-in, the Yangtze is seventy-five miles away. We're not sure how far down the river we'll get. We're carrying enough food for ten days, which means we'll have to average about eight miles a day. Very doable, if the river is flat. But if we run into road blocks, we'll run short on provisions.

Thirty-year-old Joe Dengler is the on-river leader of the trip. He and I walk along the Shiulo He for half a mile, trying to get a feel for what's to come. I ask if he is nervous. "No, I'm excited," he counters. The great-nephew of a scout on the Lewis and Clark expedition, the sinewy Californian quietly aspires to a life of big adventure. "Do you know how lucky we are, to be out here, doing this stuff, leading this life? I don't feel scared or nervous, I feel lucky."

Studying the river as it flows past rocks and trees on the far bank, Joe's calculation is that the river is running at about 1,200 cfs—quite a bit faster than the 800 cfs we'd hoped to find. It means the river is running at roughly twenty miles an hour. The faster flow means it will be easier for us to get swept into rapids we'd rather avoid, and tougher to paddle out of trouble. Gazing at the aquamarine river Joe is quiet, his silence an attempt at downplaying the fact that he wished the river was slower. The reason for concern is that within the first ten miles, according to our 1948 Russian maps, we should meet a sizable tributary, which could double the river's flow. "It's quicker than we'd hoped," Joe finally admits, "but I was also concerned we might get here and find it nearly dry. Too much water is actually an easier situation to deal with than too little water."

From where we unroll and blow up our boats we can see the river disappear around a corner into a tall, steep-walled canyon. Eighteen of us will be carried by a flotilla comprising of two safety kayakers, two fourteen-foot rubber rafts, a cataraft (two sixteen-foot-long yellow pontoons attached by an aluminum frame), and a pair of Shredders (two ten-foot-long black rubber pontoons connected by a thick rubber floor). We will carry two big bags of ropes and climbing gear, plenty of first aid (and two doctors), ten pounds of personal gear per person, a propane tank and stove, and several watertight bags of food (mostly rice and freeze-dried casseroles). All of the gear will be packed in the two rafts, which will also carry five people each.

A big, square Tibetan house overlooks our scene and a small crowd of women, dressed mostly in red, sit in a row on a bench, watching us pack. Jiyue reports they are as astonished and amazed by our colorful gear—wetsuits, life jackets, helmets—as we are by theirs. One local man tells Jiyue that he's hunted in the region for years and that there is a sheer-wall canyon and waterfall not too far downriver. We're not intimidated by the report, figuring that what might be a waterfall to him could be a simply run rapid for us.

As we pull away from shore the sun has dipped behind a trio of sunlit peaks. A dirt trail runs alongside the river for a couple miles, and a small band of kids runs after us, following until the trail peters out. Prayer flags— rectangles of white cotton cloth hung vertically on tall poles planted in the earth—line the river.

We warm up on some gentle Class III rapids and make camp after just two hours. Already there is concern—the river is too calm, not dropping fast enough. That guarantees big waterfalls ahead. Somewhere.

• • •

Up at 6:30, a quick breakfast of coffee and rice, and we're on the river by 8:30.

It's not long before we meet our first big rapid. Midway through the intial, broad, rock-choked rapid the boat guided by Beth Rypins, one of the best whitewater guides and kayakers in the States, bumps a sizable rock head-on. Harvard lung specialist John Reilly goes backward out of the boat, but is quickly pulled back in. Thirty minutes later, another big rapid, and Reilly is out again, as are New York City businessman David Larkin and Beth, who is washed over the back of the boat. Pools of calm water separate these big rapids, so self-rescue is pretty easy. Beth ends up stranded on a rock in midriver, ahead of her boat.

Then, just before noon, the river begins to narrow, as tight as twelve feet across. Fortunately after we push through a tight section the canyon opens up again. Then narrows. Then opens up. Finally we reach a spot where the river is split neatly in two by a line of rocks; the only way through is a slender slot on river left, barely big enough for the rafts to press through.

Though much of the powerful river is pushing through a thin groove, the bigger problem is that on the right border sits a giant boulder, its top edge razor-sharpened by years of slicing river. Making it even more dangerous, we can see a torrent of water being sucked beneath the rock. Avoiding this obstacle—which could slice a boat, or sever a head—is key. But there's little room to maneuver in the fifteen-foot-wide gap.

Our boat is first, and the river pushes into the sharp rock. I have to stand to avoid being guillotined. The cataraft, manned by Paulo Castillo, follows and has a rough ride. *National Geographic* photographer Ed Kashi is thrown violently from his seat on the front of the boat, just above the undercut. He surfaces, cameraless, twenty feet downriver. But the cataraft is stuck, jammed beneath the overhang, shuddering, threatening to rip apart as several tons of rushing river pound against its metal frame. Paulo strains on the left oar, desperate to free his boat, and after thirty seconds has success. "That yellow camera case of Ed's prevented me from getting sucked all the way under," he admits as we pull into shore, the boat's frame snapped in two.

While Paulo repairs, we study the maps. Jiyue interrogates the small group of Tibetans who come down to the riverside to gawk. They insist the big tributary we're expecting is just an hour away. Beyond, they continue, the river drops into a steep canyon that takes them a full day to walk around in order to reach the next village. "If they are right," says Jiyue, "we should find trouble by the end of the day."

The tributary means more water, maybe twice as much. More water pushing through a narrow canyon equals danger. Though the sun is on our backs, we are chilled by a nervous sweat. "It's possible we may need (rope expert) Bruce Smith sooner than we thought," says Hertz as we balance on a rock, trying to see far downriver. "I'd rather we have to climb out of the canyon than swim through it." Joe sidles up. "Just keep your eyes open for escape routes," he warns. "Let's be careful down there, let's not do anything stupid."

After two hours of reading and running an extensive series of Class IV and Class V rapids we still have not hit the confluence. Then, at 5 p.m., with the sun already sinking, there it is—a big, nameless river adjoining the Shuilo He on our right. We stop and scout downriver from a rocky triangle where the two meet.

The tributary adds another 500 to 600 cfs, which means the combined river is now running at close to 2,000 cfs, more than double what we would have liked. The onset of darkness doesn't make the river ahead look any more approachable. "I'll be really glad when this day is over," confides Beth as we climb back into our boats.

Worse yet, just as our informants had suggested, past the confluence the walls begin to gorge up. In a matter of minutes, before we could even think about slowing the boats and reconsidering, we're into the very situation we'd desperately hoped to avoid, floating into a sheer-wall canyon with no escape but downriver. Two-hundred-foot walls of ebony granite rise vertically on either side of us, and the black river picks up steam as it turns tight bends. There's no place to pull over, few calm eddies from which to scout or regroup.

This was our biggest fear. While confident that we'd be able to *think* our way out of even the tightest spot, our biggest concern was entering a sheer-wall canyon, with no option for escape. Now we are forced to run anything in front of us, including waterfalls.

One hundred yards ahead the river disappears around a corner, into blackness. We can hear the roar of a big drop. Desperate not to round the corner completely blind, Joe steers our boat, the lead boat, into a tiny pool on river right. He climbs hand over hand twenty feet up the slick rock wall to peek downriver. "The river turns hard right, then drops left over a ten-foot drop," he hollers down, barely audible over the roar of the river. "We've got to hug the right wall, then paddle straight over a big rock with water pouring over it. We *cannot* allow the boat to be sucked left . . . if we do, big holes will pull us under and throw us all into the river." Beth, waiting for a report, has her paddlers pulling hard against the current to keep their boat from being swept downriver. Cupping his hands around his mouth, Joe repeats what he's seen.

We are most concerned about the pair of Shredders. The name comes from their maneuverability and light weight, but their strengths are also a weakness—they may be too light to stay upright going over big drops.

We go first. All I remember from the charge is the sound of loud grunting and groaning as we sink paddles into the violent froth, trying desperately to stay to the right. Just as we begin to drop over the waterfall the front of the boat is sucked under, simultaneously burying all five of us. It feels like somebody has dumped a swimming pool on top of our heads. Despite the thrashing, we keep paddling and pop out at the bottom of the rapid like a cork. Forty feet downstream we see an indentation in the rock and pull into a shallow, cavelike inset. Beth's boat is next, makes a similar move, and ends up alongside ours. All we can do to stay out of the fast-moving current is cling to the wall by our fingertips. There are no ledges, nowhere to tie-off. "I can't hold on much longer," shouts Jon Dragan, his body hanging halfway out of the boat as he struggles to keep us next to the rock.

The Shredders are a different story. The first, manned by Hertz and fifty-six-year-old veteran river-runner Henry Black, goes first. It is buried as soon as it hits the hole, and flips. The two safety kayakers fighting the current midstream bark out a play-by-play. Both men are tossed into a washing machine of violent waves; Henry is thrown free and begins to float downriver, orange helmet barely visible above the waves, eyes wide open, hands striking out for the walled shore he cannot see.

Hertz is trapped at the bottom of the waterfall, on the verge of being sucked into the maelstrom. It is impossible for him to get back into the boat and his mind races—"Let go," or "Stay with the boat." Either option puts him at risk of being sucked into the so-called keeper hole at the bottom of the falls—once it gets you, it keeps you. His debate lasts just seconds, though to him it feels like hours. Finally the river kicks the boat free, as if it were a twig, and Hertz hangs on. But even as his minidrama is unfolding, the second Shredder attempts to run—with similar results. Leif Sloan struggles quickly to the steep wall and somehow gets half his body up the slick rock. Mike Mather, a young, experienced guide from West Virginia, hangs onto the side of the boat as it is kicked around in the powerful regurgitation. Now we've got four swimmers.

Usually with swimmers in the water the rafts would move to midriver to help scoop them up. But that's impossible here. If we let go of the wall, we're floating too, around the next unscouted corner and over whatever big drop comes next. One of the mantras we all know by heart is "Save Yourself." As paddles and various brightly colored gear floats by, we can only hope our swimmers are stroking for their lives.

Henry is the first to float past. Steve Jones, positioned in the front of Beth's boat, attempts to pull him in over the bow, but cannot. The river is moving too swiftly, the boat is not anchored, and Henry is dead weight. As he floats almost past the back of the boat Beth makes a last grasp, gets his life jacket in her hands, and struggles him in over the stern. The air is filled with tense shouts—"Get him in the boat!" "Grab the Shredder, it's getting away!"—but otherwise the interior of the canyon is deadly quiet. Mather drifts by, grasping his Shredder in one hand; it takes two safety lines to drag him into our now-crowded inlet. Hertz and Sloan come next, riding atop an overturned Shredder.

In the darkness of the cave we regroup. Nervous laughs mask grave concern. There's no time to make a plan. We just have to keep moving.

The sun is now gone and finding a camp is going to be difficult. We all know the option may be sleeping in the boats, clipped to the steep wall.

We drift out of our safe haven and sixty feet away see the river making another blind turn. As a group we peel to the right wall. Joe and Beth climb up ten feet and peer downriver. They return with thumbs up, Joe claiming, "No problem, just one big drop around the corner, followed by waves."

"It's no worse than what we just did," he reports. But his optimism rings false. I am sitting next to him in the boat and though he gives me a tight-lipped smile as he tugs on his helmet strap I have seen him in enough tough situations to recognize he hasn't told us the whole truth. "Remember, reach out of the boat and paddle hard, but be ready to throw your weight to the center in case we drop off something big," he yells in a hoarse voice. (Later, he will admit, "We couldn't see a damn thing, but we had to run, we had no choice. We got up there and we could see waves, but we just couldn't tell how big they were, or what came next.")

The next half hour is frightening. We run a trio of monstrous rapids, unable to scout any of them. In each, we round a turn and are faced by a series of five- and six-foot waves. The tall walls and setting sun mean we are now navigating in near pitch blackness. On any other river we would have scouted similar-sized rapids for fifteen or twenty minutes, trying to pick the best course. Not an option here.

At seven o'clock we come upon a giant rock slide on the river's right, which left behind a steep pile of rubble. This would be camp. Exhausted, all adrenaline drained, we pull the boats up onto the rocks. "Finally, a firm mattress," jokes John Reilly as he puts his sleeping bag out on a heap of sharp shale.

Dinner is a quiet affair. Joe makes a stab at lightening the mood, but his, "Hey, what a great day," is greeted by stony silence. For all we knew this gorge could continue for twenty more miles, meaning tomorrow and the next day could be just as frightening. Reilly, physically perhaps the least prepared to be here, stares into the fire, motionless. "This may not have been a very smart thing for a father to do," he says, thinking of his three daughters back home in Boston. David Larkin overhears him. "While I think we're all here to be scared—I think that's part of the reason we do these things—I didn't think I'd be this scared." Paulo Castillo, normally the most reserved of us all, admits the forecast for tomorrow is "ominous."

Mike Mather says he'd tried not to think most of the day, just to focus on the water dead ahead. "It's not just that we're in really wicked whitewater, in the middle of a canyon no one has ever seen, it is that we are in it in the middle of nowhere.

"When the first guys rafted the Gauly River in West Virginia, they each carried a quarter in their pockets so that if they got stuck they could hike up, find a pay phone, and call for help. We don't have any such option. We're stuck here."

Before crawling up to my rock mattress I lie beside the rushing river, on a slab of marbleized rock. I switch off my head lamp and gaze up at the steep canyon walls, which form a dark, silhouetted V where the river slices through. The sky is filled with stars. I let my hand drag in the cold, incomprehensible river, almost hoping to feel its pulse. It runs over my fingers, soft and velvety, but gives no clue of what secrets it holds. I pray that it will be kind to us tomorrow. Its response quickly lulls me into an exhausted sleep.

But I barely sleep, kept awake by a recurring nightmare: I am swept out of the raft and left behind, clinging to the sheer rock wall. No one comes back to help me. The climb out is straight up, impossible. My options are to fall back into the icy water and swim for it, most likely through several sets of big rapids. Or just to hang there on the wall, wet and cold.

• • •

"Swimmer!" Hertz and Henry Black had crashed their Shredder again, this time hitting a wall, and flipped. Henry is hanging onto the boat as it heads for a rocky drop. Our third day on the river began under a bright sun, but quickly turned . . . ominous.

"Let go of the boat, Henry," Joe yells from the rock where we had pulled over to scout. It took Henry a few seconds to realize that while saving the boat was important, saving himself was more so. Joe tosses him a safety rope, but it misses its mark. Husky Jon Dragan, a fifty-two-year-old whitewater veteran from West Virginia, tosses a second line, but Henry misses it too. Taking literally a last desperate stroke before he is swept over the drop, Henry grabs one of the floating lines and swims to shore, gasping for breath. Kayaker Brian Hulse makes a stabbing grab of the Shredder just before it plunges over the rocky rapids, an invaluable save— if the boat had disappeared, our already crowded rafts would have become even more crowded, less maneuverable.

It isn't until 2:30 that we finally emerge from the steep gorge that had almost swallowed us. A narrow valley opened up, and the geology changed. Joe studied the map taped to the back of our raft, trying to identify tributaries and mountain peaks on the muddy photocopy. "Man, I'm lost," he mutters. Joking, I ask if he is sure we are even on the right river. His look suggests now is not the time for joking. "If I'm right, we should hit a flat section pretty soon, and hopefully be able to make up some time," he says. The fact that the Chinese government has charged us a steep permit fee for access to this underexplored part of their country, and then not offered good maps, is a major irritant.

An hour later we are stopped by a halfmile of rock-choked, unrunnable canyon. The river has forced its way through soft rock, causing two-story-tall rocks to calve onto the shoreline. Boulders the size of mobile homes lie in the middle of the river, culminating in a fifteen-foot drop.

Normally, it is a rapid we would consider running. Except this one is followed by fifty more feet of roiling water, and another twenty-foot drop. Beth, Joe, Eric, and I hike to just above the lower drop and experiment, tossing small logs into the caldron. They submerge instantly, disappear for sixty seconds, before being spit out—minus bark—into broiling whitewater. As we watch, thinking about what such a ride would do to a human body, Beth says, tongue firmly in cheek, "They just didn't plan those rocks very well, did they?"

It takes only ten minutes to decide this stretch of the river is unrunnable. We can't risk a swimmer in this mess; neither can we risk losing a boat. "As much as I'd like to try and run the top part, we've got to err on the safe side," says Joe, who seems genuinely excited by the non stop problem solving. But the problems keep mounting. It would take us nearly twenty-four hours to move man, boats, and gear less than half a mile past this predicament. The next morning we will belay everything—people and gear—

by rope around a fifty-foot sheer-wall corner. Without the ropes, the trip would have been over, and we'd have been hiking out.

• • •

Day four begins with a near tragedy. As we move equipment downriver, kayaker Brian Hulse decides he will paddle his ten-foot-long plastic boat to a point just above the twenty-foot drop we'd seen strip the bark from a log. But his boat is overloaded with gear, and when he tries to pull to shore the fast current drags him back into the river. Ironically, we are standing within feet of him, carrying bags and boats around the falls, when he is swept away. We clearly hear his last word, a powerful expletive, as he realizes he is going over the falls.

Tumbling nose over end, he lands upside down, and is caught in the backwash of the waterfall. At one point the whitewater pushes his boat free—by then he is right side up—but then sucks him back under, and over. When he is finally pushed free he is swept against a giant rock and we think for sure he'll be sucked beneath it. A great athlete, he is able to power away from the rock and into a calm pool. But there is muttering from the other guides as we watch him get "washing machined." If he gets hurt, or worse, it would mean we'd most likely have to stop and hike him out. Hertz, who feels overly responsible for luring us all here, is most distraught. "Never again. I'm not doing anything like this again," he says as we push a raft up a two-story-tall rock, "I'm sticking to rivers I know, or ones I can send scouts down. This 'never-been-seen-before' stuff is just not worth it."

When we finally get around the waterfall and to the opposite shore, we are greeted by more bad news. The kayakers have scouted ahead and the next mile of river is even worse than what we'd just climbed around. And it ends in the biggest drops we'd seen yet—a pair of thirty-foot waterfalls, the second one disappearing into a cave. Fortunately there is plenty of walking room over rocks on the river's left, so we can keep moving downriver. But as we begin yet another hike around—pushing, pulling, and lugging boats up and over the rocks—I notice everyone looking up at the hills that surround us, scouting for overland escape routes. Hiking out is looking like a probability.

Our progress is not good. In the first three days we've covered twenty miles. On the fourth, less than half a mile. We are still fifty-five miles from the Yangtze. At this rate, we'll run out of food long before then.

To make matters worse, at the waterfall we run out of walking room on river left. That means that in order to continue we have to put boats in the water and cross the river, just above the falls. The opposite shore offers little reason to be optimistic. It is rocky, with few places to pull in. The rafts will never navigate this section under their own power and there isn't enough room on the other side for the kayakers to pull in and get safely out of their boats. The Shredders are out of the question. The only craft capable of making the move across the river was the cataraft. Though the boat looks like a pair of bananas tied together by aluminum poles, it is light and very manueverable. Thankfully too, Castillo is arguably the world's preeminent catarafter.

"Getting over doesn't look so tough," he says as we study for potential routes. "It's stopping once we get to the other side that worries me. I can easily envision getting to shore, thinking we're safe, and then being pulled backwards over the edge."

While we debate the best way to get across, we dub these the "Last Chance Falls." The afternoon is spent plotting how—using ropes and pulleys—to rig a system to pull the boats loaded with gear and people across. It will take a dozen trips and each will be cutting the fine edge of a deadly drop. One mistake and boats, gear—and lives—will be lost. The first challenge will be for Paulo and Joe to carry a rope across via the cataraft, then relay it back to us. Each side of the two-hundred-foot-long rope will be tethered around a rock or a tree, and hauled in via pulleys by a trio of men.

"I'm concerned there will be too much slack, though," argues Joe. "If the rope vees, we'll never be able to tighten it up enough to keep a loaded raft from falling over the edge. Remember, we'll be pulling against the current, which is strong." The solution is a pendulum, or triangle, of ropes, an idea floated by Hertz. A second line will be tied near the middle of the cross-river rope and tied off to a tree high above on the cliff. Manned by its own pair of pulley jockeys, the second line will hopefully keep enough tension in the main line to keep the boats from drifting. "It's the kind of thing you talk about in theory, or set up to try a rescue," says Joe, "but I've never had to do it with people's lives really hanging in jeopardy, on the brink of being swept to certain death."

For all the technical concern, the bottom line is that if Paulo doesn't make the ferry across the next morning we'll all be hiking out—and he and Joe will probably be dead.

At 6:30 we quit for the day. Camp is made fifty yards from where we'd spent the night before, in fact we can still see last night's camp—a bad sign. In two full days we'd traveled not even half a mile. For the third straight night our beds will be rocks. Most of our inflatable sleeping pads have been punctured by sharp rocks and we are now sleeping atop lifejackets, wetsuits, and empty dry bags.

Given our lackluster mileage, the big event of the day is the appearance in this otherwise unpopulated area of a lone Tibetan hunter. Dressed in an aged and soiled Chinese army uniform, he carries an AK-47.

With Jiyue's help, we find out his name is Shu Lunzhi. He is as amazed to see us as we are him. His first thought is that we are prospectors, come for the gold, which is abundant in the Shuilo He. He helps us all day, humping boats and bags over slippery rocks in his worn-out sneakers. His every move is gentle, nonthreatening, though he keeps his machine gun over his shoulder at all times.

Employed as a village guard, he is a four hours' walk from home. He's come to hunt mountain goats, wild pigs, and small bear—with his machine gun. When asked what we should expect from the river, he says it levels out after three more big rapids. He is familiar with the waterfalls we are trying to evade. When the river is lower he cuts young trees, lays them across the big rocks at the top of the falls, and crosses the river to hunt. If he's successful, he carries his score back across the river balanced on his shoulders. Late this night he disappears for half an hour and returns with a goat leg, which he turns into a delicious midnight stew.

• • •

Up early the next morning, sitting on the bank of the river, it is still cold. I sip warmed-up goat stew and, looking around, am reminded of one reason we had come to China. As the stars fade and the sun creeps into the canyon, a delft-blue sky is revealed. Pillowy clouds hover over golden peaks at valley's end and a single arc of sunlight spotlights the densely forested slopes. A flock of starlings rises, wings silvered by the morning's brightness.

As Paulo and Joe prepare to take the cataraft across, the sun still hadn't hit the inside of the canyon. I overhear Paulo tell his partner, "As soon as we bump a rock, jump off and pull us in. I don't want to have to bump a second one." Chief cook and safety kayaker Marco Gressi and I sit on an immense rock overlooking the scene. Knowing that he would kayak across the powerful river next, he admits, "I can't wait to be on the other side, stirring the soup."

There is nothing we can do but watch. While the cataraft is rigged—every rope tightened, pontoons pumped and repumped—I see Paulo slipping into a wetsuit and running shoes. A California-born river rat, this is a sure sign he's taking the crossing seriously. In the years I've watched him on rivers I've seen him suit up maybe once before and never before seen him wear shoes on the river.

After a big upriver push, Joe mounts the front of the cataraft like a bronco rider. The sun, now glistening off the river, highlights the red-and-yellow climbing rope hung over his shoulder. The crystal-blue river, pulsing at nearly twenty miles per hour, pours in a smooth tongue between a handful of giant rocks at the top of the falls.

While still in the safety of calm water, Paulo strokes hard upriver to set himself up to cross. He makes a couple false starts, testing the current, making sure he has enough room once into the meat of the river to get full, powerful strokes without banging his oars on exposed rocks. With no warning the boat drifts into the current. It looks like they're heading fast down the left side—the wrong side. But with a half dozen strong pushes the boat is across and into the rock-laden eddy on the opposite shore. Joe leaps off the front, stumbling briefly as he pulls the banana-boat to safety. Whoops of relief shower the air. The nerve-racking crossing took all of twenty seconds. It then takes five hours to secure the triangle of ropes and pulleys needed to safely drag the rest of us across the river.

At four o'clock on our fifth day on the river, we are still moving downriver. But getting around the falls proves as arduous as skirting them from above. As twilight sets in we stagger through a two-hour portage-from-hell, hacking a trail through the brush that lines the shore, lugging everything—bags, propane tank, kayaks—one hundred feet at a time, fire- brigade style. Dressed in wetsuits, helmets, and life jackets—no one wants to fall in the river, or crack a skull at this juncture—means raising a powerful sweat in the heat of the late afternoon.

Ironically, we do see some cracked skulls as we portage. The first belongs to a Chinese man who our pair of doctors estimate has been dead for about a month. We discover him as we pass bags along the riverside; his body is draped violently over a log, crammed between two rocks. The back of his head has been caved in by a rock. His pants and belt are intact, but his shirt has been stripped by the rushing water. We guess he got too close to the river during monsoon season, and was swept away. Within a hundred yards we find the bodies of two more men who'd suffered similar fates. Finding dead bodies in the river was prophetic for us all, a powerful reminder of just how unrelenting a powerful river can be.

• • •

Our seventh day on the river is relaxed. After portaging the boats around a narrow, "frowning" hole—the kind that swallows you and doesn't spit you out—we spend the rest of the day smoothly running Class II, III, and IV rapids beneath a bronzing sun. As we progress the valleys grow more broad and we pass one gentle tributary after another. The wide-open skies are a welcome sight after a week spent in the tight confines of the narrow canyon.

At lunch we park on a sandy beach across from a small, busy gold- mining camp. Afterward, as we peel out, the workers line the banks and wave. Some hold seining baskets, others shovels. Behind them, men cut wood to fuel the engines that suck up river water and, hopefully, spit out gold flakes.

Despite all the physical difficulties of the trip, the first real conflicts emerge that night. Joe, prompted by Eric, explains over a roaring fire that the decision has been made to end the trip roughly twenty-five miles from where we are camped, at the only village on the river, called Beiyong Ping. From there, we will climb to the last road marked on the map. That would leave us thirty miles short of the Yangtze. "We just think this is the safest way to go," says Joe. "We're all a little disappointed we won't dip our toes into the Yangtze, but realistically, if we hit another gorge or two, it could take us ten more days. And we can't afford that." We have food enough for three or four more days.

For the next fifteen hours small meetings are held up and down the sandy beach, as the decision is debated. Joe floats the idea of a small group—one raft and two kayaks—continuing. But by the middle of the next day he's withdrawn that idea. "Bad call," he admits. "We've got very little Chinese money and only one Chinese speaker. We've got to stick together. We came in as a team, I think we should go out a team." While there is some dissent, led by Jon Dragan who confides, "I've never quit anything I've started," the logic in hiking out ultimately made sense. We've dropped two thousand feet and covered forty-five miles, very similar to the first descents we'd made on the Futaleufu and the Colca. Inside the tight canyon walls of the Shuilo we'd seen a part of the globe no man had seen before.

The biggest hassle is that the trail leading to a logging road is on river left, which means we are at best a hard three-day drive away from Lijiang. That's if we can find vehicles willing to pick up eighteen hitchhikers and more than a ton of gear. As Dragan cheerfully points out, "Now the adventure begins."

Our last night on the Shuilo He is spent sleeping on sand brightened by the glimmer of gold flakes. On a sunny morning we roll up the boats, load them onto pack mules hired from a nearby mining camp, and climb three thousand feet straight up from the river. As we cross the narrow bridge over the Shuilo He we look thankfully upriver and somewhat longingly downriver. Beneath us the river twists and narrows before disappearing into another canyon. As we climb, we each to ourselves wonder exactly what lies beyond.

BIG CHOP ON THE YANGTZE

My eyes are locked on a bright red dragonfly that has lighted a foot in front of me on the edge of the yellow Lexitron raft. I focus on the bug like a madman, trying desperately to avoid looking downstream at what lies ahead, as we push the heavy rubber boat off the sand, into the fast-moving Yangtze River. It is a blazing, sunny day—it's been like that for the past week here in rural China, not far off the border of Tibet, heading south toward Vietnam. But any big geographic picture is beyond me at this instant. Basically I am filled with dread as we float through deceptively calm waters towards the biggest waves I've ever seen on a river.

Hung Men Khou is the name given this rapid when it was first attempted nine years before, also the last time it was attempted. That one had ended badly, with boats flipped and men swimming frantically for their lives.

We had scouted from shore for more than an hour, trying to read the quarter-mile-long rapid's breaks, rolls, and torrents. Initially the run looked left . . . except for those big breaking waves crashing backward about a quarter of the way in. Then we thought it looked like we should run down the right, a course that might eventually push the big boats into the center of the river, where immense rollers crashed together in a miasma of whitewater. The greatest danger was getting too far to the right, because then you'd more than likely be sucked into the wall and flipped. And a flip here meant swimming to save your life as the boat was either sucked to the bottom of the river or pulled downstream toward Shanghai, twenty-five hundred miles to the east.

That three rafts and a trio of kayakers have already run the rapid successfully is no solace. Our boat is big, heavy, weighted down by literally a ton of baggage and a creaking metal floor. We—photographer and longtime river guide Barry Tessman and I—have a plan. Our goal is to slide out into the eddy, high above the entrance to Hung Men, then "bite off" a corner of the giant entry wave at an angle. Hopefully that initial bump will turn the raft around to face the next series of waves head-on . . . from there we just hope to hang on through the giant train of waves. The key is hitting that monstrous second wave head-on. If we do, the big boat should steamroll right along. We will definitely get wet, but we should stay upright.

As we push off and drift into the fast-moving flow Barry is at the oars, thus bearing 99 percent of the responsibility for our safety. Loud grunts emanating from the back of the boat indicate he is desperately trying to row backward, across the current, valiantly trying to position the raft dead in the center of the fast-approaching two-and-a-half-story waves.

As most well-laid plans do, this one goes awry. Badly. We don't quite get enough of the initial wave to spin us around to face the wave. Instead we just get hit hard and spun sideways—depositing us in the worst possible position, heading sideways into a twenty-five-foot-tall wall of waves, in a boat rendered completely unmaneuverable.

This is where my limited role begins. It involves throwing my weight into the front tubes just as they are hit by giant waves, desperate to keep rubber on water, endeavoring to prevent the front end of the boat from getting too much air and flipping over backwards. I sneak a look back a couple times, just to make sure Barry's still in the boat. I glimpse him jerking on the oars, grunting like a man possessed, a look of confused desperation on his face, yelling out "high side," while I flop around in the bow like a drunken marionette.

It gets worse. We are sucked as if by a vacuum cleaner into the giant chop on the right, which tosses the boat dangerously close to the wall. If we so much as kiss the rock, the boat will flip and we'll be thrown into the churning maelstrom. I catch Barry's eyes and he shrugs his shoulders even as he grimaces, still struggling against the oars fruitlessly. The only thing we can do is hang on, ride it out, pray we stay upright. Vision is obscured by a wall of water pouring into the boat from all directions; I try to catch a breath and swallow a mouthful of river. I hang on to a safety line with one hand, flopping halfout of the boat.

Despite our un-effort, the big boat is finally tossed into the center of a train of smaller waves, ten feet tall, remarkably still right side up. Our tumult lasted about a minute, though it felt like an hour. Wiping the river out of my eyes, my mood changed dramatically. At the top of the rapid I felt like hiking around. Now, just a half mile downriver, I'm exhilarated, glad to be here, wouldn't want to be anywhere else in the world, looking optimistically downriver . . . and silently praying that Hung Men Kou was the last big one of the day. Of course, it is not.

• • •

The Yangtze is one of the world's great rivers. Its thirty-nine hundred-miles make it the third longest in the world (after the Nile and the Amazon, just a tad longer than the Mississippi). Originating in the snow-covered Tanggulashan mountains of southwestern Quinghai, it rises from the Quinghai-Tibetan plateau and passes through Tibet and twelve of China's twenty-nine Chinese provinces, dropping 17,600 feet before spilling into the East China Sea near Shanghai. Powered by more than seven hundred tributaries, the Yangtze supports a third of China's population.

We are attempting a section known as the Great Bend, a three hundred-mile stretch that cuts across Yunnan province, situated in the southwestern corner of China. Yunnan is the most varied of all the provinces, its geography ranging from tropical rainforests to the frozen Tibetan plateau (the so-called Roof of the World). The area has been inhabited for more than two thousand years and today thirty-four million people live within its borders. The majority are Han (who make up 93 percent of all of China), but twenty-four of the country's fifty-five minorities live there, too, making for a varied and diverse culture.

We are only the second "team" of westerners to attempt this stretch. Only a handful of Chinese have run it successfully, members of competing expeditions racing in the mid-1980s, to be the first to descend the entire Yangtze. Due to excessively high permit fees charged by a government that until very recently has discouraged tourists into China's interior, the river has been absent of river runners for a decade. This despite the fact that the scenery is majestic and the average flow of 65,000 to 70,000 cfs makes it roughly five times the power of the Colorado coursing through the Grand Canyon. (In 1987 Sobek, the California-based travel company paid the Chinese government $100,000 to run the Great Bend; our trip, organized by a small New York-based outfitter, cost a quarter of that.)

Permit fees are dropping and access to China's interior is opening up because the government is slowly recognizing that the hard currency that accompanies tourism is good. The truth is China desperately needs the foreign exchange that tourism provides; with several million tourists flocking in every year, the tallest buildings in the country are hotels. Since the early eighties individual travelers have been more or less welcome and the man-on-the-street even in small villages is quite approachable. In fact they are the first to admit that the great socialist experiment was a bust. Ask if they are communist and they look at you like you're crazy. Ask if they prefer capitalism and big smiles break out. They know on which side their *baba* (bread) is buttered. In the nineties China's GNP has grown by more than 10 percent each year. In parts of the country this swelling tide has lifted many to a level of consumerism they never imagined. But for how long? Population controls popularized in the early seventies, including such campaigns as "Longer, Later, Fewer," are working (more so in the cities than the countryside), but China's 1.2 billion population may still double in the next fifty years. Which translates into big pressure on its natural resources, especially its most powerful river.

The Great Bend is about one thousand miles from the most talked-about stretch of the Yangtze, the Three Gorges—where, as we ready to raft, mountains are disappearing and a new concrete topography is rising in their place, connected in a man-made design whose foundations are being laid across a dust bowl so broad that it seems almost planetlike in scale. More than one million people will be displaced by the dam, which will be six hundred feet tall and 1.3 miles across, creating a reservoir stretching 385 miles up the Yangtze, submerging ancient farmland, temples, wildlife habitats, and archeological treasures dating from ten thousand years. In their place will be the biggest, most expensive and perhaps most hazardous hydroelectric dam ever attempted. It is expected to be finished in 2009, at a cost of between $17 billion and $30 billion. After the Yangtze has been dammed, the world's engineers will be left with only two major rivers to plug: the Zaire and the main stem of the Amazon.

We are among just a few westerners to traverse this section of China, to ride the beautiful, mysterious Yangtze, and we are fortunate. As capitalism pokes its fingers deeper and deeper into even the most rural regions, China's few unadulterated places will soon be overexplored.

• • •

To reach our put-in we must hike through the Tiger Leaping Gorge, one of the great attractions of Yunnan province and one of the planet's most beautiful and giant natural *flaws*.

The gorge is twelve miles long and the Haba Mountains tower on both sides of the canyon, highlighted by the 18,899-foot glaciated summit of Jade Dragon Peak, or Yulongxue Shan, which looms over Lijiang. The river we can see one thousand feet below the narrow trail is not more than a narrow ribbon of continuous spit and foam. Thirty giant rapids, each one seemingly bigger than the next, disrupt the river, making it virtually un-navigable—though a half dozen Chinese have managed to run the entire length of the gorge by encapsulating themselves in rubber tire-cushioned crafts, similar to going over Niagara in a barrel. So far all but one have emerged bruised and battered, barely conscious, but successful.

The canyon's name comes from a legend. It seems that a very proud tiger was being chased by a hunting party when it reached the edge of the gorge, an apparent dead-end with the Yangtze roiling a thousand feet below. Urged on by an incredible will to live, the tiger leapt and landed safely on the other side of the river.

It takes us two days to hike the path along the canyon's edge. The morning we choose to start is cool and cloudy. Our destination is a guest house halfway through the gorge, at a tiny village called Walnut Grove. It takes five or six hours of easy, awe-inspiring walking. Chiseled marble cliffs lead up to the shimmering peaks of Black Water Snow, White Snow, and Cloud Snow, all over twelve thousand feet. We cross over rock slides, some that appear to have come down within recent hours. We shimmy across and beneath waterfalls. At some points the path is reduced to two feet wide, meaning your backpack is hanging over a thousand-foot drop as you hug the wall with your chest and chin.

Late afternoon brings us to Sean's Spring House Guest House. The lodge is set on a hill above small terraced farms that plunge directly down to the river's edge. Tattered Tibetan prayer flags hang over the stone patio; tall green corn grows behind a fieldstone wall. A heavy mist hangs over the twelve thousand-foot peaks, turning the black, tan, and forest-green walls into a muted mural. Established in 1986, Sean proudly hung the first American dollar he received in 1992. A hand-painted sign out front reads: "Best Travel Information in English. Hot and Cold Drinks. Free Hot Showers (Solar Heated)." Business must be good: Electric lines arrived three weeks earlier and Sean is building an addition to sleep twenty more, doubling his occupancy. Rooms for two, three, or four cost less than a dollar for a night. (The government has a plan to put in a road along the gorge one day soon, to provide easy tourist reach, a plan which will inevitably destroy the beauty of the very place they are trying to lure people to see.)

The place is crowded tonight, fifteen travelers of diverse nationalities, all headed for the end of the trail at the village of Dali. When we arrive we pet a goat tied to the front post and observe a couple of chickens scurrying around the yard. Not long after, I notice all three are missing (clued by one of Sean's pretty little girls walking gingerly across the patio carrying a bowl of blood in her hands). As soon as darkness falls, guess what we have for dinner? Goat liver and goat heart appetizers, followed by chicken soup, snow peas, and barbecued goat legs.

Sean sits with us after dinner. He speaks good English, a rarity in rural China, and is very helpful about the history of the incredible valley where he grew up. While he talks he points with one hand; his other is useless, attached to a deformed arm, a story he gives up with a little prodding. When he was two years old the Red Guard visited the region during the latter years of the Cultural Revolution. Ostensibly they were checking to make sure Chairman Mao's "education" program was being adhered to. As an example, they pulled young Sean from the crowd and set him afire—

this is what would happen to anyone who chose noncompliance, they warned. The example left his left arm crippled and burns covering most of his upper body. It also left him with a hatred for all things Mao and the China he represented. Thus the explanation for his giving his two daughters distinctly Anglo names—Lucy and Rosie—and why he's obviously ignored the one-child population measure.

An entrepreneur, Sean is doing alright, so he's staying put. But many of his friends are among the spectators to China's economic transformation; many have already left the countryside for bigger cities where they believe/hope there are more jobs, more opportunity. While eight hundred million peasants may have plenty of food and a small house, most have very little cash in a society that puts an increasingly high value on money and consumption. Many in the countryside get by on just $20 a month, while the national per capita wage in urban areas is $470. As a result, many are fleeing the countryside for the cities, migrant workers looking for mostly non-existent work, resulting in growing ghettos, unemployment, crime, and a steady decline in Marxist ideology. China's official news agency reports there are approximately one hundred and twenty million peasants out of work in the countryside, a number that could swell to two hundred million by the year 2000. Meanwhile, the government says transient workers roaming the country in search of work—some eighty million—are a major source of crime.

Sean is not worried about the future—his or his country's—and refuses to allow bitterness to dissuade him. He's got a growing business, dependent on a growing tourism industry, so he's in favor of opening all of China's doors. He's picked up on the lessons of capitalism well. When a guest, an innocent from Tennessee, admires his tablecloth—replete with Sean's Spring House logo—he offers to part with it for 40 yuan. "It's handmade," he says. When the happy tourist departs, Sean disappears into a storeroom and returns with an exact replica of the cloth he just sold. Turns out he's got boxes of them, made in Lijiang. "That's not a bad thing, is it?" he wonders out loud, adapting a particularly innocent look. "Isn't that how you get ahead in America?"

• • •

By midmorning on our put-in day the skies start to blue up. As the boats are rigged—oar rigs adjusted, metal boxes filled and locked down, personal bags cinched tight, water jugs filled—a couple dozen young kids watch, enchanted by a donated Frisbee. The air is filled with nervous chatter. Although not exactly unknown, our scouting report indicates the river below is big. Maybe too big. Two weeks before, California kayakers and river guides Beth Rypins and Joe Dengler had run the same stretch we're about to try. "Biggest waves I've ever seen," was Joe's report; his estimate was that the river was running at 90,000 cfs, or nearly ten times as fast as the Colorado through the Grand Canyon. When all that power hits rock-choked stretches it created waves more than 30 feet tall. Monstrous troughs that sent the kayakers cartwheeling, boils that spun their boats perpendicular to the river then back, within seconds. "I was behind Joey a couple times," says Beth, "and he simply disappeared when he dropped off the top of a couple of those waves."

If we pull this off without incident it will also prove that running the Yangtze is now a trip for just about anybody with the will and the pocketbook. While several of those along are among the best river runners in the world, lured by the chance to run one of the world's great rivers, we are joined by a cast of middle-aged adventure travelers of middling experience: three lawyers, a stockbroker, a former NFL tight end, an art director, architect, plant manager, Xerox designer, camera dealer, forensic psychologist, and nephrologist. The paying customers will ride in two rafts, eighteen- and seventeen-foot Sotars, accompanied by three safety kayaks and a small cataraft. Two big, heavy baggage boats—aging, metal-floored Moravias—will lug all the food, fuel, and personal gear. Barry and I are in the biggest, leakiest, most unmanueverable craft and will truly bring up the rear.

Our first test lay waiting less than an hour downstream. "First Blood," Sobek had dubbed it.

Twenty-foot waves pitched in every direction along the right side of a long, center wave. Sizable rolling waves would inevitably dump back on the boats as they plowed through the middle of the quarter-mile-long furrow. Most respectable was that the waves were just as big at the top of the rapid as at the bottom. Though the river had dropped since Beth and Joe had visited, we guessed it was still running high, at 60,000 cfs.

We were the last through and the first big wave stood our nineteen-foot boat literally on end. Portland lawyer Jay Waldrin and I tried to keep the front end of the boat touching water, even as the boat swamped. We were literally underwater as we pounded on the front tubes with our full weight, trying to keep the boat from flipping over backwards. Barry said later that for most of the run all he could see of us was the tops of our red helmets. This action continued for several waves, the big boat surfing right, then left, as Barry bravely but vainly attempted to point its heavy bow straight into the crashing waves.

Just when we thought we were safely at the end of the rapid, big whirlpool boils concealed just beneath the surface threatened to suck us under, as if a giant hand were reaching out from below to pull us down. I turned around and Barry was pulling on the oars as hard as he could—which is pretty damned hard if you've ever seen his biceps—with a look of shock and concern on his face.

The highlight of the afternoon was the narrowing of the gorge into tight canyon walls rising several hundred feet straight up on either side. The becalmed river was squeezed from a half mile across to just one hundred feet wide. The shiny black rock walls changed colors as we drifted with the flat current—turning tan, then a shiny off-white, sprinkled with every mineral color imaginable, gold, silver, emerald, jade, sapphire, ruby. Thankfully the wind was at our backs as we drifted out of the gorge and past the immaculately terraced fields of small villages. Even in this remote corner of the world's most populous nation it's difficult to truly get away from it all.

The lowlight of the afternoon was when we let Jay try his hand at rowing us through a sizable rapid, its most notable feature being a rock the size of a small hotel plunked right in the middle of the river. Running that rapid reminded me of landing a 747 at the Hong Kong airport—there was only one line to take and if you were off by just an oar stroke, if we so much as nipped that big rock, we'd be upside down in a second. Jay tried to assure us with tales of the big rapids he'd rowed in the past.

We were hardly convinced when we almost bought it, the big waves over-powering Jay's experience, and the boat coming within inches of nipping that rock. A relieved if slightly aggravated Barry jumped immediately back on the oars.

• • •

As well as contending with the physical challenges of running this big river, it is a job each day just to keep mental track of all the incredible visuals lining the shores. Waves this day average six to eight feet, so most of the day we luxuriate by taking in the sights. As we push off to start our second day on the river a gaggle of kids run along the banks after us, several of them carrying small rifles. Our floating idyll is interrupted in mid-afternoon when the lead raft drifts close to the one-hundred-foot-tall rock wall and a small herd of rambunctious mountain goats kick a potentially dangerous spray of rocks off the cliff edge, missiles pocking the flat water around the boat.

We make camp on a sandy beach that Beth and Joe say did not exist three weeks before, an indication of how much the river has dropped. Across the river we can make out a cluster of a dozen small houses with peaked, wooden-tiled roofs. One big house stands out because of the thirty-foot tree shading it. It is the only tree of any substance in the whole valley, the rest of the forest having long ago been cut for fuel.

During the night we can see flashlights flickering across the river; in the morning a few lone figures dressed in dark colors lean against walls, looking down on us. What must they think of this floating flotilla? Probably that we are gringo prospectors, dressed in obscenely bright colors. And what must these people think of this powerful, magnificent, river that flows in front of their homes? They surely don't use it for recreation—there's no swimming across to sunbathe on the rocks and the only boat within sight is a smashed wooden dugout canoe. Do they see the river as a threat or a source of life? A barrier? A vein, a link, transportation to another world?

On our side of the river we meet a fisherman living in cave. Though a handful of miniscule fish are lined up in front of him, he is eating bark, herbs, and corn. He explains to Jiyue and I that he comes here for three days each week to fish for his family. It takes him two days to hike here from his inland home. He wears his chopsticks tucked in his belt like a gringo would carry a knife; a blue wool cap is pulled snugly over his ears. When he smiles, I can make out just a pair of yellowed teeth. He generously shares his homemade rice wine with us, and we dig out a pack of Marlboros and a couple airplane bottles of Johnny Walker Black in return.

Food scarcity is not the only concern of the region. This night, just fifty miles away in Lijiang, a 5.8 earthquake rocks and rolls. A month later a 7.0 would jolt the same area, killing more than two hundred, collapsing two hundred thousand mud homes, seriously injuring 4,000. It was followed by one hundred and eighty-four aftershocks in the next twenty-four hours. The worst earthquake in recent history in the area was in 1976; that one killed an estimated two hundred and forty-two thousand in a tremor that registered 7.8.

The tenuousness of the housing combined with the abundant population makes for big-time disasters along the Yangtze. Flooding is an annual concern; torrential rains combined with big snow melts and even global warming are blamed. No matter how many earthen breaks are constructed, no matter how many billions spent, almost annually the big river muscles its way out of its banks to take a toll on the crowded towns that line them. In this century alone floods along the Yangtze have killed a half million people.

This night, on our little sand spit, all is peaceful. Sleeping under bright stars and a nearly full moon, it is almost too bright to sleep. When the moon finally dissolves through the V of the canyon, the night is plunged into blackness. The sky is saturated with stars, and features dozens of shooting ones as well as the occasional satellite. It is a pleasure to wake up during the night, rolling over in the soft riverside sand, an occasion to take solace in the incredible night sky.

• • •

Morning starts with a visit from a thirty-foot motorized longboat carrying a dozen miners. We'd passed their camp the previous afternoon and wondered over the campfire last night exactly how they managed to get their unwieldy boat onto this flat stretch of river, which is banked on either side by rapids that would quickly and thoroughly break that boat in two. One of my rafting partners insisted they must have brought it in by pack mule, piece by piece.

They arrive as we are packing up our boats and it is hard to judge who is more curious about the other. Once we explain we are not prospectors—the instant conclusion of all the Chinese we met, since they found it impossible to imagine that we'd come halfway around the world for a pleasure float—they give up how they'd gotten their boat here. Turns out there is a dirt road three kilometers downriver and they had brought the boat in by truck. It is used to shuttle men, equipment, and gold back and forth across the river and to the road; Lijiang is an eight- hour drive away, though just fifty miles away as the crow flies. We ask about their mining methods, concerned they might be using arsenic to help filter the gold. Turns out they do it the old-fashioned way—with a sluice and sieves.

The Yangtze is known as the "River of Golden Sands" and when we camp at night the sands literally glisten with tiny specks of gold. Until 1975 it was illegal for anyone but official government operations to take the gold. Today, individuals are not allowed to mine for gold, but must join collectively under the supervision of local authorities. There is only one hitch: Any gold taken must be sold to the government, which generously pays *half* the international market rate. Not surprisingly, there is a thriving smuggling business blooming. (Mineral smuggling isn't the only illegal business making news as China battles with encroaching capitalism. In the last few years some of the heroin heading out of Burma for the West appears to now be falling off the truck as it heads across China. Eighty percent of China's drug seizures and more than half its "registered" addicts are here in Yunnan province. Nationwide heroin addiction is becoming an unacknowledged problem. At its current growth rate China could soon have the world's highest number of heroin addicts.)

Back on the river, around noon we arrive at the confluence of the Shuilo He, a powerful tributary that joins the Yangtze at the very peak of the Great Bend. We drag the boats onto a high, sandy beach, with a purpose. The widow of a California river runner named Ron Mattson has asked that we hang a prayer flag in his honor, high in the trees above the Yangtze.

An oarsman on the first descent of the Yangtze, Mattson had recently been killed in a motorcycle accident. The vividly colored prayer flag was strung between a pair of sycamores overlooking the confluence, and a short verse was read out loud under a hot sun. It is a decent thing to do and reminds us all that this life we're living so fully at the moment is hardly guaranteed.

After lunch I row Barry and me through the biggest rapid of the day, a powerful but pretty straightforward run through choppy ten- and fifteen-foot waves. When we emerge, upright, the valley widens and the fertile valleys are more populated and heavily planted. Terraces are three hundred and four hundred feet deep, each level carefully plowed by cow power, each ledge expertly built from turf and stone. Villages sit atop the fields, one thousand feet above the river.

Closer to the river's edge the plant life is exotic—bananas grow next to tall cacti, willows next to palms. Groves of pine trees are surrounded by oaks and prickly pears. Fields of bamboo by small patches of marijuana (which the Chinese use medicinally, mostly for a tea used to cure headaches). As we enter a mini canyon, the tall rock walls curve with the river and a twenty-foot-wide waterfall shoots straight out of the rock. Of course we paddle close, for the opportunity of a shower.

• • •

On our sixth day since leaving Lijiang, dark clouds fill the up-valley crease in the canyon and a cold wind blows over camp. The sun doesn't hit our little beach until 9:30. A quick two-kilometer pull downstream brings us to Ban Jo Wa, a five-century-old stone village built fifteen hundred feet above the river. We've decided, based on Beth and Joe's scouting report, to hike up and see how these folks live.

The trail is narrow and steep, winding around terraced fields planted with corn and wheat. At several points it intersects and commingles with a quick-running stream coursing downhill, leading us beneath a couple waterfalls of icy cold freshwater. We pass a man and his daughter plowing a fresh field with a cow and a single wooden plow blade digging a deep rut into the earth. Each terrace is forty feet deep, its walls made of turf and field stone; a sophisticated irrigation system has been diverted from uphill and keeps the plantings tall and green.

Along the path we pass elderly women loaded down with bundles of vegetables in sacks on their backs, and men carrying long scythes. The women wear jade and turquoise hoop earrings and traditional square black hats. They stop and smile, politely stepping out of our way even though we are the intruders. We check out their baskets of reed, they study ours of nylon and Cordura.

Barry and I step off the trail to try and communicate with a pair of older men squatting on the edge of a terrace. With hand signals they tell us they are both sixty-three. Wizened and brown-skinned, they load a scrimshaw pipe with tobacco kept in a soiled leather pouch. They get a big kick out of the Polaroids we offer, but an even bigger charge by touching my leg. They can't get over the long hair, pulling up their blue cotton pant legs to reveal thin, virtually hairless legs.

The village is finally reached after a tough forty-five-minute climb. Below we can just make out the faint yellow of the rafts. The entrance is via stone steps leading beneath a decorative stone arch. We are met by a family of big, black pigs. In fact, there are so many pigs rooting around the streets, on the stairwells, sleeping, pissing, munching, waddling we wonder if Ban Joe Wa translates as Pig City or Hog Heaven. (In fact, it means Jade City, for the mineral that used to be here in abundance.)

Narrow cobblestone and mud walkways lead up. Electric lines hang above, strung from a mini-hydroelectric plant powered by a small tributary dropping to the Yangtze. Immense yellow and orange squash line the ledges of the stone walls, ripening. A satellite dish can be glimpsed at the very top of the hill. The town is actually two: old and new. The original houses are literally built from stone, the new from stuccoed mud. From high on the hill, looking down on the suburb of two hundred newer houses we can see two boys playing pool in a room without a roof (we never found out how the hell they got a pool table this deep into the outback, since we are five hours' walk from the nearest road). A basketball hoop hangs forlornly over a slab of cement. Excited schoolchildren clamber around us as we invade and the elders sneak long stares. They are all especially curious about two hundred and sixty-pound Bruce Bergey, a one-time NFL tight end.

We arrange lunch at a private house, and, seated on low benches in a stone courtyard, are offered generous plates of rice, squash, and potatoes. Our host and chef endures us with a big smile as he stir-fries. Two posters decorate his kitchen, one of a smiling monkey, another of a smiling Buddha. After a sumptuous lunch we waddle back down the hill, to the wide sandy beaches where our boats cook beneath a hot sun.

The afternoon is spent in mostly calm water, the only chore being paddling the heavy baggage boats through the still sections of the river. The biggest action occurs after running a simple, right-angle Class III rapid. Relaxing in the calm beneath the rapid, the rubber tube Bergey is seated on— he's in the front corner of one of the paddle rafts—is sucked under by an unseen whirlpool. The big guy goes out of the boat, sucked down by the vortex. Guide Steve Jones immediately stands up in the back of the raft, trying to spot Bergey when he resurfaces. "I could see the top of his helmet coming towards the surface," he tells us later, "but it wouldn't break the water. First he came up on one side of the boat, then the other, then disappeared again. I was getting worried when he finally popped up for good ten feet in front of the raft."

"It was as if I didn't even have a life jacket on," says Bergey, after he's been pulled back into the raft. "I started swimming for the light and something kept sucking me back down.

"I've swum rapids before, but this is something I've never experienced. And never want to again. The river held me in its mouth, trying to keep me. It felt like it was just playing with me, like a hawk with a mouse."

• • •

It isn't until our last day on the river that we meet Hung Men Kou, that quarter mile of giant, rumbling, breaking waves, crashing around in a mixmaster of human-being-keeping whitewater.

The odd thing is, though I love running rivers, I'm not a fan of big rapids. Which differentiates me from a lot of people who raft. For example, while I'm standing on a rock trying to assess Hung Men, Ed—a sixty-something nephrologist from Connecticut—sidles up and confides that this is why he comes on such trips. "I would be happy to see four or five of these monsters each day." My guess is, Ed's never been sucked deep down into a dark river in such a maelstrom. Me, while everyone else is studying waves, plotting a hopeful course, I'm looking at everything but the rapid, looking downriver to the placid waters below, anxious to be there.

Today I study the simple clothes of the group of kids and adults who have gathered on the rocks to watch these silly gringos risk life and limb. Like fans of stock-car racing, they are no doubt hoping for a spectacular crash. I investigate a bombed-out looking building nearby that resembles a Motel 6. I am told it was a school, bombed by the Red Army twenty years ago. I scramble over big boulders that dot the mouth of a sizable tributary that streams into the Yangtze just above the rapid, pumping up the river's flow, feeding the rapid. Between the boulders is a sticky black mud that threatens to rip off my shoes as I try to cross it quickly. Mostly I try and keep my gaze far downriver, to the mountains in the near distance and the flat water that lies below, to the place where, Allah willing, we will all be safe and sound and upright in just a matter of minutes.

My stomach is in a knot, my mind questioning why I am here as we push our big boat into the eddy. That's when I spot the bright red dragonfly posed calmly on the yellow raft. Focusing on the iridescent bug gives me some peace before the inevitable tempest.

MURDER IN THE KARAKORAM

Death occasionally crossed the mind of Edward "Ned" Gillette, though he didn't dwell on it, wasn't scared of dying. But like anyone who makes a career out of adventuring, he wondered how he might die. Perhaps the ultimate late-twentieth-century adventurer—renowned for the variety of his expeditions as well as a singular skill at convincing corporate sponsors to finance them, whether they be around mountains, across oceans, or through deserts—Gillette, fifty-three, had dared the gods in a variety of treacherous settings. When his time was up, he had to assume it might come beneath the coldest part of the Atlantic, or deep inside some mountain crevasse.

In his darkest moments he could never have expected to be shot-gunned to death through the wall of his tent.

On August 5, a beautiful, blue-skied summer day, he and his wife, Susie Patterson, forty-two, were camped at the base of the sixty-eight hundred-meter Laila Peak, beneath Chogolumga Glacier in the Northern District of Pakistan. They had left the U.S. in early July for two months of exploring, climbing, photographing, and writing. It was almost a holiday compared to some of the more arduous trips Gillette had made over the past thirty years.

That afternoon they had completed a tough five-day trek across the glacier; they jeeped from Gilgit around the mountains, in order to begin their climb from the small village of Daku. They had attempted the route—though in reverse—the previous September, but were turned back by deep snows. They returned early in July to spend two months, finishing this trek as well as the circling of Nanga Parvit, which they had completed just weeks before.

It was rugged, remote country. The Haramosh Valley is one of forty that carve east and west from the Karakoram Highway and the Indu River gorge, dead-ending at the glacier. Angular, jagged peaks rose all around their camp spot—the very same place they'd camped the September before—to twenty-three thousand feet. Three small villages hung precariously along the ridges of the narrow, fifteen-mile-long valley.

From their tent they were three kilometers from the nearest small village, and six hours' walking from the road that lead to the Karakoram. It was another three hours by jeep to Gilgit, eighty miles away. The Karakoram Highway is frequented by buses, trucks, military vehicles. In fact, the highway is littered with police checkpoints (where, ironically, Ned had filled in false names as they passed by.)

This trip was a goal for Ned that was much more important for him than it was for me, [says Patterson from their home in Sun Valley.] I really loved the Nanga Parvit part, the beauty of it, the goal. This thing Ned really wanted to do. We didn't know if we could get up and over the pass.

The day before it happened was such a cool day. Cloudless, blue sky. The pass was at sixteen thousand feet—which for Ned was no problem. Easy enough that we could go fast. But beautiful and fun and carefree. We were on the glacier, but going up the pass, so the crevasses were open enough at this time of year that we could see them. They weren't big. Fairly easy travel, beautiful country.

The top of the pass was good and fun; coming down was nothing but hideous loose rock. There was a faint trail. We actually ran into one local person coming the opposite way over the pass, so we knew it was doable. Ned never thought anything was impossible. He always thought he could make something work, without it being death defying.

The descent was really scary, slightly out of control, lots of loose rock. It wasn't like crampons and ice axes would work on all these slick rocks.

Another real problem that I always feared, was that even if Ned and I were roped, together, I'm so small that I might not be able to do a good belay.

We didn't see any other tourists. In the past three years people just haven't been going to Pakistan, unless they're going to climb the high mountains. Or to travel along the Karakoram Highway. So what Ned and I wanted to do was something in the middle. Which is why it was cool. We would be in really remote areas, wouldn't see any westerners. And we always liked that, especially Ned. He was always asking, "Have any westerners been here before?" I'm pretty sure no one had done this trip before.

It took us four hours to get down the pass; Ned especially was really beat. We camped in the exact same spot we'd camped when we'd come up the valley last fall, in these grassy shepherd fields. We also wanted to camp there so we could look back up at the pass we'd just crossed.

We got down in early evening, put up camp, had tea, made dinner. We put up our little green two-man tent, which blended in with the grass. Ned especially was really psyched that we'd accomplished this crossing. Exhausted, but really psyched. With night came a moon that was not quite full, kind of eery. It was pretty bright. We could see the moon's craters and it felt really close. We had a really beautiful dinner together, literally said, "I love you," and went to sleep.

The next thing I heard was a gunshot. [It was between 10 p.m. and midnight.]

The sound was piercing, loud. I woke up and Ned was wild-eyed. All he could say was, "It's my insides . . . . .I think I'm dying . . . my insides are whacked out . . . I think I'm dying." Then he passed out.

I thought he'd gone deaf, because he had ear problems, or that he was having a bad dream. I was just waking up and I didn't understand the seriousness of it right away.

There were more shots. I was yelling at him to wake up. I wasn't hysterical, I just didn't know what was going on. I think I never, ever wanted to admit to myself the seriousness of what was happening. I got him back to consciousness by shaking him and yelling at him, slapping his face. His eyes were glazed, [she starts to cry,] with such a wild look on his face . . . it was so scary. Then he came to, and seemed almost normal.

I kept saying "I've got to get help," and he kept saying to me, like a little boy, "Don't leave." But he was coherent enough to say "We've got to get out of the tent, it's dangerous."

Ned was in shock. That's the only way he was physically able to get up, because he was in such pain. We started putting our boots on . . . and then I got shot. Ned said, "Oh god, they got you, too." It felt like a sledgehammer slamming into my back—it didn't knock the wind out of me—I just felt so nauseous. I think Ned realized what was happening to us, better than I, and I think maybe then he felt better somehow, that maybe I was with him now, that we were going to die together .

We were just able to get out of the tent, to hide behind our packs, which were up against the side of the tent. We couldn't stand up, couldn't walk, couldn't travel. We couldn't see anyone.

I just got so cold, I said to Ned, "We can't go anywhere. I've got to get back in my sleeping bag." I was starting to crawl back into the tent when we saw a man, or a kid, coming out of the darkness with a big rock over his head. Somehow Ned managed to get a rock and lunge at this guy and the guy just disappeared back into the dark.

We got back in the tent. We didn't have any energy to do anything else. We couldn't really talk. Then another gunshot went off—I don't think it hit anything. Both of us were yelling now, "Please stop, we're dying, you've done enough, please stop." [She thinks about a half hour passed between the first and last gunshot.]

Ned held my hand., but he never said he was in pain. At one point he said, "I'm worried," at another point he said, "I'm losing a lot of blood." I'm sure he was in shock, and acute pain, but I was the one saying, "Please, Ned, please help me." I kept having to crawl across his head because I felt like I had to throw up, but I couldn't throw up, it was too painful.

We just focused in on getting through the night, and on being together. We both really had a lot of hope.

Dawn came and we were both still alive. Neither of us could move, we just lay there. We knew that at some point someone would come up to the meadow. Ned was still able to get his head up and look out both sides of the tent to see if anyone was coming.

We didn't have enough energy to yell any louder than we're talking now. Finally someone came and one guy spoke some basic English. Ned kept saying, "We got shot." He was really clear. Six shots, two men. Go to a phone, get a helicopter up here, go now. Then two more men came.

Eventually one guy went down, but an hour later a kid came back up and said no one had gone to phone for help. So Ned got a bunch of rupees—he zeroed in, he was really coherent—and said, "Get somebody down there, get a helicopter up here."

After that Ned started losing consciousness. [She starts to cry.] At this point I think he knew it was only a matter of time. His breathing started getting labored. I felt his stomach, I could feel the gunshots, his heart was erratic . . . during the course of the morning all he really said to me was, "I love you, I love you," that's all he said. [She stops talking, starts crying softly.]

I propped him up, cut his T-shirt off him, and he just closed his eyes . . . it was peaceful for him, but for me, I just didn't care anymore. [She is crying steadily now.] I didn't care, nothing mattered anymore . . .

After that I just laid in the tent all that day . . . I had to plead with the villagers not to leave me alone because I was terrified. They asked me if they wanted me to leave Ned in the tent . . . and I said yes, because I thought maybe he'd say something, or move . . . and finally I realized this was awful, and I had them take him out and the whole tent floor was full of blood . . . there were down feathers everywhere. That was the first time I really saw the blood, and the degree of the gunshot wounds, and just how brutal and horrible it was .

I was in a lot of pain, but I just didn't care about anything. I laid there all that day and all that night, waiting for help, but I can't tell you what I did. I was like an insane zombie. There were ten villagers around

the tent now and they did everything they could for me,
encouraging me to be strong, to have courage.

Finally the next morning—almost thirty-six hours after the shoot-
ings—I agreed to let them take me down in a stretcher. It was the most
incredibly painful ride down on this stretcher, but these
villagers were incredible. It took four hours to get down, over really rough
terrain. They used our climbing rope to strap me in; I
couldn't breathe I was tied so tight. But they didn't want me to fall out.
I could only lay on my side; I was shot on one side and my back. So they
slammed me between two big posts, in a rudimentary homemade
stretcher and tied me in. Halfway down the police were finally coming
up. There was a doctor in the car . . . they got me into what they called
an ambulance, a busted-up jeep.

She was kept in a hospital in Gilgit for five days, one lung filled with
blood, sixty to seventy buckshot in her back and side, before being allowed
to fly to Islamabad where her brother, Pete—a good friend of Ned's, who had
introduced the two—was waiting.

• • •

Two days later, on Saturday, August 8, two suspects, Abid Ilussain and Naun
Ileshel, were arrested, turned in by local villagers. A shotgun was recovered;
the pair charged with murder and assault. A trial was to be held quickly; if
found guilty the pair would be hung within a matter of weeks.

"Just a couple dimwitted kids doing a stupid robbery of the rich
Americans," says Bob Law, Gillette's brother-in-law. According to local police, Gillette was the first foreigner ever murdered in this region of Pakistan.

"The pair were turned over after 'prompting' from police," says U.S.
Embassy Counsel General Bernie Alter, from his office in Islamabad. "I suspect that the police heard rumors of who might have done it, went to that
village, and said they would make things nasty for the whole village if they
didn't help."

Patterson does not believe robbery was the motive. "I think this Muslim
stuff just makes these kids crazy. Think of it: Nothing was stolen. Why not?"

• • •

The sad irony is that at the time of his death, Gillette had moved away from the big, corporate-financed, riskier expeditions and back to simple, purer individual trips. "Ned had evolved into this incredibly beautiful person," Susie wrote in a note to Ned's family. "He got back to why this adventure stuff intrigued him in the first place. The beauty, the simplicity, the purity, yet still maintaining that desire to find a goal to explore and do incredible things in a new place, country."

His sister, Debby Law of San Francisco, confirms Gillette's evolution back to more simple trips. "He'd come around to doing small, independent, self-reliant, creative, fun trips—with Susie. Their relationship meant everything to him."

Gillette's death has fallen particularly hard on his eighty-five-year-old mother, Janet, of Quisset, Massachusetts, who lost her husband just five months before.

• • •

Ned Gillette was one of the most successful of a breed of modern-day "career adventurers." His greatest love was doing things no one had done and perhaps not even imagined. He didn't specialize in any particular region, and was the first to admit he was not the most gifted athlete. What propelled him was an incredible wanderlust and a kind of patrician, New England sense of hard work. He succeeded where so many others failed, because he knew how to work the system—how to attract sponsors, coax dollars out of their pockets, and keep them happy during and after his expeditions, by never hesitating, in his writings or lectures, to thank out loud the corporations that made his chosen lifestyle possible. "You've got to differentiate yourself from others in the field, and you've got to always remember to say thank you to the guys who sent you," he told *Outside* in a 1986 cover story. "I'm selling a product really," he admitted. "There's the adventure itself, which is why I'm in it. But it's at least half promotion. It's a funny business."

His jack-of-all-trade love for adventure and sport began early. Father Bob was chairman of the National Life Insurance Company of Vermont and his mother, Janet, took Ned and his sister, Debby, to Quissett Harbor on Cape Cod, where Ned learned to sail. He first skied at age five at Stowe;

spent summers with his family sailing off New England. Holderness School Prep school led to his being an NCAA cross-country ski champion for Dartmouth in 1967, then an alternate member of the 1968 U.S. Nordic ski team at the Grenoble Olympics in 1968. Briefly flirted with business school; worked for a year and a half in the management training program of International Paper. Entered business school at University of Colorado in Boulder. Lasted twenty-four hours.

His first jobs were working as director of skiing at Yosemite, then running the ski touring center at the Trapp Family Lodge near his birthplace in Vermont. Jan Reynolds eventually did five big expeditions with Gillette, and met him when he hired her to teach skiing at the lodge. "Ned loved bizarre characters, and they were drawn to him. He had run the ski school at Yosemite, until the Von Trapp family lured him back to Vermont to do the same job. When he came, all these wacky California characters came along with him, just to be around Ned."

He began to climb seriously in Yosemite. "I was an eastern preppie Ivy Leaguer, but at Yosemite I ricocheted off in another direction," he told *Sports Illustrated* in 1990. "I started doing things, saying things, smoking things, thinking things that were totally new to me. I opened my eyes to life as an adventure. I've always thought, if you have a solid upbringing, it allows you to be crazy by election thereafter."

In 1978 he (along with Galen Rowell) made the first one-day ascent of Mt. McKinley; in 1980 he was among the first Americans to climb in China, summiting 24,757-foot Muztagata and skiing off; in 1982 he climbed Mt. Everest; in 1984 he made the first nordic ski descent of Argentina's Mt. Aconcagua; he was the first American to climb the Himalayan peak Pumori. He led several long-distance ski trips in a wide variety of frozen places—across the Robson Channel and Ellesmere Island, and, in 1981, a first circumnavigation of Mt. Everest. He considered a 1980, three hundred-mile winter traverse of four Karakoram Himalayas, the highest mountain range on earth, the most physically challenging trip he'd undertaken. "We live in a time where you can no longer climb the highest peak, or no longer explore blank spots on a map," he told *Outside*. "Adventure is looking at old subjects in new ways.

None of us are explorers anymore. We're guys who dream up things that might be fun to do."

His 1988 voyage via the self-dubbed *Sea Tomato*—an enclosed rowing boat that resembled a bright-red pickle—was perhaps his most publicized, wackier, most death-defying adventure. During the crossing of the Drake Passage, from Cape Brecknock, Chile, sixty miles northwest of Cape Horn, to landfall near King George Island, Antarctica, the twenty-eight-foot aluminum craft, designed by Gillette, capsized three times.

The first day out, gusts were up to fifty knots. "We were shot out of there like a rocket," he said afterward. "We capsized three different times and one of us went overboard each time." They covered ninety nautical miles the first two days, without touching the oars. Squalls tossed the 1,500 pound boat around like a tomato. They had expected to be at sea for twenty days, but completed the seven hundred and twenty-mile crossing in a wind-assisted thirteen days.

Soon after, he met Susie Patterson, then thirty-five, introduced in Sun Valley by one of her brothers. A ski phenom—she made the US National Ski Team for the first time at age thirteen—Patterson was the U.S. women's slalom champion in 1974, downhill champ in 1976. After the 1976 Olympics, where she placed fourteenth in the downhill, she skied the World Cup Circuit. A self-confessed "ski princess" for the first twenty-five years of her life, she admits "I'd been up high mountains all over the world—on chairlifts. I was good and I loved what I did." She'd spent maybe one night in a tent; today she jokes she wasn't even sure where Asia was.

I didn't know who Ned was or what he did; I only knew he was the one.

We met a little more than ten years ago—shortly after he did his Sea Tomato *trip—and we fell in love in a weekend. He and my brother Pete had done a trip, they did the first ski descent down Aconcagua. He came up to visit Pete and it was the first time he had introduced me to any of his friends. Ned kept asking him, hey, what's the deal with your sister, and Pete would say 'Oh, she's trouble'."*

They were married at Sun Valley's Roundhouse restaurant on Bald Mountain, August 18, 1990. Ned now had a full-time partner: "Now I can bring my home life with me," he quipped.

What I said to Ned was, "I'd like to climb a mountain someday, a big one. Do you have any ideas?" says Susie.

Soon I was listening to a madcap scheme to sneak across a Chinese border closed to westerners, climb a peak illegally, and then escape. Because I didn't say no, I guess I said yes. In short, we agreed to climb Tibet's 25,355-foot-high Gurla Mandhata, "the Mountain of Black Herbal Medicine." It was an adventure in the tradition of a time past, when mountain climbers were romantically inclined explorers.

"So what happens if we get caught?" I asked.

"Oh, we might have to spend a few nights in jail or, worst case, get tossed out of the country," Ned answered vaguely.

"Guerrilla mountaineering," Ned called it, and I liked it.

After an oxygen-starved, stormbound honeymoon in a tent at twenty-one thousand feet while climbing Gurla Mandhata, in 1994 the pair traced five thousand miles of the Silk Road, through China and Central Asia, by camel caravan. That was Gillette's last heavily financed, heavily publicized trip.

That was the period of life where the end result of the trip was the most important thing to Ned; I went into it more just for giving it a shot. I didn't think I'd like it, but I just fell in love with that way of life.

"I had no experience outside of the ski world. Ned always called me the Ski Queen. On that trip, I expected to give in and see what his world was all about, but really didn't think I'd like it in any way. It worked the opposite way on me. It cast a spell on me. The life style became an addiction for me."

"We did a lot of small, not heavily funded, things together before the Silk Road. Like skiing in Iran. But the Silk Road caravan was the epitome of sponsoring and funding. On that trip Ned started to

realize that, god, the obligation to sponsorship was that you were, in his words, 'tied to a promise,' without any real flexibility to do what you want. It was a real turning point in his life. He thought that was not the direction he wanted to take anymore.

He made a huge evolution from then until now. Back to why he started doing this stuff, just because he loved it. The purity, the simplicity, and the honesty. The process became the essence, not the result. He evolved into that kind of person, which was beautiful for me to see. I think some people were disappointed that maybe he didn't write more, and pursue the sponsorship, but this lifestyle made him very happy. Even the day before all this happened, he said, "You know, Susie, a day hasn't gone by on this trip where one of us hasn't said how lucky we are." Because we had our love, our health, and our happiness.

"I'll speak for Ned now. He was a happy guy in the end, real happy," [her voice breaking.] *"He was dedicated to his mom and his dad, and to me, but otherwise we led a pretty private life these last few years.*

"I had ten incredible years, and the only justification for losing him is that we squeezed a lot in in a short time.

"One trip that we'd done was really special to him, I just remembered it when I was out on my run. We crossed the Indian Himalaya's by snowshoes in winter. Just the two of us. That's one thing he was really proud of; that the two of us could figure things out on our own. Find a country we wanted to go to, and go.

"We went, through the mountains in winter. up a frozen Zanskar River, crossed passes on snowshoes and ended up in Menali. I think Ned was as proud of that trip as he was of the Sea Tomato trip. Just being able to get up the frozen Zanskar River, figuring out how to do a lot of these things in winter, when it had never been done before. It took us three and a half or four weeks, in January. Physically, it was the hardest, coldest thing I'd ever done.

"Ned was a magician at creating really neat goals, without a lot of hoopla, without big sponsorships. I got much, much stronger, too, so it enabled us to carry a lot more weight, do more things. Each trip I gained more experience and became more of an equal partner."

• • •

In retrospect, what made Gillette special was his great sense of himself, his own limitations, his place. He was first in a growing breed of modern adventurers who recognized that what mattered for the contemporary adventurer was not just skill and intrepidity, but style, flair, finesse.

"Ned was very strong in an endurance sense," says Jan Reynolds. "Alan Bard, who was big and strong, used to say he'd never traveled with anyone as strong as Ned. When Galen [Rowell] and Ned climbed McKinley in one day, it was Ned who broke the trail all the way to the end.

"He always admired the good, hardcore climbers; he was more bold than fancy. Strong mentally and physically, what made him special was that he was also such a regular guy, with insecurities like the rest of us. He was always concerned that he was dressing like a dork. He really was 'everyman's' friend."

"I don't undertake these things to please my fellow skiers or my fellow climbers or my fellow rowers," Gillette said in 1986. "I do them to please myself and, I like to think, to give something back to the man in the street, the guy who sits at a desk and maybe isn't doing what he wants with his life.

"If anything, I'd just like to think I remind people that it's possible to do what you want. If adventuring is about anything, that's what it's about."

Their next trip was to be to the Dolbo region of Nepal. The air tickets for it are still on Gillette's desk.

Says Susie, "Ned's famous last words were, 'I've always wanted to do this.' And I'd say, 'But Ned, you've always wanted to do everything.'"

Jan Reynolds, who accompanied Gillette on the Southern Cross expedition in New Zealand, then climbed with him in China, Mutagada, and around Everest, puts it this way, "What made him special was his way of inspiring people. if he'd had a motto it would have been 'Dream, then do.'"

• • •

The senseless and seeming randonmness of the killing sent shockwaves through the adventuring community. The only controversy centered around just how dangerous was this region of Pakistan. Could—or should—the pair of experienced adventurers have known the area was unsafe? In March the U.S. Embassy in Islamabad had warned of threats against Americans in Pakistan, after gunmen in the southern port city of Karachi shot dead four American oil company employees apparently because a Pakistani was convicted in the United States. of murdering two CIA agents. Greg Mortenson, director of the Central Asia Institute, a private agency providing schooling and aid to poor people of the region, assures that Gillette's killing was not political. "The cold-blooded nature of it is a freak thing. It was an isolated thing, not a specific act against Americans."

How dangerous, depends on who you ask. State Department spokesman in Islamabad, Richard Hoagland, said by phone after the killings, "Though very remote, the Northern District is not especially dangerous. But it is a very traditional area, very tribal, steeped in Soviet era wars, still imbued with what is known as the 'Kalashnikov culture.' Many people there carry guns."

Mortenson goes further. "This area is totally wild. Everybody carries an AK-47. The people are very isolated, and notoriously violent and danger-ous. I would never go there myself, especially not without a local porter or a guard." He suggests that maybe this time Gillette ventured too far off the beaten path. "The foreigners who go in there are usually large groups of mountaineers, with hired local porters. You rarely see individual back-packers traveling there. Gillette was a worldwide traveler, and knew what he was doing, but I would never have gone up there without hiring a local, somebody who at least spoke the language." (Mortenson worked in the region for six years and had his own near-disastrous experience: In 1996 he was abducted and held hostage for eight days. "I got lucky, because I can speak the language and they knew who I was.")

The State Department's Bernie Alter, on his second tour in Islamabad, says that this northern region is not as dangerous as the northwestern frontier, a hundred miles away. "The area doesn't get thousands of tourists, but hundreds of trekkers each season; the only reports of violence are occasional assault and rape of woman travelers."

Patterson, recuperating at her home in Sun Valley, is adamant that the image of the area as dangerous is overblown, that it's not true that everyone has guns.

During this whole trip we were in totally open areas. Nothing was unrestricted, nothing illegal. We were not close to any dangerous borders. We would have considered a guide, but it changes things. Having someone speak the language for you, tell you what to do, where to go—after that caravan trip we both decided, god, we're adults, we'll take care of ourselves. That's half the challenge of it.

"I want to stress, this was not in a dangerous place. In our trip up the same valley last September there was nothing that said to us this was a dangerous place. Whenever you're in a border area of China, India, or Pakistan, it's always dangerous. But we weren't near a border area. Some people said we were in Kashmir, which is totally not true. A lot of Pakistan along the Indian border is restricted, because of the stuff they're going through, but we weren't near any of that.

"The only thing I'm bitter about is that it appears the police stood in the way of the military—and the military were the only people who could have dispatched a helicopter. The police were really tedious, they were really unwilling to work with the military and other people who were trying to help. If this guy had run down immediately, gotten to a police checkpost, gotten on a phone, had the military dispatch a helicopter, they could have gotten there early the morning after. But that's all woulda, coulda, shoulda. The only thing that's really saving me right now is that I've been told that even if Ned had been shot like that in his backyard, there was enough damage that he wouldn't have lived. I don't know if that's good or bad or what, but that's the fact.

Some people have said we were in a dangerous zone, that it was maybe too dangerous. A lot of people have written to me that while they could have dealt with a mountaineering accident, this was too awful, too brutal. Well, it was awful and brutal. But the nice thing is that neither of us made a mistake. Ned would never forgive himself if he got himself in this situation by having made a bad decision. This was totally out of our control.

It doesn't make it any easier, but it gets back to Ned as a person who took only calculated risks. He couldn't have done anything about this.

Gillette's body was cremated, in Pakistan, and carried back to the States by Patterson. By his request, there was no burial, no ceremony, though a private memorial was held at the Trapp Family Lodge in Vermont.

AIR ANTARCTICA

I like being places where you are forced to listen to your own heartbeat, commanded by nature to pay attention to the in and out of each breath. Antarctica is one of those places.

It was so windy last night that I thought at one point my tent was going to explode. Literally. Thanks to a trio of pinholes along one seam, the sides of the thin nylon membrane were sucked in by the forty-mile-an-hour gusts, then exploded outward, making a cracking sound, like an M-80 going off. This went on for several hours.

Such Antarctic winds have driven people mad. Last year the FBI was called into the American base at McMurdo to investigate a murder by kitchen knife, the continent's first homicide. The Brits are famous for incidents of wind-and-isolation madness: At Rothera base a few years back an engineer barricaded himself in the bar for a month, threatening anyone who tried to come through the door with a fire ax. His excuse? The sound of the winds.

When morning came this day, the winds dropped. (Note, I don't say "when the sun rose," since its up twenty-four hours in January.) By noon, they were back, gusting katabatics whipping snow across the ground at chest level at thirty to forty miles per hour. As I trudged across the crusty snow, the wind whistling inside my fur-lined hood was the sound of freedom—and frostbite.

My friend "Borneo" Steve Pinfield and I spent the afternoon kick-stepping up one thousand feet of an ice-and-snow-packed bowl, with ice axes and crampons, to the peak of the tallest of the Patriot Hills. We are four hundred miles from the sea, six hundred miles from the nearest scientific base at the South Pole, and eighteen hundred miles from the nearest town at the southern tip of Chile. Atop the ridge we are met by even bigger winds, gale force, blowing up the other side of the hills from the flat ice that separates the Patriots from the Independence Range. We look toward Mt. Vinson, Antarctica's tallest peak, down a long line of granite, snow-covered peaks separated by fields of ice and snow, suncups, sastrugi, and crevasses.

With our axes dug in for stability we continue up the knife edge of the rocky ridge to the snowy summit. Thankfully this wind is constant, not gusty. Big gusts would easily pick us off and dump us over the edge. Everywhere we look the wilderness is vast, unending. Pausing to catch our breath we talk about the slim chance of being rescued should one of us fall this far from "the world." It's very humanizing to stand so far beyond civilization, far beyond help.

Think of it this way. Imagine a land the size of the United States and Mexico covered by ice and blowing snow, where temperatures hang well below zero. Now imagine there are just six hundred people scattered across that entire land, and that you've just been dropped off in the center. That's what it is like this day, atop these Antarctic Hills, in the middle of the Heritage Range of the Ellsworth Mountains. Despite that many of these mountains have names, Antarctica is less well mapped than the moon.

But that we are here, in the middle of the last continent, suggests that it is not totally beyond reach. As far back as 1938, Australian explorer Douglas Mawson, who accomplished many firsts, wondered if "from an economic aspect, the frozen South may not attract immediate attention, but who can say what a train of entrepreneurs the future may bring?" Me, I have come South with the most audacious of Antarctica's modern entrepreneurs, a flying company, the only private business operating on the continent.

1. "IF WE DITCH AT SEA . . ."

There is only one way to reach the interior of Antarctica—unless you're a scientist or government-contracted plumber or electrician putting in time at one of the continent's bases—and that's to fly with the once seat-of-the-wind-pants air charter company called Adventure Network International. The wild-ass fantasy of a handful of dreamer/climbers a dozen years ago, the little company that began as jottings on the back of an envelope is now a multi million-dollar-a-year outfitter in its twelfth season delivering climbers, expeditioners, and fat-walleted tourists to the most remote, most potenially dangerous place on earth. Against all odds, it works.

I have known the operators of the company for many years, but it took until this past January for me to hitch a ride to Antarctica with them. On a sunny, windy day in Punta Arenas, Chile, I climbed aboard a Hercules C-130 cargo plane along with twenty other passengers, including four climbing parties and four individuals who'd paid $21,000 each to visit the South Pole for a few hours. A pair of ANI employees were along for the six-hour ride, including managing director Annie Kershaw, whose late husband Giles—perhaps the greatest polar pilot ever—trailblazed the company.

It is a weird assortment of passengers, but not unusual for ANI. It included a hardened team of veteran climbers from Croatia and Slovenia as well as a couple of doddering grandmothers incapable of putting on their own wind pants and boots. A seventy-four-year-old American woman from Michigan, who claimed she was going to the South Pole "because I've been to the North Pole," admits her friends back home can't figure out why she is so intent on "going nowhere." There were also a pair of veteran North American climbing guides, Skip Horner and Tod Burleson, escorting nine clients of differing experience headed for Mt. Vinson, Antarctica's tallest peak at just over sixteen thousand feet. As Annie Kershaw tries to squeeze an elderly German woman into a pair of wind pants, Tod Burleson, who was on Everest during last year's fatal May, watches from the edge of the cargo hold. This is his sixth trip with ANI. "It's a shame," he sighs, "it kind of takes away from the spirit of adventure, doesn't it?" Horner, who first guided with ANI in 1988, is watching too. He remembers his initial flight to Antarctica, which was quite different than this one. "When the plane landed, I think it was a DC-3, the other guide, Gordy Wiltsie, and I were completely covered with aviation fuel that was basically floating loose in the back of plane. Things have changed a lot since then."

A lot has changed since the early days of ANI. It used to be that the "boys"—veteran climbers and pilots—who ran the operation did not need a GPS to find the brothels in Punta Arenas. Today the company is run by a pretty blonde woman with a preference for paisley hairbands, who considers "gee whiz" an expletive. Probably the best word to describe Annie Kershaw is conservative. And that's probably why ANI is succeeding.

The five-man flight crew—and their Hercules—are from South Africa. This is their second season flying round-trips (at $200,000 a crack), from Punta Arenas to ANI's base camp near the Patriot Hills. They are a perfect crew for this mission, since their experience includes flying through bullets and landing on unlit runways in the dead of night across Africa. Landing a twenty-five-ton plane on a sheet of ice is a breeze, comparably speaking. "This is the kind of nonsense we love," says the captain.

A slight apprehension fills me as I wait under sunny skies on the runway, listening to the wind whistle. It's a far way we're going today, to a distant, isolated place. Planes are hardly new to Antarctica; eighty years ago the Australian Mawson brought the first aircraft to the continent—a Vicker REP monoplane. Neither are plane crashes—the skeletons of more than fifty aircraft dot the ice, all but a few military or government owned. The worst Antarctic air accident was in 1978, when an Air New Zealand jumbo jet crashed into Mt. Erebus, killing all twohundred and twenty-five aboard. My mood is not helped by the most salient piece of information passed along during a brief briefing from the co-pilot as he demonstrates safety measures onboard. "If we ditch at sea please don't inflate your Mae West's until you are *outside* of the safety door. It's a tight fit as it is."

Ditch at sea?

The flight over the Drake Passage is actually very smooth. The sea is flat and blue, the sky painted by wisps of white clouds. The drum of the twin-engined props is loud, overpowering, hypnotic. Annie, her blue down jacket pulled up around her head, naps in the last row. She barely slept last night, typical of the night before one of the dozen flights the Herc will make each season. This is the first time she's visited Antarctica this season, and she's going to check on the camp and eighteen-person crew, which is based on the continent from November through early

February. ANI's eleventh season is almost complete; this is the second-to-last passenger flight. She wants to gauge firsthand how the season's gone based on conversations with her on-ice team. A couple weeks from now the camp's kitchen, meteorology, and radio tents will be packed and stored in an underground cave—as will its bright orange Cessna 185—until next season.

Any apprehension diminishes, perhaps falsely, after we cross over the first ice sheet. The bright light reflected off the surface of the ice blazes through the tiny portholes in the cargo hold, illuminating the cabin's dark interior with blinding streaks of white. An occasional crack in the ice sheet exposes blue-black waters.

After six hours we near the three-mile stretch of rippled blue ice that is the landing strip at the base of the Patriot Hills. I sit in the cockpit for the landing. One of two copilots, standing, shouts over the roar of the engines: "See those hills, to our right? How far away do you think they are?" I guess a few miles.

"Try fifty miles. It is so big down there it is impossible to judge perspective from up here." One result is that in order to set the big plane down it must be guided in by a pair of mirrors held by camp crew on the ground—one at the threshold of the runway, a second near its end. "Everything is so white, so bright, that it is virtually impossible to distinguish where the ice begins. So we just line up those mirrors, drop straight down, and pray."

At the trio of small peaks known as the Three Sails we make a hard right-hand turn. As the plane drops, the captain "quacks" hello over the radio to the base camp with a small rubber ducky. He and one copilot are strapped in, as is the navigator sitting just behind. A second copilot and engineer stand, unbuckled, bracing themselves for what could be a rough landing, holding on to the metal frame with one hand, bucking-bronco style. There's no use for brakes on the ice; stopping requires throwing the big engines immediately into reverse, then skidding for half a mile, desperately trying to keep the nose straight-on.

The landing is smoother than I expected, in part because I can see it coming. For the rest, strapped down in back, unable to see the ice as it approaches, it comes as a bigger shock, jolt, surprise. When the wheels hit for the first time I hear a few squeals from the cargo hold. We skid for nearly a mile.

"That was smooth enough I'd think you did it every day," I say to the captain, who has actually done it fewer than ten times.

"Highest compliment, mate, highest compliment," he replies.

2. THE MOST REMOTE CAMP IN THE WORLD

We are steered to a stop carefully by a man in blue fleece and a jester's hat. The back cargo chute is dropped and bright sunlight and cold, cold air rush in. The plane's engines keep a steady beat—to shut them down in this cold risks not being able to start them again. The camp manager, in the faded orange polar gear of the British Antarctic Survey, strides aboard, wearing a Viking's horns with the word MENTAL printed across its brow. The rush is on to unload the green barrels of fuel, bags, snowmobile, and food, and a crew of a dozen has come out to help.

It is zero degrees Fahrenheit; January, midsummer. By the end of the half-mile walk to the dozen tents that are the base camp some of the over-dressed climbers are sweating, pulling off layers of clothing. Eighteen persons live here from November to early February, including the camp's manager (who when employed by the BAS spent two and a half years straight on the continent), two mountain guides, four pilots, two engineers, radio and weather operators, two cooks, a trio of Chilean military men on assignment, and a "client relations" person. It is a true melting pot of nationalities—this season's crew hails from the United Kingdom, New Zealand, Canada, the United States, Australia, Chile, and Uruguay. Also in camp are a pair of Poles and a Norwegian, who are handling logistics for expeditions under way. (Adventure Network provides logistical support for every expedition that comes to Antarctica, which this season includes seven ranging from solo efforts by a Norwegian, a Pole, a Brit, a French woman, and teams from Korea, and the United Kingdom.)

After a massive dinner for fifty in a double Jamesway tent that serves as the kitchen, two Twin Otters are loaded with climbers and gear to be shuttled to ANI's base camp at Vinson. No wasting time when the skies are bright and winds are down. As the planes are fueled I walk out for a look around. It is 9 PM but as bright as noon. Camp sits at twenty-five hundred feet, on the edge of the blue-ice runway, facing the Patriot Hills, which climb to four thousand feet.

Back in the mid-1980s, Adventure Network knew that to accommodate climbers and tourists it needed a semipermanent base camp near Vinson, a place to store fuel and food and bodies while they waited to climb. No one besides a government had ever considered building a station in the interior. Siple, the American base one hundred and fifty miles from the South Pole, was closed in 1986 because the National Science Foundation that runs the U.S. bases decided it was too expensive to maintain a base so far from everything. Nearby is where ANI decided to plant its camp.

The first challenge was finding a good spot. Giles Kershaw—who came to Antarctica with the BAS in 1972 and had since flown more hours over both poles than any man—had done numerous studies with BAS expert Charles Swithinback on the blue-ice areas around the continent, looking for those that would make for perfect natural runways. Searching satellite photos they decided a four-mile long stretch of flat ice near the Patriot Hills would be perfect. It sat at eighty degrees south, eighteen hundred miles from the nearest city or town, on a plain where the wind came off the mountain and cleared the flats of snow. Brakes would be worthless on such ice; the pilots would have to throw the engines into reverse to slow their aircraft, then pray. By comparison, the runways at Antarctica's big government bases are constructed from packed snow, using bulldozers and teams of men with picks and shovels. For Giles the challenges were numerous: No one—not even the best government pilots—had ever tried to land the big planes he was considering (C-130s, DC-4s, DC-6s) on such conditions. And he intended to land on wheels, not skis, another first.

Once the site was chosen, and after Giles relayed hundreds of tons of fuel, supplies, and two smaller planes to the foot of the Patriot Hills, they constructed a completely removable weatherproof tented camp, stocked with enough sustenance to feed three dozen people for a month or more. The camp consisted of a half dozen sturdy WeatherHaven tents with cots and thermopane windows. Two tents were joined together to make a kitchen/dining room, complete with heaters, gas cookstove, and sporadic radio contact. Months of meat and vegetables were deep-frozen in pits. Every move was made difficult by the katabatic winds that roared across the flat ice up to one hundred miles an hour and a windchill factor that dropped below minus one hundred degrees.

All this was done in preparation for the 1987 season, which despite the company's efforts, was nearly a disaster. They had leased a DC-4, which arrived in Chile and immediately had to have all four engines replaced. Essential parts languished in customs, so fuel-caching flights were delayed. Clients who had paid $35,000 to be flown to Vinson arrived in Punta Arenas, waited and went home. To top it off, for a month the NSF and BAS successfully pressured Chile to stop selling the company fuel.

Repaired and fully loaded with seventy-three thousand pounds of fuel, gear, and passengers, the DC-4 took off on its maiden voyage in December 1987. A few miles over the Drake Passage, the Omega long-range navigation system broke; thankfully Giles had already flown the route twenty times and found Patriot Hills by dead reckoning. After seven hours he touched down on the sheet of ripply blue ice, the first solid-ice runway in Antarctica. Three weeks later—in January 1988—ANI flew its first two planes loaded with tourists to the South Pole.

3. INTO THE HEART

I have come for a couple weeks of sled-pulling, climbing, and skiing. I was hooked up with ANI guide Borneo Steve—who proved to be a perfect traveling partner, in both the tough conditions and the many hours spent inside a small tent. After a couple days testing equipment, we skied away from base camp pulling sleds loaded with seventy-five pounds of tents, sleeping bags, food, ice axes, climbing rope, and fuel for an extended camping trip in the middle of the ice.

Now, some of my best friends are polar robots, men and women who have skied, man-hauled, dogsledded, and walked across the coldest parts of the globe. Put them in minus fifty degree temperatures and big winds and they just turn on, as if some key inside their minds had been switched. I'm not like that. I've spent a fair amount of days in some truly cold places, but usually with the promise of a short-lived adventure. I keep going back to cold places for one reason, because of the incredible wilderness that opens up if you are willing to put up with a reasonable amount of discomfort.

Here in Antarctica, just beyond the Patriot Hills, is a perfect example of just such underexplored terrain. At this moment, there were fewer than a dozen people doing the same as we. And no wonder. It's fucking cold. On the day we set out temperatures are minus ten degrees, crosswinds blowing at 10 mph, equaling a wind chill of around minus thirty degrees. The wind, thankfully, is across us, though it nearly blows us off our feet a few times, gusting to 25 mph.

Pulling the sleds is not so difficult . . . at first. We glide smoothly over the lumpen ice and the scenery changes slowly, but dramatically. After five kilometers, base camp has disappeared and the flat plains prove to be more rolling; we drop over a ten-foot descent and an entirely new panorama of rugged, snow-peaked mountains—dozens in a row—is unveiled. We are heading for a small, snowy plateau above an icefield at the foot of a hill that leads to the Minaret, an unclimbed, five thousand-foot jewel that Steve would love to try and find a route up. If we kept skiing we'd eventually hit the base of Mt. Vinson, an overland trip that's never been attempted due to an abundance of nasty crevasses.

The exercise layers me with a coat of perspiration, which quickly chills when I stop for a breather or just to gawk at the surroundings—which I try and do with regularity. I don't want to have this experience without looking up occasionally to admire and wonder about where I am at, a mistake made by some of the more driven polar explorers. After ten kilometers we stop for lunch, and the cold and exertion begin to take a toll. Sitting on our gloves, drinking hot water, and chewing chocolate bars, Steve takes our minds off the cold with a tale about a New York society lady who came to Antarctica with ANI a couple seasons ago and insisted on being flown back immediately after visiting the South Pole, "because it was too cold." She was met in Punta Arenas by her hairdresser, who'd flown down from Manhattan.

After lunch we ski more directly into the wind—did we shift direction, or did it?—and the problem of vision surfaces. With my hood up, its fur-ruff flapping across my face, I can see out of only one eye. Then, thanks to the inverted humidity inside the hood, my glacier glasses fog. I experiment with putting the hood down and my nose begins to frostbite. Neither option is comfortable and for much of the afternoon I see basically just my ski tips.

One mile from where we will make camp the surface compounds the difficulties, becoming a mix of blue ice and a crusty layer of snow. We are on a slight descent and it is tricky to ski across the patches of ice without the sled—connected around my waist by a harness—banging hard into my back, throwing everything off balance. It is late in the day, we've traveled sixteen kilometers, and it ain't getting any warmer. The toes on my left foot—the foot facing the wind—are beginning to tingle.

Camp is on a flat span at the bottom of our descent, in the shadow of the Minaret.

We put up a new Kelty tent, stick it down with bamboo stakes, ice axes, and skis. Extra ice axes are thrust through the harnesses to keep the sleds from skittering off during the day/night.

4. AGAINST ALL ODDS

Adventure Network's short history is inextricably linked with the tallest mountain on the continent, Vinson Massif. Dominating the Sentinel Range of the Ellsworth Mountains, 2,000 miles from the tip of South America, 800 miles from the South Pole, Vinson has a plateau fifteen miles long and ten miles wide, all above 12,000 feet. In rapid succession are five peaks just one hundred feet smaller than the 16,067-foot main summit. First seen from the air in 1959, it was named after U.S. Congressman Carl Vinson, a strong proponent of Antarctica research and exploration. In 1983 it had been climbed only twice: The first was in 1966 by the American Alpine Club Official Expedition, a mega-dollar deal supported by the National Science Foundation, the second in 1968 by a team of German and Russian geologists, which the NSF termed "illegal."

By the early eighties Vinson had become the object of desire of a handful of the world's best mountaineers, each with their sites set on becoming the first to climb the tallest peak on each continent. Reinhold Messner, Gerhard Schmatz, Naomi Uemura, and Pat Morrow were among those racing, which in Antarctica meant first conquering the logistical nightmare of reaching the foot of the mountain.

In 1983 an unlikely pair of climbers entered the unofficial contest— movie mogul Frank Wells and Snowbird Ski Resort owner Dick Bass. They too set out to climb the seven tallest peaks, but with an added twist: They hoped to accomplish the feat in one year. Their advantage over more experienced climbers was simple: They had a lot of money. Wells and Bass hired the best guides and support crews possible and in quick succession knocked off five of the seven tallest peaks in the world, before turning their sites on Antarctica.

"Once Wells put the word out that he was trying to figure out a way to get to Antarctica all calls eventually led to Giles Kershaw," says Rick Ridgeway, who along with Chris Bonington Vemura had been hired to help. "So he got hold of Giles."

Giles Kershaw was already something of a legend in polar flying circles. He had flown for the British Antarctic Survey from 1974 to 1979 and since then had been freelancing in both the Arctic and Antarctic. He had flown around the world, over both poles, and provided air support for several major expeditions. In 1983 alone he landed at the North Pole twenty-three times. In 1980 he was awarded a medal from the Queen of England, after he flew across a thousand miles of trackless white to rescue three South African scientists who had been marooned on an iceberg for eight days. Even among his adventuring peers Giles was considered the most adventuresome, the most curious, the most visionary.

He was more than happy to assist Wells. Together they found and leased a Tri-Turbo DC-3 in California. Owned by a defense contractor, it was an oddball aircraft ideally suited to the short runways and long distances of polar air travel. Wells also initiated talks with the Chilean Air Force, who agreed to airdrop necessary barrels of refueling gas near the British base at Rothera.

Simultaneously, in Vancouver, Pat Morrow was trying to raise money to climb Vinson. A veteran climber—only the second Canadian to top Everest—and accomplished photojournalist, Morrow was more than a little pissed that his competition was a pair of fat cats. He wrote of their effort with thinly disguised disdain. "In this age of jets, the financially independent Bass and Wells are able to take an important time-saving shortcut because they do not have to search for sponsors. They surrounded themselves with the best climbing guides available, who led them in safety up the mountains and prepared their camps and meals." Such criticism notwithstanding, the Wells/Bass team topped Vinson in November 1983, only the third ascent of the mountain and the first without government support or cooperation.

Morrow wasn't yet beaten; if he could get to Vinson the next season he might still beat Wells and Bass in the race to be the first to climb all seven continental summits. He raised $250,000 from friends, family, sponsors, and three climbing partners and in October 1984 chartered the same Tri-Turbo DC-3—and hired the same pilot, Giles Kershaw—that Wells had. His coleader on the trip was Martyn Williams. The soft-spoken redhead was born in Liverpool but moved to the Yukon in his early twenties to teach and explore. A veteran of dozens of arctic climbs, just prior to hooking up with Morrow, Williams had skied across Greenland. They were a good match: experienced adventurers with big dreams.

Unfortunately their climb never materialized. The seven-man team got as far as Argentina's Esperanza station, where the plane was blown down a glacier and nearly dumped into the Southern Ocean. Giles flew it back to Argentina for repair, while the team waited in Antarctica. Upon landing Kershaw was placed under house arrest for three days, essentially for carrying a British passport (this was soon after the Falklands war). After flying back to Antarctica he discovered severe ice damage to the plane's engine and the Morrow/Williams ascent was called off. Four months later Wells and Bass made Everest and won the seven summits race.

The next year, 1985, Morrow and Williams decided to try to top Vinson again, even though the big sponsorships were lost with the Wells/Bass "victory." This time out they were motivated by the knowledge that, with Kershaw, they had blueprinted a system for flying eager climbers to the most out-of-the-reach mountain in the world. (Frank Wells of course takes credit for laying the path.) Morrow and Williams set up a corporation—joined by Morrow's wife, Baiba; Williams's girlfriend, Maureen Garrity; Bart Lewis;

and Mike Dunn—and in the midsummer of 1985 Adventure Network International was official.

Morrow and Williams—joined by Kershaw, whose vision and risk-taking were essential if the company was to work—scraped together $30,000 for insurance and partial downpayment on a leased Twin Otter. They had made a key contact in Chile with a former Pinochet military man, retired Air Force General Don Javier Lopategui, who offered to airdrop thirty-six drums of fuel at $40 per gallon to the base camp. The Chileans also promised rescue help. Morrow and Mike Dunn then found two teams of climbers willing to pay big bucks to be flown to Vinson's base. One was South Korean, the other American, led by veteran California climber Dan Emmett and including Yvon Chouinard and Doug Tompkins. By charging the two climbing teams more than $20,000 per man, ANI was able to finance three trips to Vinson—including its own. "It sounds easy in retrospect," says Morrow, "but we worked for a year without wages and were at risk personally for everything."

They learned valuable lessons that season about the hassle of running a business thousands of miles from civilization. Logistics and expense were incredible. The Tri-Turbo was no longer available, so they leased the Twin Otter instead. Insurance for the plane wasn't secured until the eleventh hour, and cost $60,000. The plane would need additional fuel, which cost another $70,000. They had to pay the Chilean Air Force a fortune to airdrop aviation fuel and a month's food at the Vinson base camp. En route to Vinson when the plane stopped to refuel from a cache near the British base at Rothera, the novice entrepreneurs were handed a telex that would also set a precedent for their future: The British Antarctic Survey had been warned by the National Science Foundation not to assist the private company.

It was the flying of Giles Kershaw that ensured the success of that first season. After dropping Morrow, Williams, and four others at the base of Vinson, Giles flew back to Punta Arenas for the Koreans, a seven-hour flight each way. Upon delivering them to Vinson, he joined the Canadian team for its successful ascent. Then he flew back to Punta Arenas to pick up the American team. Chouinard remembers the flight as "the riskiest thing I've ever done."

That first season was a success in Antarctic terms, that is, no one died. "The amazing part is that it paid for itself," says Martyn Williams, the first to admit he and his partners knew little about running a business. "Everything was done on the back of an envelope at the bar of the Navagantes Hotel in Punta Arenas. To our amazement at the end of that first season we had $50,000 left over." On his way back to Canada he passed through Santiago, where he met with Chilean Air Force officials. They told him they had fuel cached halfway down the peninsula that they would be glad to sell him—for $50,000. "I knew then that if the thing was to have a future fuel was the key, so I gave them the money," says Williams.

Over the next two seasons ANI escorted two dozen of the world's best (and wealthiest) climbers to Vinson, including Messner, Arne Naess, and Paul Pfua. The business was loosely administered by Williams in Punta Arenas and Hugh Culver in Vancouver (Culver was made business manager because he had previously run a river-rafting company). A full partnership in the company was awarded Giles, to keep him on board. The only money the partners made were guide wages. The continued support of the Chileans—who presciently saw Antarctica as a growing source of tourist revenue—was crucial. The Chileans even allowed Adventure Network to construct the only private house in Antarctica, on King George Island. But they have never been allowed to use it due to the protest of other governments. From day one the company's biggest stumbling block was the National Science Foundation, which ever since the Antarctic Treaty was signed in 1961 has publicly and voraciously discouraged any private business or expedition from coming to the continent. "They tried to thwart us by discouraging the Chileans—or any other country—from helping us," remembers Williams. The NSF's tactics were not subtle: At one point the Chilean base at Marsh was running out of fuel and the NSF refused to sell to them if any was to be later sold to Adventure Network. Its overarching rationale was simply that if ANI or its clients ever got in trouble and had to call for rescue, the NSF would most likely have to come bail them out, which would be expensive, inconvenient to its mission of science, and dangerous.

"But we always felt it was really a territorial thing," says Williams.

"They just didn't want anybody else down there." He is most amazed that the little company actually worked.

"We knew there was a demand among climbers to get to Antarctica," he says, "so we figured we'd have some fun for a year or two and that would be it. We didn't realize at the time that we were opening the door to anybody who had ever dreamed of going to the interior."

5. SOUTH TO THE POLE

On January 11, 1988, Adventure Network made history when it sent a pair of Twin Otters loaded with fifteen well-heeled passengers to the South Pole. Most of them were Americans, who had paid $25,000 each for the honor of being the first tourists flown to ninety degrees south. The seven aboard the first plane—which landed fifteen minutes before the second—paid an extra $10,000 premium for the privilege, and prior to takeoff a fight nearly broke out among the passengers arguing over who and who had not paid the premium.

When the passengers emerged into the bright sunlight a few were woozy and required oxygen. An eighty-year-old man turned a frightening shade of blue and a real estate man with a drinking problem nearly passed out from lack of a bracer. Those passengers still conscious traded ball caps and T-shirts with the U.S. government crew stationed at the Amundsen-Scott South Pole base and planted local Lions Club flags in the ice.

Several were "competitive" travelers, who had come this far south—nearly two thousand miles from the nearest town—to check several countries off their "Places I've Been" lists. Most headed straight for the barber's pole that marks the South Pole and fast-walked around it. Members or aspiring members of the Century Club—membership requires having visited at least one hundred countries—they "captured" eight countries by walking twenty paces around the pole. But arguments erupted among the country collectors. Exactly which countries could they count? Only those with territorial claims reaching the South Pole were official, and Norway's Antarctic claim has an undefined southern border. By walking around the South Pole had they really been to Norway? Or not?

"For some it was a life-changing experience," remembers Gordy Wiltsie, one of ANI's first guides. "They would go back and spread the word about the importance of preserving this pristine place to an important segment of the population. But most of these folks, once they'd seen the Pole, couldn't get out of there fast enough."

6. THE ONLY REAL BLONDE IN PUNTA ARENAS

Early in my visit I fly to the Vinson base camp with Annie Kershaw, under a bright, midnight sun. "It truly is God's country," she repeats, as we gawk out the windows at the light glinting off snow-crested peaks, rocky ridges, deep crevasses, blue ice, and tall sastrugi. She points out a small, sunlit range called Kershaw's Rumpoles, one of several mountains named after her late husband.

She tells me about the first time she came to Antarctica. "Giles and I, and an old friend of his named Mike McDowell, flew to the base of Vinson in 1989 and landed. They set up a tent for me, gave me a thermos of hot tea, and flew off to look for other possible landing strips. I'd never been inside a tent before and had never drank from a thermos. I was not really scared, but it did dawn on me 'What if they don't come back?' Here I am in the middle of nowhere, with no food, no radio . . ."

Perhaps the most amazing thing about this tiny company—though it bills millions each season, it carries just a few more than one hundred passengers a year—is that it is run not by some tough mountaineer or veteran climber, but by a petite blonde who admits that not that long ago she did not know where Antarctica was, north or south.

Anne Campbell Kershaw came to Punta Arenas in 1990 to run the local office of the Vancouver-based company. She also came to the isolated tip of the Americas to grieve. Her husband had been killed a few months before, flying a gyrocopter off the Antarctic Coast.

She and Giles met in 1985, when she was a twenty-five-year old s tewardess. She'd led a sheltered life prior to that; at home in Glasgow her father had driven her on dates until she was in her early twenties. Giles was her first real boyfriend. After they married she moved to Hong Kong where he was based part-time, flying 747s for Cathay Pacific. She got a job as a kindergarten teacher. When he was killed she was just thirty and considered herself too young to be a widow. Though she knew little about Antarctica, and had been there just once, she assumed Giles's share in the business and moved to Chile. Today she jokes she is the only real blonde in Punta Arenas and is known around town for her Scottish brogue, charm, and frugality. She favors preppy velour headbands, Patagonia jackets, and pumps. With her in control in Punta Arenas the mood of the operation is decidedly different from the days when ANI's customers, mostly climbers, came south knowing its managers had a keen, almost familial relationship with the local barrooms and brothels. Under Annie's guidance the company now passes out a cheery handout on arrival called "101 Things to Do in Punta Arenas."

As we talk on a bright, windy afternoon, she is in the process of closing down after ANI's twelfth season—her sixth as managing director. Just thirty-six, she sighs when she considers the outsized logistical woes that are her daily headaches. "I guess every season has been better than the last, which often means simply there have been fewer near catastrophes," she confesses.

When she took over the company after a disastrous 1989-90 season in which it took on too much and failed a couple of big expeditions, ANI was $600,000 in debt. But her reasons for joining the company were more personal than economic. "After Giles died I felt like ANI was an abandoned child. I thought it needed to be taken care of, and I wanted to be in Punta Arenas as a kind of caretaker—to try and make sure nobody else died." Today she owns 37.5 percent of the company—the rest is owned by Mike McDowell (50 percent), and Martyn Williams (13.5 percent).

While ANI's first seasons were judged successes (basically because no one was killed), nothing has come easily. Aircraft, its biggest single cost, are expensive: the company now spends $2.5 million leasing aircraft for the four-month-long season. Locating, caching, and paying for fuel is a constant struggle; transporting fuel to the interior is the biggest reason that a round-trip aboard the Hercules costs $200,000. The company's biggest asset is the couple of thousand fifty-five-gallon barrel drums of fuel they have stashed at Patriot Hills, Vassal (on King George Island), near the Thiel Mountains, the South Pole, and McMurdo, delivered over the years by airplane and ship. (Patriot Hills also serves as a cache for the U.S. and British governments, indicating a warming of relationships between them and Antarctica's only private business.) Annie calculates that each drum of aviation fuel flown to Antarctica, costing $150 in Punta Arenas, is worth $6,000 by the time it gets to Patriot Hills. Those at the South Pole are valued at $24,000. Given that the company's assets are so intangible—and are located in the middle of the most forbidding continent—has meant it's never been able to get a bank or operating loan.

Ironically, the company's reputation has grown even as its primary source of passengers has slackened. Climbers are grateful for the service, but the numbers who can afford such a trip—now priced at more than $25,000—are limited. Early on ANI realized climbers were not enough and expanded; today they deliver tourists to the Antarctic Peninsula to see penguins and to the South Pole and guide skiers around Patriot Hills. Filmmakers, scientists, explorers, even governments have all hired the company. Adventure travel companies also use ANI's flying service to help coordinate logistics for their own Antarctic offerings, most notably Mountain Travel's somewhat ostentatious 1988-89, $91,000-per-person "Ski to the South Pole." Next season they will have more planes in Antarctica than any of the government bases.

Annie is concerned they may have tapped out on South Polers, too. The first season they flew to the Pole they took thirty-three; two years ago forty-eight. This season just twelve. "I'm afraid that many of those who can afford it have already gone," she rationalizes. To counteract this potential loss, she has pushed the company to open a new route, in a new section of Antarctica. A new base camp dubbed Blue One was initiated this past season, near Dronning Maude Land, within easy distance of spectacular, never-before-attempted climbs. Two groups— a Norwegian climbing team and a *National Geographic* writing and film crew—spent a month there this season. For next, some of the big hitters of the climbing world, including Chris Bonington and Reinhold Messner, are lined up. But she knows she won't get rich off climbers.

With eight government bases within easy flying reach of Blue One, she is contacting their various Antarctic representatives, selling an air delivery service to the difficult-to-access bases. "The Japanese now, for example, send a ship with personnel and supplies, and it takes them seven weeks to reach Antarctica. ANI—or Polar Logistics, as the new company is called—is offering to fly them down from Cape Town, South Africa, cutting both time and expense at a moment in history where every Antarctic base is suffering from budget cuts.

"We need this economic boost and I've been pushing it with my partners. The biggest misconception about ANI is that we make tons of money. It is not true, since everything we do is so expensive. Believe me, I'd probably make more working as a checkout girl at K-Mart."

But what confounds her most is how people have come to think of ANI's service with such complacency. "Most people still don't understand the dangers of what we do everyday. I am constantly amazed that people don't take Antarctica seriously enough. We had one expedition that showed up and the only map they had was printed on their promotional t-shirts. Passengers get on the Hercules and breathe a big sigh of relief, as if they were perfectly safe. Me, I'm back in Punta Arenas, nervous until that plane touches down on the tarmac again."

7. FORE!

Last season more than eight thousand tourists visited the coast of Antarctica by cruise ship (just more than one hundred traveled to the interior with ANI). Each January now the peninsula resembles the French Riviera, thick with casino love boats discharging passengers by Zodiac to visit the shores. Many of them are captained by crews inexperienced in Antarctic waters, guided by photocopied charts. *A Guide to Yachting Antarctica* has been published, encouraging private visits. One result of all this increased traffic is continual talk among Antarctic Treaty members and environmentalists about how to police or regulate visitors. There is talk of amending the environmental protocol to the Antarctic Treaty to include an annex specifically addressing tourism. "These are the last wild days," writes American scientist David Campbell. "Antarctica can no longer have an icy indifference to humans."

The future of Antarctic tourism is ANI's future. Though the company's partners considered walking away from the risky business after a disastrous 1989–1990 season, the decision was made to keep on, in part to help earn back the money they'd lost. But changes were in order. A new emphasis on grabbing a bigger chunk of the adventure travel trade has meant softening the pitch.

One result is that Martyn Williams is spending less time with the company; Pat Morrow sold his shares a few years back. Both admit that some of the thrill that motivated them initially is gone. Williams has climbed Mt. Vinson four times, been to the South Pole a dozen times, skied halfway across Antarctica and to the North Pole. Morrow has been to the top of the tallest peaks on each continent and continues to climb new mountains, new routes. They started the company to provide their equally crazed adventuring friends with a way to access one of the last great unknowns. Now at ANI's annual board meetings the partners debate the pros and cons of flying fanatical golfers to the South Pole to hit multicolored balls. Morrow winces at the notion that the company's future lies in supporting stunts like golfing and motorcycling to the South Pole. "They do not meet with my personal philosophy of adventure and that was certainly not our original intent," says Morrow, as he packs for a forty-day climb in the Yukon. "But decisions are made for economic reasons these days."

"There is a huge market out there of people who want to get a taste of adventure without getting their hands dirty," says Hugh Culver, a one-time ANI partner who now manages a Vancouver construction company. "So the more Adventure Network can pasteurize the programs, the more attractive they're going to be to the guy who's got $15,000 or $20,000, the guy that wants a taste of Antarctica but doesn't want to freeze his buns off."

With even the South Pole now within relatively easy reach of any armchair adventurer with a fat bank account and a parka, is this a good thing?

Mike McDowell thinks it is. President and half-owner of ANI since 1990, McDowell is a veteran Antarctic and Arctic tour operator and himself something of an adventurer (though open-heart surgery last year has slowed him). A big, bold, brash Australian, McDowell has been to Antarctica more than forty times since 1978; for a year he lived on a sub-Antarctic island working as a geophysicist. He's pulled a sled four hundred miles from the South Pole (with Martyn Williams) and climbed Vinson. He founded Quark Expeditions in 1985 and since then has taken several hundred passengers around the Antarctic coastline; a few years later Quark made the first commercial voyage to the North Pole, on a nuclear-powered icebreaker McDowell leased from the Russians. Ironically McDowell was along on Adventure Network's first flight to the South Pole.

"I don't think we'll ever run out of adventures," he explains by phone, the day after he and Williams returned from a successful fifty-three-day ski to the North Pole. "There are dozens of big mountains that have never been attempted, and many, many skiddoo trips, skiing trips, and layabout trips we've only imagined." Flying people from Patriot Hills to emperor penguin rookeries on the coast, a popular ANI trip, was McDowell's idea.

But while McDowell implies the company is looking for more adventurous trips, its efforts are mostly aimed at luring less adventurous types. "We recognize that we have a different kind of passenger now," says Annie Kershaw. "They are slightly older, not interested in an 'activity' kind of trip. In the past when we took people to Patriot Hills they did a little bit of skiing, climbing, hiking, and navigation, a variation of what you can do in Antarctica. Now, with the clients a little older, we're having to look more to the sort of cruise-ship type of program, where they have slide shows, videos, volleyball, aerobics, and lectures." The company's new promotional pieces are slick. They advertise trips ranging from ski safaris ($12,500) to visits to the South Pole ($21,000) to Vinson climbs ($27,500).

Despite the maturation of its clientele, wild-ass pitches continue to come over the transom and they get more and more inquiries from expeditioners seeking air support. They recently had an inquiry from a Hong Kong man who wants to parachute into the South Pole. "We will consider it," says Annie, "and I can't wait to hear what the NSF says when they get wind of it." And flying in golfers is still discussed

"Definitely we would take golfers," says McDowell. "Our operating costs are so high we have to entertain almost any scheme, any madness that comes across the desk. The more bodies we can pump through the system, whether they're playing golf or whatever, the better."

I ask Annie Kershaw what Giles would think about today's ANI. "He would think it too sophisticated . . . and at the same time he would be trying to figure out ways to land jets at Patriot Hills," she says with a smile. And about golfers at the South Pole? She smiles again, and avoids the question. "Honestly, we'd like to be able to turn some of these down," she admits, "but they help pay the bills. This is a business after all."

8. SOUNDS OF SILENCE

My sled-and-ski trip was one of the great, small adventures of a lifetime, and I thought often about the variety of friends who would love to come South for this one-of-a-kind experience—if they could scrape up the bucks. We saw all weather—bright sunshine, calm, big winds, snowstorms and white-outs, freezing temps. One night it was so warm in our solar-heated tent we slept on top of our sleeping bags; the next, it was so cold we kept our gloves on inside. One afternoon, coming down a knife-edge slope, our sole map blew out of my pack and is probably still blowing across Antarctica. This was just a few minutes after we each fell, briefly, into narrow crevasses. We skied across slick blue ice, climbed magnificently carved wind scoops, hunted for fossils in piles of rocks, and came down a steep hill with visibility at zero, sleds threatening to slide ahead and pull us down behind them. On our last day out it was snowing so hard we had to use the GPS to find base camp. It was Antarctica at its best—trying, yet ultimately rewarding.

Back at Patriot Hill's, inside my pink and yellow tent, faded from hundreds of days under twenty-four-hour sun, the walls heave and snug with the 40 mph gusts of wind that ripple then expand it. Snow pelts the tent and the wind alternately whistles, hums, and roars. A heavy wash of blowing snow breaks over the tent, leaking an occasional fine spray of powder through small holes along the tent's seams. When the wind pauses, it is deathly quiet.

It's comforting to be in a tent during a winter storm. Inside, it seems like nothing can hurt or harm you. But if that thin nylon membrane were to disappear, if through a small slit those fierce winds were allowed inside, or if one of the aluminum poles snapped, it would mean big trouble. On this day I thought about what it would be like to be stranded in the middle of Antarctica in my long johns. I also thought back to the recent late afternoon Borneo Steve and I had shared soaking up rays, shirtless beneath a bright Antarctic afternoon sun.

Fifteen days after I arrived—the final three stuck in place because the blue-ice runway was covered with snow—the Hercules returned at two o'clock in the morning. Out of the back chute stumbled a whole new flock of urban penguins, decked out in bright, clean fleece and wind-stopping Gore-Tex, shading their eyes and stumbling stiffly in boots made for steep slopes not flat blue ice.

Within minutes after boarding the Hercules for the return flight, I fell fast asleep. My hood pulled tight around my face, I could still smell the smells of Antarctica, feel the winds and the cold. I didn't budge until we touched down, hard, on the cement runway in Punta Arenas, eighteen hundred miles, six hours, and many many worlds away.

ON THIN ICE, ONE LAST TIME

"I wonder what Johnny Carson is doing today?"

The question comes out of the clear blue. I have no response to the query posed by my travelmate Will Steger. In part because it's difficult to say much of anything when the wind in your face is blowing at fifty below, the dog's are running slightly out of control, and you're doing the best you can to stay upright on your skis. While I had no idea what prompted the question, it somehow made sense; I'm never surprised by how far the mind will wander when you're in the middle of nowhere.

The day started in a swirling groundstorm of snow, as had most days on a three-month-long "training trip" across the Northwest Territories. I'd come along for three hundred of the 1,000 miles, to spend time with an old friend, perhaps America's best-known polar adventurer.

It is very cold and we are on the last of three sleds, making our way from frozen lake, up and over portages, to the next frozen lake, and so on through the nine-hour travel day. It is too easy to describe this barren, ice-and-snow-cloaked landscape as alien. But late this morning, with blowing snow whipping at knee height, the blue-black lake frozen beneath, the horizon aglow by a sun barely visible through the haze, it felt as if we were traveling across another planet. As we skied away after a fifteen-minute lunch, the sun appeared perfectly round against the bright blue sky. Blowing snow still swirled around our feet. Below our skis were patches of the deep, frozen blue Asiak River, which drains into the Coronation Gulf of the Arctic Ocean. I watched the ever-changing ridges rimming the lakes, still pondering the question of "Where's Johnny?" and listening to Steger encourage his dogs. Each driver has his own tone and rhythm and words to keep the eleven-dog teams straining at their harnesses; Steger's encouragements sound like Saturday morning cartoons crossed with Beatles songs, something like "scoobee-doo, flub-a-dub, kip, kip, kip, obla-di." His dogs must like what they hear, because they pull harder when he sings out to them.

All afternoon the Carson question dogged me, in part because it came from a guy who has never owned a television set. I'm not sure if Steger knows Johnny no longer reigns on late night. While he may not keep up with rating wars, what he does know is how to travel and survive in the most arduous, frozen places on the planet. His public recognition—numerous awards and support from the National Geographic Society, the Explorer's Club, teacher's groups, scientific associations, honorary doctorates—has come from his 1986 leading of the first unsupported trip by dog team to the North Pole and in 1989–1990 leading a team of six men 3,741 miles by dogsled across Antarctica. Before and since he has covered thousands of miles across the Arctic, Canada, and Greenland at the back of a sled, sometimes with a partner, occasionally alone. Now, age fifty, he is preparing this team for another Arctic assault, a crossing of the Arctic Ocean, from Siberia to Canada, via the North Pole, a dangerous seventeen hundred-mile trip they hope to make in one hundred days. It is no easier for Steger to answer the question he's asked most—"Why?"—today than it was when he was making solo trips in his twenties. What he does know firsthand is how much the Arctic has changed in the past thirty years. A few days before we had stopped at a five-hundred-employee gold mine, Lupin, risen from the ice in the middle of the frozen nowhere.

"I first started coming up here in the 1960s, as a teenager," he remembers one night, squeezed inside the yellow North Face tent, heating some leftover oatmeal. "I would arrive at a camp in my kayak and most of the men I would meet had considerable Arctic experience. I would sit up all night listening to tales of adventure. Thirty years later we pass a giant gold mine in the middle of nowhere and meet men and women who work in the middle of the Arctic and have never been more than one hundred meters from camp. It's like a space colony. To me, that represents the typical way of life for most westerners today. People have stopped feeling, stopped knowing the place they live and work—whether it's a suburb of Minneapolis or the High Arctic. We are losing touch."

He is an oddity, Will Steger, in many ways a throwback to an earlier day and one of the last of a breed of men (and women) enticed by adventuring and exploring the frozen corners of the globe. Eccentric, scattered, and absentminded, he can be simultaneously ferociously focused, quick-witted, and charismatic. Over the years—we first met in 1986, just after he returned from his first North Pole trip—I've seen him greet with élan the prime minister of Japan at the Royal Palace in Tokyo, make small talk with the Bushes in the Rose Garden, talk politics and the environment with then-Senator Al Gore, and testify before Congress on the same. Smarter than most suspect, his charisma is proven by the fact that he's charmed millions of dollars from corporate sponsors over the years and thousands of hours of volunteer time from people who see his overriding causes—educating people about the frozen world—as true and important.

Because of his focus on education, teachers and schoolkids around the globe see him as a hero, thanks to classroom curriculum and computer linkups the one-time elementary school science teacher helped develop. He knows meteorology and the night skies like most know the way from their house to the local 7-11. While he has learned to give a black-tie lecture to a crowd of patricians, he is most at home in the wild, where he takes on animal-like characteristics, such as peeing as he walks or drinking water from the lake on his hands and knees, as a wolf would. His favorite meal is raw caribou. In his hand-built cabin in the Boundary Waters of northern Minnesota, are hundreds of books. On one shelf, stacked next to one another sit *Silent Spring, How to Dynamite, Kerouac's On the Road,* and a text on canning fruit. There is another side to Steger, too, what we'll call "the child within."

I've seen him, after a couple too many pisco sours, loft butter patties off the end of a spoon toward the mayor of Punta Arenas, Chile. Just before going to Antarctica he blew off the tips of two fingers by holding on to an M-80 seconds too long. I've watched him gleefully dynamite irrigation ditches and dance, furiously, by himself on his birthday. I've seen him weep when one of his dogs died and also beat one of his team for disobeying. Perhaps what irks him most is when he is dubbed a loner, since he insists he is not. He loves people, in fact loves nothing more than organizing big parties—then disappearing once everybody has shown up. Out of the dozens who have traveled with him over the years some regard him as egocentric, motivated by seeing his name in the headlines. But perhaps the highest compliment ever paid him came from Anne Bancroft, a member of his 1986 North Pole team. She told a reporter a few years back that, if lost in the Arctic in the middle of a storm, the one person in the world she would want to be with was Steger.

Bill Graves, the recently retired editor of *National Geographic* magazine, brought Steger into the society's historical fold in the mid-1980s and has helped fund each of his expeditions since. He calls Steger "the most unprepossessing, most humble hero of exploration I have ever met. I've never known anybody—and I've known a lot of them having run the so-called 'nut squad' at the Geographic for many years—with less apparent ego and more absolute determination and courage, a man of incredible strength of purpose and spirit and determination. He does what he says he's going to do. There was no question after talking to him for five minutes that he was going to get to the North Pole. Yet he's such a tiny little guy, until you look at his record you can't believe he is actually fifteen times the size of the rest of us—and he is."

The seventh (of nine) children born to William and Margaret Steger of St. Paul, his has not always been a charmed existence. There is a haunted past that is not part of his press kit. Twice married, twice divorced, in his twenties he endured a typical period of youthful unrest that saw him hopping freights, drugging, living on the streets of Los Angeles, before finally seeking solace—and finding his life's focus—at a Zen monastery in the Sierras.

"We didn't put any restrictions on any of our kids," says Will Steger Sr., an engineer and inventor. "We encouraged them to do whatever they wanted. Will just happened to stretch every limit."

The core of his life has always been adventuring. At twelve he volunteered to help chart the northern lights as part of the 1957–1958 International Geophysical Year project. (His job was to write a report every third night on what he saw in the skies and send them on to IGY headquarters in New York.) When he was fourteen, he and brother Tom built a raft and "Huck Finned" down the Mississippi. In 1964, age twenty, he made a three-thousand-mile kayak trip from southern Alberta to northern Alaska; the next year he made three first ascents by new routes of peaks over 18,900 feet in the Peruvian Andes. In 1969 he led a four-thousand-mile kayak expedition on the MacKenzie, Peace, and Yukon Rivers, taking time off from his job teaching elementary-school science in St. Paul.

In 1970 he started buying land on the edge of the Boundary Waters outside Ely, Minnesota, and organizing winter skills trips, initially for juvenile delinquents out of the Twin Cities. He built a small cabin by hand, miles from the road, and slowly bought neighboring land as it was available. Today his Homestead is a sprawling four hundred acres, with a dozen small cabins, a main lodge, guest cabin, the original cabin, and a five-story-tall "castle" on a hill that he designed in his head while traveling across Antarctica (and built mostly with monies made licensing his name to Target, for things like Will Steger band-aids, lunch buckets, and fireplace logs). He envisions the Homestead's future as a kind of enviro/educational think tank in the wilderness, accessible to corporations, non-profits, educators.

He slowly bred a sturdy breed of "Steger" huskies and started taking extended trips—with just one friend, his second wife, Patti, or alone— deep into the High Arctic. Those early trips were launched out the back- door of the Homestead, and he dressed in $30 worth of Salvation Army clothes. He remembers those trips as the best days of his life, "leaving and not telling anyone, coming home and not telling anyone." One trip across the Arctic by dogsled, dog pack, and raft covered seventy-eight hundred miles. In 1985 he traveled another five thousand miles from Duluth to Point Barrow, Alaska, to test equipment, procedures, and teammates for the next year's successful run at the North Pole. Along the way he accumulated hundreds of true adventures. Like running out of food six hundred miles from the nearest town; one day unzipping his coat and having it freeze, unable to be rezipped as temperatures dropped toward minus forty degrees; falling chest-deep through thin ice into freezing waters more times than he cares to recall; pulling man and dog out of crevasses; disguised in a sealskin cape shooting seals for dog food when there was nothing else to eat.

Patti Steger, though no longer his wife, remains one of his best friends. "What makes Will Will is that he simply does not see barriers. He is the most persistent man I know. As a result, when he has an idea or a vision and others say it's not possible, he simply doesn't hear them."

Now, at fifty, a time when most men his age are worrying about college tuitions and planning for retirement, and the most strenuous thing they do in the cold is pull-start the snowblower, Steger is packing his dogsleds for what may be the most dangerous, arduous expedition of his life. Why?

Some days, he admits, he wonders too. This current International Arctic Project has consumed him for four years, seven days a week, sixteen hour days, and cost $250,000 out of his own pocket. Fund-raising for such adventure has become nearly impossible as corporations with the money see less and less return on "investing" in polar expeditions. Virtually all the big "firsts" have been done. The advantages of high technology—from improved clothing systems to GPS, which essentially eliminates the option of being "lost"—have changed adventuring.

Still, there are believers. More than fifty companies have donated to this trip, from Adidas to Yamamoto Kogaku Co., Ltd, providing everything from dog food to long underwear, batteries to M&M's. Shaklee, 3M and Lands' End are the biggest donors to the $1 million pot—three-quarters of which has gone into the educational component. Charlie Orr, CEO of the San Francisco-based Shaklee Company, which has put up $100,000 for this trip, is one of Steger's most ardent supporters. In the United States, adventurers—sailors, climbers, ski racers, polar men and women—get attention in one of two ways: Either they win something, or they die. Simply being "the best" garners them little; there are way too many Michael Jordans and Joe Montanas to compete with. Steger has made a name and a career out of a seemingly antiquated pursuit by pure determination.

In 1984 I gave Bill Graves, then expedition editor at National Geographic, *a list of four expeditions I hoped to do." I wanted to go to the North Pole, I wanted to make a five-thousand-mile trip by dogsled to Alaska, I wanted to do a north-south traverse of Greenland, and I wanted to kayak the Northwest Passage. Crossing Antarctica wasn't even on the list. So though this is my last big expedition, I'm not even done yet. I have yet to kayak the Northwest Passage." For the record, he is and will remain the only man to dogsled to both poles, in part because dogs have now been banned from Antarctica. "I'm still in favor of some adventure for adventure's sake," he says, "though such efforts are becoming increasingly difficult to fund. I'm reminded of one of our most loyal patrons during our efforts to raise money to go to the North Pole in 1986. Julia Marshall was an eighty-five-year-old woman from Duluth whose family owned a big department store. She bailed us out twice with $5,000 checks, at times when we literally had $20 in the bank. When her second check arrived it was accompanied by a scribbled note in her hard-to-read handwriting that said simply 'We need adventure now.' I have always agreed. But adventure today demands more creativity, and more responsibility, than it did twenty years ago.*

Since we returned from Antarctica in 1990 thousands of people have come up to me and said thanks for what we had done for them. They weren't patting me on the back for being a great guy, they were simply saying thanks for motivating them, inspiring them to overcome some barriers of their own, to try something they'd always wanted to try. If you want to know "why" I do these things, I guess that's why.

Tomorrow, March 7, the team—four men, two women, thirty-three sled dogs—will leave the Russian Arctic island of Severnaya Zemlya. They hope to reach the North Pole by April 22, the twenty-fifth anniversary of Earth Day, and then continue south across the Arctic Ocean to Resolute, the northernmost town in the Canadian Arctic. The plan is to arrive by unique sled canoes at the end of June or early July. (About two-thirds of the way through, the dogs will be flown out and the man-hauled sled canoes dropped off.) Such a crossing has never been achieved in one season because the ice melts in late spring, turning the seas into a cold wash laden with thin crusty ice and icebergs. While the subject of not making it is rarely broached, two major obstacles could stop them: Warm temperatures, which mean more open water, and uncooperative winds, which could force them far off path.

Steger is most concerned about the first forty miles. "The real challenge is going to be literally getting onto the ice—because at that point it is moving by the island, even at the coldest temperatures, at five to eight miles a day. We could get there and be looking at forty miles of open ocean." If that's the case, all they can do is wait until it freezes enough to run nine-hundred-pound dogsleds over, or until the wind shifts and blows in moving ice. Other big risks are storms that might cause the ice to break up around them while they're encamped at night and the ever-present danger of losing sled or man through thin ice. Errant, hungry polar bears are also a concern, and why each sled carries a rifle. All of this excites Steger. "This area is the most dynamic, moving surface on earth. From day to day you don't know what to expect. It could be perfectly clear in the morning and then by afternoon you've reached another stretch of open water. In the Arctic, unlike much of Antarctica, each day is different, monotony is not an issue. In simple terms, the challenge is for us to get across the Arctic before the breakup begins."

The team is a mix of young and old, of wide-ranging experience. Russian Victory Boyarsky, forty-four, PhD in mathematics and physics, is a returnee from the Antarctica crossing; Julie Hanson, forty-one, a longtime Outward Bound instructor in Ely, Minnesota; Martin Hignell, thirty-three, from the United Kingdom, a former dog trainer with the British Antarctic Survey; Takano Takako, a Japanese journalist and athlete, whose inclusion helps introduce the effort to a big Japanese audience; and Ulrik Vedel, twenty-eight, an officer with the Danish Military who has worked for years patrolling Greenland.

The "first" involved is "dogsledding, in one season," since the Arctic has been crossed twice before: The first time it was over two seasons by British explorer Wally Herbert, who camped for more than a year while waiting for the seas to refreeze so he could continue, and in 1988 by a Canadian-Russian expedition on skis hauling sleds over a shorter, one-thousand-mile route. "In the past, experts, people I've respected, have advised me I was taking too great a risk," says Steger. "I've gotten used to people saying 'You won't make it.' But I study these routes for years in advance, I've spent long months traveling in the Arctic. I know things about these conditions, these places that others do not. In terms of risk, we're up in the ninetieth percentile. So it's a very feasible trip—if everything goes as planned. Which it rarely does."

In part the trip is intended to help draw attention to the importance of the Arctic's ecosystem and the critical role it plays in sustaining a healthy global environment. The Arctic is not a body of land—it is an ocean that freezes and thaws. Its winds strongly affect the temperature and currents of the world's oceans and exerts a powerful influence on the weather patterns of the entire northern hemisphere. Around its periphery are found the world's most productive fisheries. It is home to one of the world's last remaining migratory herds—the caribou. It is also rapidly becoming a repository for a wide range of contaminants from the world's industries, and the same qualities that make the Arctic unique in our imaginations—extreme cold and long periods of darkness—also act to extend the shelf life of pollutants deposited there.

But it is the high-tech communications ability—links to global computer systems, thus classrooms, scientists, and armchair adventurers— that has Steger most excited about this trip. When Admiral Robert E. Peary reached the North Pole in 1909, it took months before the news could travel to New York and London via telegraph. In 1986, when Steger and team reached the North Pole unassisted for the first time since Peary's day, news traveled by radio to Resolute Bay about twelve hundred miles away, then by telephone and fax to Steger's home office in St. Paul. This team expects to arrive at the North Pole to be greeted by live TV cameras, a joint effort between ABC's *Good Morning America* and Japan's NHK Broadcasting Corporation. "This is where adventure has gone," says Steger. "Tying high technology into adventure is a must if you expect sponsorship, and if you want to grab media attention, [and] thus keep your sponsors. Funding expeditions has never been easy, but now you have to be a lot smarter than just climbing a wall."

In many ways, things haven't changed that much since Columbus whee-
dled advance monies out of Queen Isabella. All the early polar
explorers financed their expeditions with advances from book sales and
promises of magazine articles, films, photos, lectures, appearances,
testimonials, and so on. (In 1908 the *New York Times* paid Commodore Peary
a $4,000 advance for his story.) None of Steger's predecessors, though, were
greeted by Joan Lunden live. More interesting than live television, is the access to classrooms new technology creates. When Steger and team crossed
Antarctica, hundreds of thousands of students around the world were able to
follow them, day by day, via satellite correspondence. This International
Arctic Project has built on the success of that program, developing curriculum and study guides, enlisting schools and teachers, arranging for computers, modems, and other materials, so that classrooms from Japan to
California, Northwest Territories to Brazil, can click on their Macs every
morning for a report on how the team is progressing. It is expected that 20
million to 25 million children will follow the expedition by computer.

The team will radio positions and observations about what they're seeing,
what they're doing, how the dogs are faring, how's the weather, to a base about
two hundred and fifty miles north of the Arctic Circle in Resolute. Details
will be sent on, via Internet. Updates will also be posted on ECONET, and
the Scholastic Network, a comprehensive online service for K-12 teachers and
students available on America Online, will be tracking the expedition daily
and provide extensive background resources. For schools without high-tech
equipment, e-mail reports and weekly fax updates will be available.

It is kids who are most turned on by Steger. When he shows up in a classroom with a slide show and a dog, they are rapt. Despite the growing fixation
kids have with computer games, real-life heroes still mean something to them.
In return, Steger likes kids, in part because in many ways he's just a big one
himself. When a ten-year-old asks him a question, he responds as an equal,
not as a teacher.

*I wrote my master's thesis in education in 1970 on the basic philos-
ophy that real education comes from within the students. That it's
not something you put into them, it's something you draw out of*

them. I almost flunked because the professor didn't see my point. A lot has changed in twenty-five years and I'm even more convinced that via this telecommunication the world—the kids—are going to see what we're doing, they're going to interact with us, it's going to draw them out. Our goal is not just to entice them into following our expedition, but into continuing to use these resources as an educational tool.

These technologies represent the future of education and a revolution in the way we teach. I spent three years teaching science to students in a classroom and I always found the process to be somewhat stagnant. Other than taking students out on a field trip, it was always very difficult to bring an event into the students lives as it was happening. Now, with computers and telecommunications, we can connect students to events in "real time," person to person, school to school, student to adventure. I would not have done this trip without the Internet, without the high-tech educational component. It just wouldn't make sense; the economic climate is not right to support "just" an adventure.

Not surprisingly, when Steger fills out a form with a blank for "Occupation" he puts a single word: Teacher. On a sunny, windy January day, six weeks before departing on what he says will be his last big expedition, Steger is kneeled on the floor of his cabin looking at maps, looking for the few white spots left where he still hopes to go.

Steger represents the last of a breed—adventurer, explorer, writer, teacher. While each season there are more and more teams and individuals making attempts on the poles, very few are attempting big, team-effort expeditions anymore. Even some of his own teammates wonder why Steger continues. On our trip last spring, on a day when Steger seemed like he'd rather be anywhere else, Ulrik Vredel wondered, "Maybe this was just one too many." Personally, I think one reason he's doing this last big trip is as simple as because he said he would.

He readily admits this will be his last big expedition. "Pursuing these firsts introduces a lot of tension into your life. But in order to raise the money and interest the media, you've got to take on big challenges, attempt big things. Virtually everything we've done in the past ten years has been a first. I want my next challenges to be building a garden, writing a book, kayaking around Ellsemere Island. To be honest, I'm sick of firsts."

He is silent for a minute or two, listening to the wind whip outside his cabin. "I'm making a ninety degree turn after this one. I'm giving my dogs to my teammates. I want to get away from the 'dairy farm' aspect, the responsibility of the office and employees. I want to start over again. Build a small team of dogs, go out and travel by myself or with one other person. Mostly into the north. I want to go on teaching. And I want to live a quieter life. I'm very happy to step out of the limelight. I've had my time."

THE ICEMAN TURNS TO WATER

On a perfect autumn day, my friend Will Steger and I begin a one-hundred-twenty-five-mile traverse by canoe—via a clear-blue string of twenty-one lakes and four rivers—for Lake Superior. It is the day after Labor Day and the skies are cobalt, the wind at our back. A smattering of red maple leaves stands out among the preponderance of tall green jack pines lining the granite shores of Canada (on our right) and the United States (on our left).

We have set out to retrace, from Lake Saganaga, literally along the U.S./Canada border, the route carved more than two centuries before by the so-called voyageurs, the canoeing adventurers who plunged deep into the woods west of Lake Superior to barter household goods, tobacco, and liquor for furs with the Indians. We know from historical accounts that we'd run into many portages during our ten-day trip. Many of them were marked on the maps, in bright red, usually next to uppercase letters reading "DANGEROUS WATERS." What we could not have predicted was that by the end of our first day of paddling Will would be mumbling a word I'd never heard him use before, no matter the setting: "This is preposterous," he muttered over and over.

Our first portage, at the southern tip of Gneiss Lake, arrived just fifteen minutes after we'd set out for the day. Though short, just twenty-five rods (inexplicably, the bizarre British measurement is still used today—three hundred and twenty rods equaling a mile), it did not bode well. Rather than pull up to nice, sturdy sand or rock, the bow of our Kevlar canoe terminated abruptly in a soft quagmire of earthy mud and loon excrement, a good twenty feet from shore. A haphazard trail of foot-sized stones led to dry land. Slide off the stepping stones and you'd find your- self at least knee-deep in the tangy mix.

Sure enough, as soon as I heaved the "Big Pig"—our nickname for the forest-green, canvas Duluth Pack loaded with eighty pounds of food and fuel—onto my back, its swinging weight carried me directly off the stepping stones and into the muck. Only one leg sank in, but my ankle-high boot threatened to be sucked off by the gravity of the mud. Will was no help. Watching from the safety of hard ground he couldn't stop laughing. I was sure the voyageurs above were laughing, too.

It turned into a long first day, including ten portages, most unmarked on the map. The longest was saved for day's end. After lugging our gear, in two trips, up and over a five-hundred-foot climb we arrived at Magnetic Lake, where, once again an accidental stepping-stone path lead through the muck to the water's edge.

This time it was my turn to chortle. Will—the canoe balanced pre- cariously on his head—lost his footing as he stretched a toe for a piece of driftwood stuck to the surface of the muck. But it was an inch too far away, and he slipped—the canoe still somehow precariously balanced on his head—into the muck

"This is preposterous," he shouted at the ghosts of the voyageurs, as we both nearly choked from laughter.

• • •

Each year for the past ten, Will and I have tried to make time to spend a week or more together in some wilderness setting. We met in 1986, shortly after he'd returned from leading the first confirmed, unaided trip by dogsled to the North Pole. In the following years we collaborated on a trio of books and numerous magazine stories and we have always found the best time to concoct plans for getting rich and retiring (isn't that what most men talk about when they're together, when not pondering that other dominant male mystery . . . baseball?) was out in the woods, deep in the barrens, no matter the season. Which over the years has led us to Antarctica, the Northwest Territories, Greenland, the forests lining the

Great Lakes, and all over the Boundary Waters that surround his four-hundred-acre complex on the outskirts of Ely, Minnesota.

When he first suggested retracing the Voyageurs Highway I was equal-parts uneducated and excited. I knew little of the history of the canoe-borne fur trade that had boomed in the 1700s, and though I grew up in the Midwest had not spent a lot of time paddling the Boundary Waters. An educational adventure? The best kind.

As we planned the trip Will kept bringing up the so-called grand portage—a nine-mile hike at our trip's end—I was sure he was exaggerating, for effect. He loves to make even the simplest adventures sound larger-than-life. I assumed that ultimately we'd arrange a floatplane to get us out, or maybe run into an ambitious Indian with an ATV. No way, I thought, would we hump a couple hundred pounds of telecommunication gear and a canoe down a narrow track, up and down hills, over nine miles. Not even Will would be into that, I thought.

• • •

In the 1700s these boundary lakes were once part of a busy thoroughfare, teeming with Sioux, Cree, and Chippewa Indians, dashing French explorers, humble but vivacious voyageurs in gay sashes singing songs from medieval France, dour Scotsmen, scions of old English houses, and, ultimately, canny Yankees.

In French, *voyageur* means simply "traveler." Along these Boundary Waters, it became synonymous with the men who made their livelihoods paddling canoes from lake to lake carrying trading goods in and bundles of furs out. Generally small rugged outdoorsmen, they lived on peas, lard, and pipe tobacco during spring-summer seasons that saw them push hundreds of miles into the wilderness west from Lake Superior.

"Sweating, panting, dark with mud and covered with mosquito and fly bites, the voyageurs dogtrotted the portages, punctuating the carriage with many a *sacré*. Two or three bales, or 180 to 270 pounds of goods were held on the bent back by a portage strap, which passed around the voyageurs forehead and reached to the small of his back," recounts Grace Lee Nute in her *Voyageur's Highway*. "We seldom eat, but we often drink," was their watchword. Time was money and the best voyageurs got back to the forts fastest, carrying the heaviest loads. The most common cause of death? Ruptured hernias.

• • •

Our third night out we made camp on a jewel of an island at the west end of Mountain Lake. With views east and west down the long lake we were able to swim off both sides of the island. After consecutive long days of paddling and portaging it was a deserved five-star hideaway; we guessed we were halfway through our retracing.

As the sun went down and Will cooked our nightly pasta feast, I wrote in my journal seated among sweet-smelling pine cones, lulled by a warm breeze moving through the tops of the trees. Blessed by Indian summer days—we paddled shirtless today, and swam in the late afternoon, unheard of for Border Country in September—we were traveling essentially alone through one of North America's great wildernesses. (How great? Remember those old Hamm's beer commercials, with the bear and the "Sky blue waters?" Filmed right here, on Lake Saganaga.)

After dinner, we talked about how amazing it was that all this land— some 4.2 million acres, protected by the twin governments of the United States and Canada—had been set aside from development. That it is shared so amicably is remarkable, too. Though these boundary lands have passed over the centuries from Indians to French to British to Yankee, for the past one hundred years or so it's been mostly peace and love all along this border line. What other nations can boast that? Think about borders in South America, Europe, Africa, the Soviet Union, Asia, even our own with Mexico. Where else in the world has there been so little conflict than along this very thin line we're following?

Under a sky filled with late-summer stars—the triangle of Vega, Deneb, and Altair is high and bright, with Jupiter rising low over the hills to the east—we wonder about how this land will change over the next one or two hundred years. Will it remain as wild, or might it one day become home to a new generation of loggers and/or second-home owners?

The only certainty we could arrive at this night is that for sure, global warming will mean longer portages.

• • •

Steger and I talked about future plans as we paddled. After a thirty-year adventuring career filled with success and accolades, he has definitely downshifted. In 1986 he led the first expedition to achieve the North Pole without resupply; five years later he led a six-man team by dogsled across Antarctica, 3,900 miles in 221 days; in 1995 he led a five-person team from Russia, to the North Pole and down to Canada, by dogsled and canoe. Later that year the National Geographic Society, which has supported each of his expeditions with money and reports, awarded him the prestigious Hubbard prize, adding him to a list of only nineteen other recipients, ranging from Roald Amundsen to Jacques Cousteau. For the moment he is content exploring the deep wilderness, reaching into Canada, surrounding his Minnesota compound. After the 1995 expedition he gave his forty sled dogs to his teammates; two weeks before we set out he turned fifty-four.

"I can confidently say that I won't be putting together any more big expeditions," he said as we paddled across North Lake under gathering clouds. "They simply take too much time to organize, and cost too much. That's not to say I won't be going back to the Arctic. I'm sure I will. But it will be solo, or with one other person."

In 1997 we had spent the Fourth of July together in Helsinki. It was the most stressful time we'd spent together. He was on his way to the North Pole by Russian icebreaker; there he would be dropped off and attempt, by himself, to pull and paddle a canoe full of gear back to Canada. He expected the arduous trip to take sixty days. Immediately after being left on the ice he was stuck in thick fog. He floated on an iceberg for twelve days, surrounded by the Arctic Ocean and deep, slushy ice, before being rescued, by Russian icebreaker. Since that disappointment—his first very public setback in three decades of hard-core polar adventuring—he says he's happy to have the big, heavily sponsored and heavily-publicized trips behind him. "I want to get back to doing the kind of smaller, low-tech trips I did when I first started out in the late 1970s, taking trips into Canada and the Arctic simply by walking out my back door, with no announcements, no hoopla."

Still, like adventurers of all centuries, the question he gets most often is, "What's next?" His primary income these days comes from writing a thrice-weekly "Wilderness Journal" report for the Lands' End Web site. He's at work on a book about his early travels with dogs in the Canadian Arctic. He's bought an island on the Canadian side of the border and will start building a cabin there next spring. And he's plotting more trips, by dog and canoe, but those kind of trips he can make just walking out his backdoor.

• • •

For all the complaining about our many portages, it was easy to forget the many hours we spent paddling. The trip wasn't only about walking, grunting, sweating, and toiling. Truth is, we were blessed by unseasonably warm days and the wind literally at our backs. We cleared Gunflint Lake, our longest straight stretch at 8.5 miles, in an hour and forty-five minutes. Same with Mountain Lake, nearly the same length. At moments it was as if we were being pushed, coasting. Some of the fluidity had to do with a good rhythm, a team effort. Will in the bow, me in the stern, and the sparkling conversation that inevitably accompanies men in the woods for ten days.

Conversation? When it's just two of you for an extended, concentrated time, it runs the gamut. From small talk (Will: What's the name of that baseball player, Mark McGwire?) to big talk (Will: What do you think is going to happen to Russia?) to no talk at all. We brushed the subject of spouses on several occasions (Will's happily married, for the third time, to a twenty-eight-year-old Filipino, Elsa). We discussed at length how lucky we'd been with our chosen careers. We even got around to closest calls with death: Will's dropping his Bobcat through the ice at his Minnesota compound and having to kick out the windows as it began to sink me swimming from an overturned sailboat on a midwestern lake, the last day of October, sans life jacket.

(We probably weren't far from the "barbaric jargon" used by the voyageurs while they crossed these same pathways. "All of their chat is about Horses, Dogs, Canoes, Women, and strong Men who can fight a good battle," is how one Englishman of the times described the limits of conversation in those days.)

All of this copacetic travel was accompanied by one lurking unknown. Waiting for us around the last bend was the Pigeon River, which would take us from the final lake to Fort Charlotte. From there we would, after all, have to walk out along the nine-mile Grand Portage that leads to Lake Superior. We knew the Pigeon would be low, but we had no clue how low. We hoped we wouldn't be walking its twelve-mile length, dragging the canoe behind us. Or worse, carrying it.

What we found was a mixed blessing. For the first couple miles the river was shallow, but flowing. Then we hit the first beaver dam spanning its width. When we pushed the canoe over the sticks-and-stones dam we discovered our second-to-worst nightmare. Below, the river was reduced to a shallow, narrow, boulder-studded stream. (Our worst nightmare? The same, minus moving water.)

Which meant that for the rest of the day we, like twelve-year-old boys, waded through calf-deep waters pulling the canoe behind us, pushing it up and over rocks. A pattern soon developed—we'd push and pull for fifteen minutes, hop back in, and paddle through a short section of deep water, then jump back out of the boat as it dragged on rocks. Will's sole complaint as we kicked through the warm water under a high, hot sun was that we hadn't brought along a couple dog harnesses, so we could just shoulder-up and pull.

By midafternoon the river thankfully deepened and we were able to get back in the boat for good. The rest of the day—before arriving at the five-hundred-foot Partridge Falls, which required a sizable portage—was spent peacefully paddling down a wide river banked by wild rice. Herons, loons, and ducks, caught off guard by our sudden presence, bolted out of the tall grass that lined the river banks, our only companions on this sunny fall day.

• • •

Our last day on the trail dawned ominously. Not just because of the gray skies, but more from inherent trepidation: Would we be able to haul all this stuff out of here? Will we fail in the eyes of the voyageurs above if we are not able to carry our one hundred and eighty-five pounds of gear and canoe down the nine-mile portage back to civilization.

The main impediment was all the high-tech gear we'd used for sending up daily reports to Lands' End—satellite phone, computer, heavy lithium battery packs, external floppy drive, bunches of wires and cables.

Unlike the extra oatmeal, those things could not be buried and left behind. By the time we compressed the electronic tools into one backpack and everything else into the Duluth pack, soaring is not exactly the word I would use to describe our departure from camp. Blundering, perhaps, plodding at best. The overstuffed Duluth pack weighed about one hundred pounds; the other had to carry a forty-five-pound backpack with the forty-two-pound canoe balanced on his head. We agreed to stop and trade loads every half hour.

Will volunteered to be the first to carry the one-hundred-pound pack. Together we lifted it onto a nearby stump and he struggled into the shoulder straps, fitting the tumpline around his forehead. He stumbled out of camp; from behind he resembled a drunken sailor, or some kind of Dickensian beggar. (We were sheepish, too, in the eyes of history, since we knew the voyageurs had used this exact trail, many of them carrying a *pair* of ninety-pound bales at once. "He is not looked upon as 'a man' who cannot carry two pieces," wrote one trader.)

When not racing each other the fastest voyageurs had made this trip in six hours. Leaving at midmorning we figured we'd be lucky to reach Lake Superior before dark. As we lurched up the trail—the canoe-carrier bringing up the rear, just in case the man lugging the Pig faltered, or fell. Will received a high compliment from a couple on a day-hike passing us from the other direction. "You look like a real voyageur," the man said to Will. The tumpline so tight around his forehead, threatening his oxygen supply, Will could only mutter, "Thanks," and plunge on.

Despite his vow to stay away from big organized expeditions, Steger, in December 2003, led a six-person team and thirty-six dogs on a six-month expedition across Nunavut, the indigenous province of northern Canada. One big difference: His transantarctica expedition had cost in the neighborhood of $12 million; for this one, he raised and spent less than $100,000.

SACRIFICIAL PEOPLE

The single-engine Otter banks hard in a tight circle over an explosive, one-hundred-foot waterfall along the Eau Clair River. The pilot, a classically daring French Canadian named Pierre, dangles a burning cigarette out his vent with one hand as he drops the plane ever lower over the sprawling tundra of the Canadian Shield, giving his half dozen passengers a first-class gaze at a wilderness few people have seen by land or air. The hilltops below are smoothed from centuries of grinding of glacier ice and plates of sand and stone. The granite plateaus are riven by crater lakes, meteor holes, fields of lichen, and three-hundred-foot tall pines.

Flying into the sun, the late afternoon light dances off the surface of a hundred rivers and their thousands of tributaries. It looks like I envision a moonscape would, except these pockets and furrows are filled with pure Arctic melt. On the left are the Hudson and James Bays that separate Ontario and Quebec. Guarded by barrier islands, sandy gravel banks lead from the blue-green shallows to whitewashed cliffs that line the coast. It is a landscape so raw, so untouched, you can literally see the etchings of the retreat of the last great glaciers, 3.5 billion years ago.

Continuing north we cross river after river the breadth of the Hudson. Robbie Niquanicappo, deputy chief of the Great Whale Cree, points out and names a dozen of them—the Coats, Nomission, the Great Whale, the Little Whale, Nastapoka. Each curves around and through lichen-covered meadows and past sheer rock cliffs and bowers of century-old pines.

Because it is so cold most of the year—we're at fifty-five degrees north, on the edge of the tree line—there is little evaporation so the rivers are always high and run fast. As they gain speed, dropping ten feet per mile toward the bays, they are increasingly pocked by falls and whitewater. From one thousand feet above, each waterfall starts out in variant shades of brown and green, before turning into burst after burst of violent white as they plunges into rock-littered rapids below. Though we can't pick them out from the air, the woods along the river's banks hide the game trails, traplines, and winter tepees that Cree hunters have used for generations.

This northernmost wilderness of Quebec is a geologist's dream, a landscape contoured over millions of years. Now, somewhat predictably, man threatens to alter it radically in less than thirty. Its proposed hydropower project—phase one is nearly complete and has already flooded or dewatered tens of thousands of acres—is the largest construction project ever undertaken in North America. If the government and its provincially owned power company have their way, much of what we have seen from the air will be buried forever under man-created reservoirs.

Quebec's twelve thousand Cree are fighting to keep their wilderness wild. We fly on, circling back slowly to a spot on the Great Whale River where we had left behind a pair of rafts and a half dozen companions. As the small plane arcs slowly out over James Bay, we get one last glimpse of the wilderness that has become the setting for a classic late-twentieth century conflict, a struggle between man's desire to create ever more "power" and his simultaneous inclination to preserve wilderness. Unfortunately for both man and nature, the two goals are usually incompatible.

• • •

The smartest gear we packed for this river expedition were mosquito headnets. Though wearing brown netting wrapped around our faces makes us look like bank robbers from another planet, the $2 investments offer some protection from the voracious black flies and mosquitoes. It is rare that human flesh and blood visit these wilds and they feast hungrily on any exposed skin.

Our first night on the river we set up camp in the dark. Though thoroughly scouted by the trip's organizer, logistics are always iffy on a first descent. The two-hundred-mile-long Great Whale River, dotted by Class III and IV rapids, had never been rafted before. As a result, it had taken us quite a bit longer than expected our first day on the river to line the rafts around perilous-looking whitewater. That meant lugging gear and food up rocky cliffs, through thick brambles and back down to the river, time-consuming, arduous tasks that showed us quickly why the Cree had over the years learned to use paralleling lakes and rivers in order to avoid these turbulent waters.

This was actually the second of such fact-finding "adventures" organized by my friend Eric Hertz and his Earth River Expeditions. A half-dozen New England states are considering buying power from the proposed hydroelectric plant, and Hertz and the Cree have brought state legislators from various states up to see the wilderness that will be lost if the project is built, to see exactly what is at risk. The village of Great Whale, one of nine Cree communities in northern Quebec and the one that would be most effected by the coming dams and reservoirs, sits at the mouth of the Great Whale River where it dumps into the Hudson Bay. It has become headquarters for the fight, visited by journalists and activists from around the globe. In Cree the village is called Whapmagoostui, the place of whales.

This month, November, was to have been a big one for Hydro-Québec, with New York state expected to sign a contract to buy $13.6 billion worth of power from the proposed James Bay plant over twenty years. But last year's visit to the area by state legislators proved effective. One of the New York state assemblymen who rafted the river and met with the Cree, William Hoyt from Buffalo, succeeded in getting the house to pass legislation forbidding the state to buy power from a foreign nation without sufficient environmental assessment. Before the bill could be considered by the state Senate (and sadly, two days after Hoyt unexpectedly passed away), Governor Mario Cuomo canceled his state's contract to buy power from Hydro-Québec, thus depriving Hydro-Québec of much-needed start-up money. Soon after, Vermont also canceled its plans to buy HQ power; today only Massachusetts and Maine are still considering such a purchase. As a result of the loss of all those hoped-for export dollars, Hydro-Quebec has slowed the project into three phases, hoping to build one at a time while it secures financing.

This year's contingency of rafters includes a foursome of New York state legislators, several staffers, head of the Natural Resource Defense Council's international program, Robert F. Kennedy Jr.—an NRDC attorney and key opponent of the James Bay project—and eight Cree from Great Whale and nearby Wapisitich. The legislators came armed with open minds and reams of white papers; the Cree brought fishing gear, guns, and traditional canvas tepees; Bobby Kennedy brought an encyclopedic knowledge of the issues as well as a fishing pole and plastic football. Our first night's camp sat high on a cliff overlooking a plunging waterfall.

While dinner was cooked by flashlight, and by the illumination of a display of spectacular northern lights, I sat on the banks of the river with Robbie Niquanicappo. Articulate and good-humored, like most of today's Cree leaders he was schooled in southern Canada. After university he worked around urban Canada before returning home to Great Whale eight years ago. His job as deputy chief is an elected one, but his plea to save this wilderness is more than a job. He and his people simply do not want to sacrifice this place; Cree homeland already provides 40 percent of Quebec's power.

Dressed in running shoes, sweat suit, a camouflaged "Save James Bay" ball cap, and wearing tinted glasses, Robbie, thirty-two, sounds like an elder statesmen when he insists, "We've been here for five thousand years. We're not going anywhere." If you listen to the Cree and their supporters it is war in which they are engaged and the battle lines are firmly etched. Hydro-Québec, the government-owned power company, wants to flood an area of Cree land the size of France. Behind its determination lie two key economic objectives: an eightfold increase in power exports, worth billions of dollars, and the availability of huge quantities of electricity for a series of new aluminum smelters under construction along the St. Lawrence River.

From the Cree's perspective James Bay is one of Canada's greatest wildernesses. But Quebec's Prime Minister Robert Bourassa views the area quite differently. He sees the James Bay watershed, which runs all the way to the St. Lawrence River, as a vast hydroelectric plant in the making, where every day millions of potential kilowatt-hours flow downhill and out to sea. "What a waste!" he wrote in 1985. The government's plan is to start building more roads, dams, and dikes as soon as it can wrangle environmental approval.

The $50 billion hydroelectric scheme has been dubbed by Bourassa "the project of the century," and its two phases are the largest development project ever undertaken in North America. Bourassa's "vision" calls for dozens of relatively small rivers to be diverted into larger ones, creating sufficient water volume to power a network of dams that would produce enough electricity to meet all of Quebec's needs, with plenty left over for export to the northeastern United States. The development would extend over three hundred and Fifty square kilometers, encompassing the largest remaining unspoiled wilderness area in the eastern half of North America. The list of what would be lost if the project proceeds is long. Entire ecosystems would be destroyed, the flow of rivers changed one hundred and eighty degrees. Ghost towns would spring up; wildlife, spawning grounds, migratory routes, farm and hunting lands would disappear. Vast wetlands and coastal marshes, important staging grounds for migratory waterfowl would be flooded or dewatered.

The region is home to rare and endangered freshwater seals, beluga whales, polar bears, walruses, anadromous fish like the brook trout and lake whitefish, and herds of caribou. The delicate balance of forest, flowing water, and marsh that support this rich web of life has evolved over tens of thousands of years, and it is threatened. But what worries the Cree most is the "cultural genocide" the project will inevitably induce. National Audubon scientist Jan Beyea calls the "project of the century" "the northern equivalent of the destruction of the tropical rain forests." Phase one of the James Bay project is already a reality. Begun in 1971 and only now nearing completion, it flooded more than forty-five hundred square miles.

What the Cree are trying to stop is the second phase, known as James Bay II or the Great Whale River Project. If this second phase gets the go-ahead it isn't only the village of Great Whale (pop. 1,000) that will be affected. So will Chisasibi, Waskaganish, Nemaska, Waswanipi,

Mistisini, Umiuyak, and Ouje-Bougoumou. And Hydro-Québec does not intend to stop: Next on the boards is the Nottaway-Broadback-Rupert Project—fourteen hydroelectric centrals, sixteen dams, ten major storage reservoirs, and more than seventy dikes diverting eight more rivers.

To the government's annoyance there is much opposition to James Bay II. Motivating the unions, environmentalists, and natives who are fighting phase two is the fact that there has never been an environmental audit or damage assessment conducted of the first phase. Hydro-Québec has conducted the only "scientific" studies to date and they claim damages from James Bay II will be "local." (That's hard to believe, considering they are planning to flood an area the size of France.) Nonetheless, Hydro-Québec has proven quite able in the past to streamroller its path. While such a project could never earn approval in the united States, the Quebec environmental commission and federal government have waffled on demanding environmental review or enforcing existing agreements between the Cree and the government.

It is not just the environment that is threatened. Natives, both Cree and Inuit, fear they are being pushed into a new era of even greater pollution, a mercury age. Since the flooding of land for James Bay I began in 1971, high levels of methylmercury have been found in the livers of seals and beluga whales, both native delicacies. Neurological disorders have already surfaced among the Cree. The high rate of mercury poisoning is due to a complex and poorly understood biochemical chain reaction set off by impounding waters on the Precambrian rocks of the Canadian Shield. Hydro-Quebec claims the problem is "temporary" and will disappear within a few decades. Critics maintain this unpredicted outcome of the first phase is just one sign the mammoth dam project amounts to environmental folly on a grand scale.

What's worse, there is a kind of double environmental whammy waiting in the wings. Electricity from James Bay II is seen as an important lever for stimulating economic development in Quebec. During the past two years Hydro-Québec has used the prospect of cheap electricity to develop an aluminum and magnesium industry along the St. Lawrence, agreeing to sell electricity to the smelters based on world prices for their products, rather than at fixed rates. Two new aluminum smelters, worth $2.2 billion, are already under construction and a third is being expanded at a cost of $500 million. The double whammy is that after the ecosystems are destroyed, up go the aluminum smelters, which create perhaps the most destructive environmental waste known to man.

The twelve thousand Cree (and seven thousand Inuit) who live in Quebec feel like they have given up enough; in 1975 they sold 80 percent of their land to Hydro-Québec so it could build James Bay I. The $135 million settlement bought them education, health care, a police force, a guaranteed income program for Cree hunters who stay in the bush one hundred and twenty-five days a year, and new opportunities like a regional airline, Air Creebec. That agreement was negotiated by laymen, the first generation of Cree to graduate from high school; like many white man/Indian agreements that came before, much of it has been ignored. For this new fight they've hired expensive lawyers and public relations advisers and claim cashing out is not an option.

"Our future is very much in doubt," admits Robbie. "We do not value this place for its economic potential; our culture is based on the land. If it is destroyed that is genocide." Recent years have been traumatic for the Cree. Just twenty years ago most lived the traditional life of nomadic hunters. Their movements were determined by the habits of animals on their traplines, except in summer, when they gathered with other families in makeshift villages for religious and cultural activities. Today Great Whale's teenagers are as familiar with shopping malls as traplines. The Cree insist they simply want to be left alone, albeit with the modern conveniences—"tools"—they've become accustomed to, like VCRs, snowmobiles, and chain saws. If Hydro-Québec gets its way a couple thousand construction workers and ancillary hangers-on would soon be living cheek by jowl with the Cree, arrived via an expanded airport and an asphalt highway through the tundra from Radisson. They'll bring with them the bane of all small Arctic villages—booze, drugs, prostitutes, venereal disease. The government argues the project will create sixty-two thousand jobs; the Cree contend that is six thousand jobs spread over the project's ten-year life and half of those will be secondary. "And those jobs won't last long," says Great Whale native son John Petagumskum, "and then the land will be gone."

Ironically a bigger problem for Quebec's Cree may not be the threat of dams and dikes, but the diminishing role traditional life plays in villages infected by encroaching westernization. In Great Whale the Cree have pre-fab houses (built with money from the JB I settlement), a new multi-million dollar hockey rink, a grocery/videotape rental store, but few jobs. A handful work for the tribe office or on temporary construction projects. A few spend their days drinking, most kibbitz and watch videotapes. While hunting, fishing, and trapping are still the cornerstones of the Cree economy, fewer and fewer young people are satisfied following in their elders' footsteps. The unemployment rate among tribe members aged fifteen to twenty-one is 55 percent and many are leaving their villages for big cities.

It is a modern dilemma, played out previously in small communities across the subarctic: Do we stay, or do we go? In many ways the James Bay project epitomizes the fate of the whole North and prompts bigger questions. Is all the additional power even necessary? Quebec's population is expected to decline shortly after the turn of the century; conservation and economic recession in the United States are lessening demand for electricity. At the same time, just how much wilderness can we expect to protect as the twenty-first century dawns, given the continual demands mankind's exploding population makes on the planet? Until the population stabilizes, aren't we going to have to continue to sacrifice wilderness for energy?

• • •

Our days on the river are spent paddling hard into the wind, thundering through monstrous whitewater and occasionally floating with the current at our back. Great herons leap from the shore and flap gracefully overhead; arm-length fish jump alongside the rafts; traces of caribou and deer are spotted onshore. Lunches are made on granite outcroppings jutting into the river and eaten beneath centuries-old puckerbrush. The Cree packed delicacies of caribou tongue and goose bannock, which we augment with grilled cheese sandwiches and canned tuna. The Cree catch a halfdozen sizable bass that we smoke over the fire and devour. Late into the night the legislators quiz the Cree on the history and future of the river we are exploring. Each day a Hydro-Québec helicopter buzzed overhead several times. Company employees are not used to "traffic" on this underexplored river and are no doubt curious about this bunch of floaters. The rafting was particularly enlightening for the Cree. All their lives they had been taught that the rapids were life-threatening and that they should walk around them, not plunge through them. In the rafts they dig fingers deep into the rubber and grimace as waves swamp the boats.

But they are thrilled by the new experience. "The white man has finally taught us something fun," laughs Robbie Niquanicappo. At each campsite the Cree make a point of predicting the future of that particular spot on the river if James Bay II is built. Where we'd camped the first night would be flooded; where we'd spent the second, in spongy, calf-deep lichen, the river would dry up. From thirty miles above the village of Great Whale the river would become undistinguishable beneath a string of reservoirs.

Government officials in Quebec cynically contend that all the Cree's posturing and protest is merely an avenue to eventually negotiating a bigger settlement for the rights to their land. But Robbie insists while there may be a handful of Cree willing to settle for the highest dollar, most would prefer to keep their land. "If not here, where are we to live?" he wonders late over a blazing campfire.

The Cree insist it is more than the wilderness they are trying to preserve, but a quality of life as well. They don't want roads, construction workers, gas stations, supermarkets, more video stores. They like their isolation. They like the fact that for three weeks each fall the villages shut down when whole families go into the bush for goose-hunting season. They like walking (or snowmobiling) the five-hundred-mile-long traplines established by their grandfather's grandfathers. They get pleasure out of ice fishing by net, and caribou hunting for subsistence, not pleasure.

But the bureaucratic vision of the place is as a dammed-up flooded bastion of power, not a life-support system for the natives who have populated these woods for the past 5,000 years. The government's argument is why should six million Quebecois suffer the loss of inexpensive hydropower simply to benefit twelve thousand Cree. Prime Minister Bourassa insists that the natives fighting James Bay II are "anti-Quebec" and that he fully anticipates a "deal" will be struck with the Cree. Bourassa's tough talk smacks of desperation and of a belated realization that a sophisticated public relations campaign by the Cree and their environmentalist allies outside Quebec, which he has ignored, seriously jeopardizes the Great Whale project. Ironically, Hydro-Québec and the government brought many of the current troubles on themselves by trying to go too fast with too little public debate, information, or consultation. Now they're fighting on several fronts and the Cree have the advantage of being in a position to pick their fights. Hydro-Québec's back is against the wall. The company has a mountain of debt and was depending on the U.S. contracts to keep it solvent. That is still a possibility: an oil shortage or other economic energy dilemma and, Hydro-Québec's power could loom as a cheap alternative. Mario Cuomo and New York state backed out of their contract on economic and environmental terms; if offered a better deal New York could easily sign a new contract with Hydro Quebec. For now the key to the project's proceeding is environmental approval, approval that is currently hung up in Cree-initiated court battles.

• • •

Forty-year-old Mathew Mukash returned to his hometown of Great Whale after college in Montreal six years ago. He ran for chief twice unsuccessfully before winning last February. He now works full-time for the tribe, fighting Hydro-Québec. Dressed in army camouflage, his long hair braided down his back, he casts for brook trout and talks about the determination he hears from his fellow Cree. "Our position has not changed," he says. "We simply do not think the project is necessary. But the only way to prove it requires an objective and open examination of Quebec's real energy needs. That is where the assessment must begin and I don't think Hydro-Québec is interested in such a study.

"Ultimately," he continues, "we want just two things from Hydro-Québec and the government. To be included and consulted in the process." He admits one of the pitfalls in any relationship between the Cree and the white man is that there is no word for "politics" in his language. But the natives in Canada are learning the game pretty well; as we speak, in Montreal, a self-rule deal is being hammered out between the government and the aboriginals. The sticking point is land rights, specifically the James Bay hydropower project. The key to success or failure of the project remains environmental assessments; without fully documenting the environmental impact of James Bay II, Hydro-Québec cannot begin. In 1991 the company gambled by trying to proceed with separate Environmental Impact Statement's: one for the roads, airports, and marine terminals, a second for the dams, dikes, reservoirs, and powerhouses. Its rationale was that if it could get the first package approved it could start building roads and expanding airports, thus making it more difficult to stop it from building dams and powerhouses. But the Cree went to federal court in Toronto to force any environmental assessment to consider the whole project at once. In September of last year a federal court judge ruled that the federal government must force a combined environmental review.

As a result of that decision Quebec's environment minister conceded that construction slated to begin last winter was postponed. It appeared the first battle had been won by the Cree. But if they have learned one thing from their experience with encroaching western civilization, it is: Don't trust the establishment. They have precedent for their pessimism. Nearly seventy tribes and bands of American Indians were officially "abolished" in the fifties as part of a Canadian government policy known as termination, which took their land, their sovereign status, and their tribal identity. In return, the government made cash payments to the Indians . . . and ignored many of its promises.

Hydro-Québec, which has invested hundreds of millions in James Bay II, is not about to give up without a fight. In an effort to sully the Cree company, representatives told animal rights groups in Vermont that the natives use illegal leg traps in the bush. They do not. The company has also encouraged rumors in the United States and Canada that the Cree are secretly negotiating a settlement with the government. They are not.

To stem a rash of bad publicity for its handling of the Cree, Hydro-Québec has sent a permanent representative to Europe to try and defuse the company's failing reputation there. Though insiders admit the government bungled its own case by expecting separate environmental assessments to be approved, Hydro-Québec is appealing the federal court's decision. And despite the court's decision, the Cree are concerned the powerful power company may start building the road from Radisson to Great Whale anyway, if simply to provoke a fight. "We don't see how they can start, given the political fallout that would surely follow, but you never know," says Luis Eguren, a veteran organizer working for the Cree in Great Whale.

"But we don't trust them at all. As for the Cree's resolve, it is firm. They're trappers and hunters and they've tasted blood. They sense the kill and they're going after it." Matthew Mukash is not worried about the Cree losing their spirit, and vows they will fight rather than fail. "This dam will not be built," he warns late one night as a tepee fire turns to ash. "It is not a matter of 'if'—it will not be built. We will prevent them, physically if we have to, from even starting that road." He expects up to three thousand Cree to join him near Radisson at the first rumble of a Hydro-Québec bulldozer. If the Cree begin disobedience, Ovide Mercredi, leader of the Assembly of First Nations, the political voice of Canada's five hundred thousand Indians, says his group will throw its weight behind them. The end of this war is not even close. And even if it is won to the Cree's satisfaction, their future remains sketchy.

With the roar of the Great Whale River threatening to drown out our conversation, Mathew Mukash echoes a sentiment I heard from several Great Whale residents. "Dam or no dam," he said, "things are going to change here, and fast. Many of us would prefer change to come slowly. But so much is out of our hands."

Eventually Cree leadership dropped its resistance to Quebec and secretly negotiated an agreement to drop their legal claims—in exchange for $2.2 billion over the next fifty years (roughly $70 million a year) and eight thousand construction jobs. Quebec will also have forestry and mining rights to Cree land, which could be significant, as diamonds have been found. While some Cree support the agreement as a panacea for severe unemployment and poverty among its changing demographic, others lament the destruction of ancestral land and a traditional way of life.

POSTCARDS FROM NEWFOUNDLAND

GOOSE BAY, LABRADOR (September 9)—Standing on a rain-slicked dock on Otter Creek, 5:30 in the morning. Pilot Ed Williams mumbles over his cup of coffee, "So, you're going up to the Middle of Nowhere, eh?"

The way he says it, I suspect he's talking literally about a town so named. I ask.

"Nope, no town. That's just the way it is out there," he says, sipping out of his Styrofoam. "Big. And empty."

He's right. As soon as the fog lifts we're heading into The Big Empty, into the heart of an isolated three hundred thousand square kilometers of starkly beautiful hard rock and icy water, home to the biggest herd of caribou on the planet—and very little else. The land of "bared boughs and grieving winds" is how turn-of-the-century explorer Dillon Wallace described Labrador. But we're not going anytime soon. I can barely make out a pair of small sailboats moored just offshore.

An hour later, Williams walks into the airport shack where we munch muffins. "Heavy weather," he announces, with understatement. "Thick as tar out there." They need five hundred feet visibility upward and three miles out. We still can't see across the bay. As morning grows, so does the fog. The downtime allows for an hour spent shooting the breeze with some of the Labrador Fish and Wildlife "b'ays" (Labradorian for guys, boys, men). A low-slung white metal building next to the docks is their headquarters. An adjoining garage is laden with the accoutrements of work in the north woods: Moose jaws on a display board, blaze-orange chain-saw cases, stump samples, soil samples. A sign on the refrigerator reads: "For staff use only, no specimens." Snowmobiles and outboard motors, radio collars for wolves, bears, caribou. Worn backpacks are permanently rigged with stout axes. Wooden snowshoes hang on the wall, red-plaid jackets from hooks, and a couple Sunshine Girl calendars are nailed to the plywood. The smell is of gasoline and pine tar. Frank Phillips, conservation officer with Fish and Wildlife, picks up a slice cut from a spruce tree no wider than his hand. "I don't know if you'll believe it, but this comes from a tree just ten feet tall—but it's more than five hundred years old. It's a tough place for things to grow."

It is a *tough* place, a stark landscape of stone and stubborn vegetation. Trees and moss grow out of sand atop the oldest unexposed rock in the world, unchanged since long before any hooves set foot on this planet. While there are an abundance of animals—seven hundred and fifty caribou for example, the largest herd in the world—there are only about thirty species of animal in the entire country. Compare that to a hectare in an equatorial rainforest, where you can find hundreds of different living things.

Thanks in part to its remoteness and isolation, Labrador is also one of North America's best-kept wilderness secrets. Miles and miles of largely unexplored and unfinished pristine beauty. It looks a lot like southern Alaska, or northern Patagonia. Its rivers and lakes hold sea-run and landlocked Atlantic salmon, arctic char, lake trout, pike, whitefish, and the world's largest eastern brook trout. Sailors and canoeists come in small number, but are hypnotized by the size, the quiet . . . the emptiness.

"The barren lands of Labrador are one of the least explored places on the planet," confirms Jim Schaefer, head of Fish and Wildlife, standing in front of a map in his office. The he turns confessional. "That's in part because it's also the least hospitable."

• • •

We've come to Newfoundland Province—Canada's easternmost, comprising simply the island of Newfoundland and the far bigger, but less populated Labrador—for an intensive, extensive two-week tour. Choppering around the fjords of northern Labrador, fly-fishing Newfoundland's Humber River, and climbing in its biggest national park, Gros Morne. A few days touring the province's capital of St. John's, winding up with a sea kayak around Newfoundland's southeastern Placentia Bay.

Though physically far larger, Labrador is kind of the bastard brother of the two regions. Unique, alienated, it wasn't so long ago that the Newfoundland schooners that visited its coast in the summer were Labrador's only links to the outside world.

Labrador's reputation as the Middle of Nowhere goes way back. During a voyage in AD 1000, Leif, son of Erik the Red, dismissed the land as unfit for habitation. Jacques Cartier, in a famous put down in 1534, dubbed it "the land God gave to Cain." In 1773, Lt. Roger Curtis of the Royal Navy was more succinct. After surveying the Labrador coast from aboard the sloop *Otter,* he wrote: "The barrenness of the country explains why it has been so seldom frequented. Here avarice has but little to feed on."

Today only thirty thousand people are scattered across Labrador—twenty-four thousand whites, five thousand Inuit, and one thousand Innu—supported by a variety of economies. Western Labrador has mining, the Churchill region a big hydroelectric plant, Goose Bay and Happy Valley a giant military base. Many are subsistence livers, hunting in the winters, fishing in the summers. Approximately four-fifths of those born here remain here, with strong ties to family and neighbors. Most of the land is left to caribou and moose, black bear and wolves . . . and trillions of black-flies.

• • •

When our Air Labrador Twin Otter finally lifts—four hours delayed—it is still foggy, but we can make out for the first time the far side of the bay.

The trees—boreal forests of black and white spruce, balsam fir, and birch—reach north for half an hour before giving out over the subarctic barren grounds. Smooth brown-rock plateaus, scarred and scratched and etched by the retreat of the ice, just fifteen thousand years ago. Sloping walls, wearing patches of last year's snow, drop dramatically to rivers and lakes. Rivers are rimmed by sandy beaches, surrounded by bogs and fields of lichen.

It is ancient land up here. The base stone of the Kaumajet Mountains is thought to be the oldest stone on earth—3.7 billion years old. The northern peaks, the Torngats, are the tallest in Canada east of the Rockies. Separated from Greenland sixty-five million years ago, the Inuits call the Torngats "Home of the Spirits."

The human population ends in Nain, a third of the way up the coast. Up here snows begin in October and can continue into June. "One thing for sure, I've never seen snow in July," says Frank Phillips, conservation officer for the Labrador Fish and Wildlife Service who's joining us for a couple days in the wilds. We're flying to a Fish and Wildlife cabin on Hebron Lake, just a few miles inland off the Atlantic Ocean.

Phillips points at a map as we fly. He gets real excited showing us the butter-knife-shaped Harp Lake, set amid fifteen hundred- to two thousnd-foot sheer-rock cliffs. The surrounding tundra, with its small mirror lakes mixed with barren rock and sphagnum reminds me of some kind of prehistoric golf course, dotted with boulders left behind by the melt of the glaciers. A now bright morning sun reflects off the shallow sand rivers, which head off in every direction. Their routes are impossible to determine, meandering river leading to meandering river, to small twisting lake to yet another, as far as we can see.

We fly over the headwaters of the Naskaupi River. It is most famous for a trio of explorers who never saw it. In 1903, twenty-nine-year-old New York journalist Leonidas "Laddie" Hubbard and a lawyer buddy, forty-year-old Dillon Wallace, along with a Cree guide named Elson they had arranged by mail, attempted to cross Labrador via the Naskaupi. Their goal was the George River, which they hoped would lead them to caribou hunting grounds and Indian villages never before seen by white man. Hubbard hoped his story for *Outing* magazine would propel him to adventuring fame, similar to Robert Peary, another *Outing* contributor.

Unfortunately, just a few days into their trip—already consumed by blackflies and mosquitoes, carrying far too much weight—they missed the opening of the Naskapi, one of five rivers exiting Grand Lake. Instead, they carried on due west, through swamps, bogs, up and over tall mountains, always frustratingly on the lookout for the bigger waters they knew were out there. After Hope Lake (which they named), followed by Disappointment Lake (which they also named), then Windswept Lake (ditto), they turned back. It was autumn, snowing, and they were literally starving to death, reduced to gnawing on maggot-covered caribou hooves and dried caribou skin. They attempted to reverse their tracks. Hubbard didn't make it; Wallace and Elson, did, barely.

As we fly over the Napkaupi it is easy for us to see how Hubbard got so confused. It is difficult to impossible, even with the help of a plane, to decipher ingress and egress of these myriad rivers. Staring out the small plane's window, Phillips shouts over the roar of the twin engines, "Those b'ays sure had some bad luck. They left us a lesson, for sure—always take a really good map."

• • •

HEBRON LAKE, LABRADOR—It was a wildlife day. After breakfast, dozens of caribou, in groups of six or eight, wander along the beach, twenty feet in front of our lakeside log cabin. After lunch, a four-hundred-pound black bear, distinguished by a big white spot on his chest, walked by out back, standing up on his hind legs to sniff us out. In the afternoon, helicoptering back from an excursion up to the Nachvak Fjord, two hundred miles to the north, we spot a pod of minke whales, a company of harp seals, a pair of bull moose standing up to their knees in lake water, and fly over one lone golden eagle. Just before sunset, a sizable gaggle of Canadian geese wing overhead.

Early in the day, Frank Phillips sits in the sea grass in front of the cabin, filleting an arctic char. A native of Newfoundland, Frank moved to Labrador twenty years ago to work as an environmental consultant for a mining company. He liked the isolated beauty here, met and married an Inuit woman, and now has three boys. University educated, he lives an almost-subsistence life, taking nine or ten caribou a season to feed his family and relatives, fishing whenever he can. He's already on the lookout for a Christmas goose.

"Sometimes we buy hamburger or chicken nuggets for the children, because it's easy. But the rest of the time we eat food we catch or hunt. I'd say 75 percent of the meat we eat, I've hunted." Tough and conservative, Frank is well aware of the struggle the aboriginal peoples have here in the north, trying to meld a life out of new and old ways. Like many spots in the arctic and subarctic, debates over land ownership and just how responsible the government should be for its native people are loud, long, and lingering. "I don't take sides in those fights, even though I think I understand them pretty well," says Frank."It's clear though that there is no easy way to get to right or wrong." In Labrador the biggest current controversies are over a proposed national park, the moratorium on commercial cod fishing, and a multibillion-dollar mineral find at Voisey's Bay, near the last town north, Nain. Inuit and Innu associations are fighting hard to make sure their people participate in, and profit from, decisions affecting what they see as "their" lands. As we talk, the air is suddenly alive with the whir of a chopper. Minutes later we are joined by Harold Marshall, right-hand man to the prime minister of Newfoundland, and Malcolm Rowe, the province's top bureaucrat. They've come from St. John's, to scope out boundaries of the proposed Torngat Mountains National Park. They stand around over a coffee, explain their mission north, and then they're off.

As the rotor of their chopper starts to whir, another helicopter sits down. This one carries Lawrence O'Brien, recently elected liberal member of Parliament, Labrador's only representative. Inside the cabin I ask him about the relationship between Labrador and Newfoundland. "I have no hesitation saying I think we're treated like third or fourth cousins by the provincial government, and I would have said the same in front of Mr. Marshall and Mr. Rowe. They know how I feel."

His opinion is that Labrador gets short shrift from the politicians in St. John's, and there is a growing sentiment that Labrador would like to be separate—a province, like the Yukon—with its own government. "Right now the Yukon gets about $1 billion dollars a year in federal monies. In Labrador, we get less than $50 million. Yet we've got a similar-sized territory, the same number of people. What sense does that make?"

Working with Innu and Inuit associations, he and others are trying to work with the provincial powers that be to ensure a solid future for Labrador. "We would rather work together," he says, "but if it comes to it, I guess secession, if that's the right word, would be alright."

• • •

Our chopper pilot, Henry Blake—from a long line of Labradorean Blakes come over from England in the early 1700s—has been flying birds for seventeen of his thirty-seven years. He's never lived anywhere but Labrador, born and raised in North West River, a town of one thousand Inuit and five hundred "settlers." Though he's never lived anywhere else, he's still excited everyday to be up here, in the Big Empty.

We stop to refuel at Saglek, site of a North American Defense station, one of a string of early warning radar stations built during the Cold War by Americans and Canadians to monitor the Russians. Today it's abandoned; bulldozers work cleaning up a mess of PCBs, left behind by the American military.

Loaded with nine hundred pounds of jet fuel, we're off, swooping low up Saglek Fjord, Tallek Arm, and around Nachvak Fjord, the grandest of all the Labrador inlets. Icebergs, floated down from Greenland and Ellesmere Island, dot the saltwater bays. We put down next to Nachvak Fjord. Henry smokes and we talk about what it would be like to sail around these inlets. His family came to Labrador from England in 1700. Though he looks a lot like a balding, late-thirties white guy, he assures me he's got a percentage of Indian blood, maybe one quarter. "Looking at the old family pictures, you can definitely see Inuit in there," he insists.

Back in the bird, we are up to fifty-four hundred feet, ripping at 110 mph, heading out over the Labrador Sea, sun glistening off the flat salt water. The geography is subtle, monochromatic—always big. We stop on the way back along the Ramah stream, to fish for arctic char. No luck, until Randy Kerr, Mungo Park's technical wizard, finds a small riverside pool just offshore. I cast once, then twice, and get a strike. The eighteen-incher was so close, I think we could have kicked it ashore.

• • •

Despite all its emptiness, Labrador has been inhabited for thousands of years. The Innu (Indian) culture datas from eight thousand years; the Inuit (Esquimaux) four thousand years. It was the first part of the North American mainland to be seen by white men, the Vikings, who sighted it in AD 986, but did not come ashore until 1010. The sixteenth century brought the Basque whalers, as many as two thousand of them in twenty galleons; they returned to Europe with twenty thousand barrels of whale oil. Next came the British and French fisherman, fur traders, and missionaries. By 1870, most of the fishermen were local, and their supplies came from Halifax or St. John's. Many of the Europeans married Innu and Inuit women.

Moravian missionaries from Germany arrived at Hebron, at the head of the lake where we're camped, in the mid-1800s. They chose a magnificent point, built a giant wooden church and mission, a dozen wooden houses, greenhouses, and a cemetery. The place was an instant magnet for the scattered Innu people who lived around the valley. Within a few years two hundred native peoples called Hebron home, the northernmost settlement in the country.

Today, all that's left is a beautifully abandoned ghost town. The fence surrounding the cemetery is flattened, several of the homes have fallen where they stood. Rusted oil barrels, borne by the wind, are scattered across the point.

In 1959 the Labrador government, with the cooperation of the powerful church, announced that the community would be relocated. It was too remote, said the government, too difficult to provide services like health care. The announcement was made inside the church, where natives were hesitant to speak up against the plan. At that time there was no aboriginal association they could appeal to. Soon after, all of the peoples were moved south, to Hopedale, Makkovik, Rigolet, and Nain. Extended families were split up, resettled in communities where they knew no one, had no hunting rights, no jobs. As a result, many Hebron residents suffered depression, turned to alcohol, attempted suicide.

The tragedy was that the government offered no options, didn't consider moving all the people together to a place all their own, where they could continue the same way of life. Instead, they relocated without consultation, without input from the people who would be affected.

Frank's wife, Sarah, was the very last child born at Hebron; her family left for Makkovik when she was two months old. She returned for the first time last year. "It was quite emotional as we pulled into the harbor," says Frank. Today, as part of a new aboriginal agreement, there are some who would like to see the former residents of

Hebron living in Nain be given a new homeland all their own, outside the community.

"But if it happens, the first thing they must do is sign an anti-alcohol agreement. That's key," says Frank, referring to one of the diseases that affects native peoples across North America. "They could go back to hunting, fishing, living off the land, living a simple life without alcohol, without TV. They could work for the new park. It's a plan that offers them hope.

"They could go back to where they belong," he says.

• • •

Back at the cabin, Frank has set up a traditional white canvas summer tent. Its walls are squared, topped by a shallow peak and tied off to barrels and rocks, weighted down at the corners by four-by-fours. Inside the floor is covered with pine boughs Frank carried up from Goose Bay. He sleeps on an ultrasoft pad made from caribou skins.

A candle burns atop a stripped branch, its sharpened point jammed into the sandy ground. Henry, Frank, trip outfitter Rich Deacon, and I cook strips of fresh caribou on the stout metal stove, fed with small branches (also carried along, since there is virtually no wood here, north of the tree line) and drink icy Molsons refrigerating in the stream nearby.

"You know the best days up here," says Henry. Frank nods. He knows what his friend is going to say before he says it. "Spring days. In March, when the sun is out and the temperatures in the teens. It's too hot some days." They load up snow mobiles out of Goose Bay and drive forty miles across the frozen ice to where the harp seals swim. They make camp there, in tents like the one we're in, and during the days sit for hours, waiting for seals to pop up through blow holes; when they do, they try to stick them fast with home-cut spears.

As the pair of local b'ays weave their stories, outside, broad green bands of the aurora borealis sway over a starry backdrop, while dark clouds race before a chinook wind. In the morning, fresh caribou and bear and wolf tracks surround the tent.

• • •

WOODY ISLAND, NEWFOUNDLAND—Sitting at a small wooden table at a rustic wooden inn, typing, I look out over Old Cove. The sky is a milky patina of gray; mottled white clouds hang over the White Hills across the strait. It is a cool, fall night.

I am good tired, thanks to a combination of several nights running with fewer than five hours of sleep and a half day of sea kayaking into the wind. First thing this morning we left St. John's and drove across the Avalon Peninsula, past the towns of Conception Harbor, Whitbourne, Dildo, and South Dildo (I kid you not). At Garden Cove, a sleepy village of one hundred and twenty, we met Jim Price and his son Jamie, who'd brought a dozen sea kayaks. By eleven o'clock, we were on the water, paddling for Woody Island, a halfdozen miles away.

It was revitalizing to be moving with some alacrity inches above the saltwater. I'm not a big climber; fishing is not a passion for me. But I love to paddle big boats on open water. This day had it all: Fresh air, continually changing skies, saltwater spray, foot-tall waves, wind in the face.

The coastline is so omnipresent here that it is virtually impossible to forget that Newfoundland is an island, the tenth largest in the world. It's bigger than Ireland, just slightly smaller than England. Its coastline is ringed by hundreds of smaller islands. Our route carries us west from Garden Cove to Bloody Point at the tip of the uninhabited Sound Island. By taking a strait between the island and mainland we are protected from the bigger seas, and winds, of Placentia Bay. We are just about as far east as you can go in North America—next stop would be Ireland, or the Azores.

From this vantage the landscape appears ever more green. Sun-dappled forested hills line the shores and a multilayered charcoal sky reaches from horizon to horizon, like a thick wool blanket pulled over the land. Like the aurora borealis, the midday sky changes shades constantly with the winds. As afternoon breaks, so does the gray. With the clear and blue come a strong headwind, making paddling more concentrated. A light sweat breaks on my back as I paddle, far ahead of the others. I dip my fingers into the crosshatch of salty waters at my bow, and touch them to my lips for a taste. By the time I round the southern tip of Sound Island at Upper Sandy Point, the sea is perfectly calm.

It's good to be on the sea, finally. I say finally because though we've seen an incredible array of landscapes across the province, and have always been within a few miles of a coastline, this is the first time we've actually been *on the sea*. And in Newfoundland the sea is all, the island's raison d'entre. It's the reason people came here, and it is still its shrine, defining all culture, affecting every life. The sea is the single element that binds all Newfoundlanders, whether they're from the Northern Peninsula or Burin Peninsula. You hear it in their folksongs—"Let Me Fish Off Cape St. Mary's," "Jack Was Every Inch a Sailor," and "The Squid Jigging Song"— see it in their art and read about it in the daily headlines.

I paddle alongside Jim Price for a while. He tells me he's been a resource planner for the government for twenty-eight years; his kayaking company is a sideline, a passion. He gets five weeks' vacation a year and schedules his three- and four-day tours around them. He is an unusual Newfoundlander, in that he uses the sea for his passion rather than livelihood. He's traveled all over the east coast of North America whitewater kayaking, and has made several first descents of Newfoundland's toughest rivers. Fifty years old, he didn't start paddling until he was in his late thirties.

"Kayaking has been slow to catch on here," he explains as we paddle. "Like a busman's holiday. People who live in Florida go to Canada for vacation, and vice versa. Here in Newfoundland, the last thing a fisherman wants to do after a long day on the sea is go back out on the sea. But that's changed as fishing has slowed as a way of life. Now I give fishermen lessons. I've got fishermen going on tours. I've even got fishermen who want to set up kayaking companies." When he started his business nine years ago he was the only kayaking operator in the country. Today there are five more, scattered around the coastline.

The cove on the north end of Woody Island, protected from Placentia Bay by a fat thumb of a point, is dotted with a few residual fishing shacks, reminders of both when it was a lively little fishing village and when later it was abandoned due to resettlement in the late 1960s. As I paddle towards a beach of smooth stone and amber kelp, I can see six feet down into the clear water. The sandy bottom is littered with rust-colored rocks and luminous white clam shells, opened.

In the cove, beneath the hillside inn called Island Rendezvous, wood-plank docks ride on empty green fuel drums and stout pilings. A handful of fishing shacks hang over the water. It is picturesque, a stereotypically perfect fishing harbor. The only thing missing are boats, people, and fish.

Thirty years ago Woody Island—two miles long by a mile and a half wide—boasted a church, a post office, a health clinic, a four-room school-house and a general store, which served as a courtroom, Sunday school, and gossip center. Daily passenger boats carried people to the mainland at Swift Current. Most everyone on the island was a fisherman, and the town had a mayor, a town council, a school board. With organization came better roads, garbage collection, electricity, and jobs. The irony is that improvements meant more government involvement, which ultimately led to resettlement. The province argued it could not afford to continue to support all of these tiny, remote villages, so it paid people to move inland.

Beginning in 1968, Woody Island's population was removed. Its school was torn down, the boards from the United Church were carried to the mainland and two homes were built from them. Today it is home to a few shacks kept by seasonal fishermen.

Loyola Pomery grew up on nearby Merasheen Island and built the Island Rendevous in 1989. "It's mostly Newfoundlanders we get here, come back to see a bit of their past," he tells me over a late-night drink. "Often the talk turns to the resettlement, which can get a bit sad. I mean my grandfather and others his age were literally dragged from their homes, leaving fingernail marks in the rock. But for me and my generation, the truth is we probably would have left the islands anyway. There was little future for us here. In that way, the resettlement was probably inevitable, a good thing."

• • •

TACK'S HARBOR, NEWFOUNDLAND—I'm a Newfoundlander born and bred, and I'll be one until I die. I'm proud to be an islander and here's the reason why, I'm free as the wind and the waves that wash the sand. There's no place I'd rather be than here in Newfoundland.

—Bruce Moss, "The Islander"

The day dawned *mauzy,* a perfectly Newfoundlandic adjective to describe a wet, gray day—which could describe most days along the seacoast here.

It is a flawless word—gauzy crossed with moist, I presumed, since no one was able to come up with the word's origin—for a morning where the air was damp, winds were steady out of the south, fog hovered, and the chance of precipitation was high.

Last night I had a conversation with Roy Wareham, who keeps a charter boat across the channel from Woody Island, in Arnold's Cove. He agreed—for a price—to carry us, and our kayaks, south for a day of paddling around the inlets and coves that rim King and Merasheen Islands. His only small hesitation were the southerly winds that were predicted, which could make crossing the western channel of Placentia Bay dicey. But if we were willing to put up with a few swells, he was happy to motor across.

A soft-spoken, forty-six-year-old, Roy comes from a long line of Wareham businessmen. His great-grandfather bought a cod-distributing business on Merasheen Island back in the early 1900s. His father later ran the business, and after university, Roy went back to work for the family. "I was one of the lucky ones, to go back home and have a job," he says in the kitchen of the Island Reservoir Inn. "Most of the friends I went to school with couldn't stay on the island because there was no work, except fishing.

"But I didn't want to stay on the island all my life. And neither did my wife, Rowena. So we moved off ". Together they run a charter boat business, ferrying tourists, photographers, and geologists around Placentia Bay. He shows me his brochure, in which Arnold Cove is referred to as the "Economic Hub of the Isthmus." It's true, if partially built on hope, since Argentia, an hour's ferry away, is slated to be the site of the smelter the government hopes will be built in the next couple years to process the minerals mined near Nain in Labrador. The idea is to keep as much of the money generated by those twin businesses in the province as possible. The downside is that smelters are some of the most polluting industries on the planet.

With kayaks aboard the thirty-eight-foot *Lori Rose,* we set out around nine o'clock across the western channel for Merasheen Island. Just as we ready to traverse, the southeasterly wind picks up and waves grow. Within half an hour we're pulling uneventfully into a one-dock cove near Tack's Beach.

Kayaks in the water—the boats are red and so is my paddling jacket, better to be spotted by our pickup boat on a day where the fog will descend by several feet an hour until the shoreline finally vanishes in the soup—we set out through the inside pass of Long Reach, paralleling King Island. The winds and tide are at our back; the few times we round a landmark and chance the sea it is rough and windy.

Paddling close to the shore the colors are majestically sober. Crystalline clear, nut-brown seas roll up onto amber kelp and whitened bedrock and driftwood. Tall, thin spruces grow out of a salt-enriched soil on a cliff edge above, half of their roots exposed and dangling. Every quarter mile the bright orange fruits of a codberry tree provide random jolts of brightness. There's not much wildlife on these islands, but we have some fun sightings. Placentia Bay has the largest population of bald eagles in the province and as we stroke along the shoreline a lone eagle swoops out of a spruce, directly over our heads, headed out to sea. A few minutes later a seal pops his head up, curious about our intrusion. A dozen merganser ducks take flight from inside a protected inlet, the last one providing comic relief as it tries and tries and trie to get airborne.

It has been exactly two weeks since we arrived in Newfoundland and this is a perfect way to wind down our ramble. A solitary drift through the pristine sounds of Placentia Bay, on the kind of weather day Newfoundlanders regard as common.

Like a lot of people from "away," prior to this trip my impressions of Newfoundland were shaped largely by Annie Proulx's prize-winning novel, *The Shipping News.* An American writer with a house on the northern shore of Newfoundland, her lyrical, sardonic book is set in a one-time fishing town very much like those we have seen along the coast. The characters who populate her fictional town—Quoyle, Mavis Bangs, Nutbeem, Jack Buggit, and Tert Card—are flimsy caricatures of some of the people whose paths we have crossed. In Newfoundland the book received mixed reviews due to its perceived exaggerations, the embroiderings of which probably hit a little too close to home.

Few writings have done a better job of describing the beloved and dreary beauty that Newfoundlanders miss most when they're away from their home. This day, on a Saturday late in September, I pull my boat ashore, onto a thick bank of rubbery kelp, and hike to its flat crest.

As I look out over the sea I think about the newspaperman/antihero of Proulx's imagination—Quoyle—who had relocated from New York to his family's long-abandoned homesite on the northern coast of Newfoundland. On a Saturday late in September he'd gone for a walk along the rough shore lining the Atlantic.

"At last the end of the world, a wild place that seemed poised on the lip of the abyss. No human sign, nothing, no ship, no plane, no animal, no bird, no bobbing trap marker or buoy. As though he stood alone on the planet. The immensity of sky roared at him and instinctively he raised his hands to keep it off. Translucent thirty-foot combers the color of bottles crashed onto stone, coursed bubbles into a churning lake of milk shot with cream. Even hundreds of feet above the sea the salt mist stung his eyes and beaded his face and jacket with fine droplets. Waves struck with the hollowed basso peculiar to ovens and mouseholes. . . . It was a rare place."

That it is, I thought as I slipped down wet rocks back to my boat and pushed off into now thick fog. A rare—and mauzy—place.

ALONE AGAINST THE SEA

"*In the next instant, a wilderness of foam hurled us upon our beam-ends, and, rushing over us fore and aft, swept the entire deck from stem to stern . . . beyond the wildest imagination, was the whirlpool of mountainous and foaming ocean within which we were engulfed. A gleaming fiery froth on the ship intensified the black night. Sleet, cutting like flying icicles, shot over the prostrate vessel. The noise was so great that it numbed the ears. No one could shout and be heard. We were . . . alone.*

—Edgar Allen Poe, on rounding Cape Horn on a sailboat, from *Ms. Found in a Bottle.*

Sailing around the world—alone, without stopping—has to be the greatest adventure of our time, as measured by both risk and reward. An indefensible claim? Perhaps. Mountaineers will make their own assertions. As will deep-ocean divers. Those who've crossed Antarctica or the Sahara on foot, or slogged to the North Pole and back, can argue that their accomplishment, and suffering, is unrivaled. (I'm talking Planet Earth stuff here, not even thinking about what's involved in rocketing off to Mars.)

But I remain convinced. Consider the combined trio of factors grinding against the success of the solo round-the-worlder: The elements—endless storms and winds, cold, snow, sleet, fog, icebergs. The surface—traveling on a constantly shifting, treacherous ocean highlighted by weeks-long stretches where fifty to sixty foot–tall waves dump on you from several angles simultaneously, knocking the fifteen-ton boat onto its side every thirty minutes or so. The isolation—one hundred and five to one hundred and fifty days at sea, 24/7. Alone, not one second of relief, including more than forty days spent farther from land than anywhere on the planet (not to mention the sleep deprivation that results from grabbing sleep in fifteen-minute segments for four straight months).

Author Derek Lundy's *Godforsaken Sea* documented the 1996 Vendée Globe, the quadrennial solo, nonstop race. He suggests the only person who might understand the circumstances of a solo sailor is a political prisoner held in solitary confinement.

• • •

Solo, round-the-world records go back more than one hundred years, to Canadian Joshua Slocum. Aboard the thirty-seven-foot *The Spray* he was the first to sail around alone. Leaving from Boston it took him three years. In 1942, Argentine farmer Vito Dumas lowered the mark, taking just two hundred and seventy-two days, and stopping only three times. In 1966, Brit Sir Francis Chichester sailed his *Gipsy Moth III* around in 270 days. Two years later a group of British seamen organized the Golden Globe, the first round-the-world, nonstop solo race, won by Robin Knox-Johnston in three hundred and twelve days, covering 30,123 miles.

In the 1980s American Dodge Morgan lowered the mark to one hundred and fifty days, then Frenchman Olivier de Kersauson dropped it to one hundred and twenty-five. In 1982 the British Oxygen Corporation organized a new round-the-world, single-handed race. It departed from Newport, RI, and made stops in Capetown, Sydney, and Rio de Janeiro. The winner of the first BOC was Philippe Jeantot, an unknown professional diver from Comex, France. He won each of the four stages, covering the 27,500-mile course in one hundred and fifty-nine days, two hours, twenty-six minutes, winning by eleven days. He won the second version in 1986, in 134 days. On the heels of his BOC successes Jeantot created the Vendée Globe. The rules were straightforward and few. Each boat had to be fifty to sixty feet long, and the sailor had to be more than twenty-one years old. All yachts had to be self-righting. The only contact with land would be via radio, satellite phone, or e-mail. The winner would be the first to cross the finish line after sailing from west to east, past the three capes. It was instantly dubbed the most difficult race ever devised. "The ultimate in human endurance, a sporting challenge unparalleled in the world of adventure sports," bragged one sailing publication. At the time Jeantot said simply that he hoped to create a pure race. "One man, one boat, first home," was—and is—the race's motto.

I have several friends, mostly Frenchmen, who have sailed once, twice, three times in the Vendée Globe. To a one they are stoic, seemingly unimpressed by their own accomplishment (though ambitious and even egotistical on other fronts). My impression is that to do that thing is so humbling, and so incomprehensible to someone who's never done it— namely, the rest of the human race—that the only option they have is to play it down. Act as if it's no big deal. "Brilliant, just brilliant!" is how Englishman Pete Goss remembers his near-death experience during the 1996 Vendée Globe. In the next breath he admits he's happy to have that race behind him.

Titouan Lamazou, a Frenchman born in Morocco, won the very first Vendée Globe in 1989–1990. He did it in one hundred and nine days, eight hours, forty-eight minutes. (The previous record had been one hundred and twenty-five days.) On his sixty-foot boat he carried premade casts for his arms and legs so that in case he snapped a bone he could continue sailing. When he sailed into Brittany one hundred thousand people greeted him. Two days later he was feted by a ticker-tape parade down the Champs-Élysées. Today, a decade later, he's basically stopped sailing, to travel and paint. All he says about that race is, "I experienced things that changed me forever, for good and bad." Christophe Auguin broke Lamazou's record in the 1996 Vendée Globe (one hundred and five days and twenty hours). He is very direct about the effects of the experience. "We don't come back intact from a race like this."

• • •

Four months before the start of the 2000 version of the Vendée Globe, Philippe Jeantot sits in his small home office in Les Sables d'Olonne, a sunny resort town on the western coast of France. The fourth edition of the Vendée Globe sets out on November 5, from Les Sables. It is a cool, early summer day. "Few sailors can go head to head for one hundred days with the sea," he's explaining. I trust him, given that he's sailed solo around the planet four times. "*La mer n'aime pas la surenchère*. The sea does not like to be challenged."

A record number of sailors, perhaps as many as twenty-five, will depart, planning on returning to the same spot three and a half to four months later. Given the percentages of the previous races, one or two of them will never be seen again.

Lamazou, winner of the first Vendée Globe, was one of thirteen starters; only seven finished. American Mike Plant and his *Coyote* disappeared in the Atlantic en route to the start of the race. *Coyote* was eventually found afloat in the eastern Atlantic, its six-ton keel ripped off, no sign of the sailor.

The 1992–1993 version was won in one hundred and ten days by Frenchman Alain Gautier. Fourteen racers started, seven finished. Englishman Nigel Burgess's boat was found in the oceans off Australia, upright and intact, no sign of the sailor. In 1996, sixteen boats left Les Sables d'Olonne and nine finished. Frenchman Auguin won. One boat disappeared, that of Canadian Gerry Roufs. Despite several false sightings near the coast of Argentina, neither he nor his boat was ever seen again.

Surrounded by mementos of a sailing life—trophies, boat parts, weather-beaten waterproof jackets, and bibs—Jeantot is tall, mustachioed, forty-seven. Retired from competitive sailing since the first Vendée Globe, he now sails mostly with his wife and two kids. Last year they circumnavigated, through the tropics. This spring he's fended off criticism that he's been an absent organizer. "There is no adventure where you spend so much time *in* the adventure," he says. "You really have to do *everything* yourself. Nowhere else in the world can you find yourself in a similar situation. If you climb Everest, you have the support of sherpas and a team. Ballooning around the world—and only two men have done that—lasted only three weeks." In his hand he holds a list of the racers he's expecting for this fourth version, twenty-eight in all. "I like to keep it to twenty," he admits. "It's easier to keep track of everyone that way. But if there are more at the starting line, they will all go." We look at the list together. Several of the names are fixtures of the big, single-handed races, the various transatlantics, transpacifics and more. Several are coming back for a second, or third crack at the Vendée Globe. Eighteen of the twenty-eight are French. Thirty-nine-year-old Yves Parlier is starting for the third time. Catherine Chabaud, the first woman to finish the race, in 1996, is back. Eric Dumont is back for his second try, as are Marc Thiercelin and Herve Laurent. Thierry Dubois lost his boat—and nearly his life—during the last Vendée Globe, but he'll try again.

Almost half of the field are newcomers to the Vendée Globe. Brit Mike Golding won a stage of the last Around Alone (the new moniker for the BOC). Fedor Konyoukhov will be making his third round-the-world try, after one Around Alone and having circumnavigated the bottom of the world from Australia to Australia. Dominique Wavre has been a team member in the Whitbrea, a crewed, three-stop circumnavigation race. One second-timer's name jumps off the page: Rafaël Dinelli, the Frenchman who spent forty-eight hours afloat on a shredded life raft in the Southern Ocean during the last race after his *Algimouss* sank beneath him. He was rescued in dramatic fashion thanks to the twin efforts of the Australian Defence Forces and Vendée racer Pete Goss, who turned his boat around and fought back one hundred and sixty miles into a fierce storm to find the near-dead Dinelli clinging to his raft. (As he turned back into the storm Goss explained to Jeantot by sat-phone, "I have no choice. I'll do it.")

• • •

When the Vendée sailors depart Les Sablles it is usually smooth sailing for the first couple weeks. A lack of wind is often more of a problem than too much. It's a good time to tune up the boat and communications equipment, and prepare mentally for the isolation—and inevitable boat-wrecking storms—that will occupy them for forty days when they hit the Southern Ocean that surrounds the bottom of the planet.

Frenchman Yves Parlier led the '96 Vendée Globe during its first weeks; he was eventually forced to drop out after his rudder broke. It was not his first attempt; in 1992–1993 he finished fourth, even though he had to turn around at the very beginning to replace a broken mast. "So you can see, I am obliged to try again, to win it. I have no choice . . . I have to go. I want to go. It's a choice I make." He has only a goal this time out: To win.

Now thirty-nine, Parlier began sailing when he was eight years old. Today he is one of France's best and best-known racers, an engineer, and father of two small children. His résumé is filled with records and victories. Of his first eight single-handed races, he won seven. In 1998 he set a record in the Route de l'Or, sailing from San Francisco to New York around Cape Horn, that still stands. In 1999 he teamed with young New Zealander Ellen MacArthur in 1999 to win the two-handed Transat Jacques Vabre, forty-five hundred miles between the United Kingdon and Colombia.

He says this Vendée Globe will be his last big solo race. "I know my boat very well, and feel very confident on her, even when knocked over. But I find myself wearing a harness most of the time now when I'm on the bridge in a storm. I have a need to be very safe these days. I have two young children and I want to come back . . . and my wife wants me to come back." In July Parlier's boat was dismasted while sailing from the US to the United Kingdom. His *Aquitaine Innovations*—the same boat he raced in the last Vendée Globe—flew off a twenty-foot wave, landed in the trough as if it were hitting cement, and the mast snapped.

Thousands of miles west of Ireland he jury-rigged a replacement from his spare boom and jib, put up the gennaker as his main sail, and nine days later limped into port. That kind of resourcefulness and ingenuity is key to finishing the Vendée Globe. Taxed by storms, bored by the monotony of sailing alone day after day after day, sleep deprived, constantly worried about what's going to break next, a race like this requires a special kind of mental "resourcefulness and ingenuity." The kind necessary to take down a mainsail in a sixty-mile-an-hour wind or turn a spare boom into a jib.

I ask Parlier if during the big blows, with mountainous waves chasing him and hurricane winds knocking his boat over, if he doesn't sometimes wish he was back home washing his car, or playing with his kids? "No, I like strong winds and big seas. During the Vendée the strong winds are most of the time downwind, which means you sail very fast. Maybe sometimes it's a bit long, and you get tired because of the constant tension. But I love that feeling." Typically understated.

And at the start of the Vendée Globe does he look around at his fellow racers and think to himself, somebody is not going to come back? "At the very first Vendée Globe I was not a competitor, just a spectator, and I remember feeling that at the start of the race. But when you are in the race it is very different, you don't think of it that way. You just sail."

• • •

Two things make solo sailing more arduous than staggering up Everest or avoiding the crevasses that dot the Antarctic plateau: Rolling a sixty-foot sailboat, most often in a raging tempest, and spending forty days—or more—in the Southern Ocean, the planet's wickedest body of water. By the middle of the race both start taking their toll. The boats that are raced single-handedly around the world today are little more than sixty-foot-long surfboards: broad deck, tall mast, slender keel. Theoretically, the heavy keel that guides them is also supposed to right the boats when they are knocked over. Sometimes they are flattened by wave and wind onto their sides. Other times the mast dips deep into the sea. Still other times the big boats turtle—go completely upside down. Theory doesn't always pan out and the upside-down boats end up sinking, leaving their navigators either afloat in a dinky life raft, or trapped inside the cabin—during the last Vendée Globe four sailors had to be rescued from their upside-down, sinking crafts.

When a boat is knocked over the sailors are most often in their cabins taking shelter from a nasty storm. Sometimes they're drinking tea, other times trying to steal a ten-minute nap or studying a chart. Next thing they know, they're upside down, with the contents of their cabin—fuel oil, food, spare parts, computers, CDs—ricocheting off the walls and their heads. "Like a ping-pong ball in a washing machine," is how Englishman Tony Bullimore describes it (he was one plucked from the sea last time, frostbitten, near dead).

Brit Robin Knox-Johnston won the first round-the-world, solo, non-stop race, the 1968 Golden Globe race. That race set out from Plymouth, England, and rounded the three great capes of Good Hope, Leeuwin, and Horn. It took him just shy of a year—three hundred and twelve days—in a leaky thirty-two-foot boat. He was the only one of nine starters to even finish the race. He wrote about the sensation of being tossed upside down in roaring seas:

I dropped off to sleep with the wind howling a lullaby in the rigging and the sound of the water rushing past the hull. The next thing I remember is being jerked awake by a combination of a mass of heavy objects falling on me and the knowledge that my world had turned on its side. I lay for a moment trying to gather my wits but as it was pitch black and the lantern I kept hanging in the cabin had gone out, I had to rely on my senses. I started to climb out of my bunk, but the canvas which I had pulled over me for warmth was so weighted down that this was far from easy.

As I got clear Suhali lurched upright and I was thrown off balance and cannoned over to the other side of the cabin, accompanied by a mass of boxes, tools, tins and clothing. I got up again and climbed through the debris and out onto the deck, half expecting that the masts would be missing and that I should have to spend the rest of the night fighting to keep the boat afloat.

"The future [did] not look particularly bright. I have bruises all over from being thrown about. . . . I feel altogether mentally and physically exhausted and I've been in the Southern Ocean only a week, and I have another 150 days of it. I shall be a Zombie in that time."

The Southern Ocean. The most inhospitable place on earth. That's right, the *most inhospitable place on earth*. Worse than the Antarctic Peninsula during a forty-day winter storm. Worse than Everest's high camp at its coldest.

The Southern Ocean is not officially named. Combining parts of the extreme southern portions of the Pacific, Indian, and South Atlantic Oceans its official boundary is forty degrees south latitude, and includes the latitudes sailors long ago nicknamed the Roaring Forties, the Furious Fifties, and the Screaming Sixties. More than twelve hundred miles southwest of Australia, barely One thousand miles north of Antarctica, an area of almost constant high wind and frequent gales, often exceeding hurricane strength. Unimpeded by land the waves of the Southern Ocean roll around the world, dotted by icebergs and small "growlers"—small bergs named for the sound sailors hear just as they rip into their boats.

In storms, the waves build and build until they are as tall as ten-story buildings. The highest wave ever reliably recorded (forget that computer-generated Light & Magic stuff)—one hundred and twenty feet high—was encountered there.

"The Southern Ocean contains that point on earth farthest from any land, 1,660 miles equidistant from Pitcairn Island and Cape Dart on Antarctica. Many of the Vendée Globe boats sail close by it, or right through it, headed for Cape Horn. Only a few astronauts have been farther from land," writes Derek Lundy.

The most famous of all French sailors—inarguably the best sailor in the world—was Bernard Moitessier. The navigator/poet spent years sailing across the oceans, and aboard his *Joshua* he once spent more than one hundred days in the Southern Ocean. (He raced against Robin Knox-Johnston in that first Golden Globe race, but once successfully through the Southern Ocean, rather than head north to the finish line, he simply kept on going, landing finally in Tahiti.) He remembered the Southern Ocean for its "exhausting gales, dangerous waves, dark clouds scudding across the sea with all the world's sadness and despair . . . and continuing anyway because you know you must, even if you no longer understand why. Sailing in these waters, if man is crushed by his feeling of significance, he is borne up and protected by that of his greatness. It is here, in the immense desert of the Southern Ocean, that I feel most strongly how much man is both atom and god. . . . And when I go on deck at dawn, I sometimes shout my joy at being alive, watching the sky turning white above the long streaks of foam on this colossal powerful, beautiful sea, that tries to kill you at times. I am alive, with all my being. Truly alive."

• • •

One veteran whose name I don't see on Jeantot's list is Frenchwoman Isabelle Autissier. The world's best, and best-known, woman sailor, she led the last Vendée Globe during its first month, until the mast was ripped from her boat, twice. Last I heard of her she was backpacking in Antarctica, both feet firmly planted on terra firma. There will be two women in this version. Catherine Chabaud was the biggest surprise of the 1996 race. Less known and less experienced than Autissier, she managed to survive the race intact and finish in one hundred and forty days—on the exact same day as Pete Goss. In the four years since, she's become a well-known face in French media, written two well-received books about her experiences and has built one of the fastest boats to be entered in the new race.

I find her a few hours after arriving in France from Newport; with a friend she'd sailed her new boat back across the Atlantic at a leisurely eleven-day pace. She plans on spending the end of the summer working with her team on slowing her boat down. "This new boat is very fast. It's very hard to control right now. And I am worried that it will be very dangerous in the Southern Ocean," she says.

I'm most curious what's motivating her to try this most-brutal of all adventures a second time. Isn't once enough? "When I arrived last time I said never again. Never again alone, never again in the south. The Vendée Globe is an experience of extremes and it tests your emotions as well as your sportive skills. But one or two months after I returned I began to forget the hardest part of the race and remembered only the pleasures. And the competitor in me was a little disappointed. I decided I wanted to go back to the Southern Ocean, and to go faster. I'm happy to go back, even if I am a bit scared of it. It's breathtaking, very exciting. But every second you're asking yourself 'What's going to break next, What's going to go wrong now?' It's very hard for the head. You feel that you are a little, little speck on that boat and that the sea can do whatever it wants with you."

In the last race, even though she skirted the northern edge of the Southern Ocean, she was knocked down many times. Once she was on deck trying to take down the mainsail in hurricane-force winds, during the same storm that sunk Dinelli's boat and nearly did in Tony Bullimore and Thierry Dubois. "I heard the noise of the wave behind me, a very big one," she remembers. "I looked around and as soon as I saw it I knew it was going to knock the boat upside down. I just had time to think perhaps it would be the end for me."

Grabbing the mast in two hands she rode the boat as it flipped over into the cold sea, almost completely upside down. Seconds later, which seemed like hours, the boat popped back upright. "It's a strange experience because you go there because of those sixty-foot waves. For the spectacle, the experience, the feeling. At the same time you have never before been so impressed by nature, never felt so small."

Having experienced the full spectrum of the race four years ago, including the loss in the recent years of several sailing friends, including Gerry Roufs and Éric Tabarly, she is more circumspect about her own chances of surviving the race this time out. "Four years ago, at the start of the race, it did not cross my mind that someone might not come back. Four years ago I was sure I would come back. I don't know how I will feel on the fifth of November; I hope I will feel as confident as four years ago. But with all the friends we have lost during the past few years probably I will also think that this time it could be me. I mean, why not me?"

This time around the youngest, and least experienced entrant is the other woman, Ellen MacArthur, from Whatstandwell, New Zealand. The diminutive twenty-four-year-old's experience is scant, understandable given her age. She's sailed two-handed across the Atlantic and this summer won her class in a solo crossing of the Atlantic. The Vendée Globe will be her biggest sailing challenge, by one hundred-fold. Thanks to Kingfisher, a giant European retailer, she's got an impressive Open 60 boat and a multimillion dollar campaign behind her. But the reality is if she finishes the Vendée Globe it will more than double her days spent solo sailing on big oceans. (Compare that with second-time Vendée sailor Eric Dumont, who's crossed the Atlantic thirty times.) Sailing since she was four years old, MacArthur crossed the Atlantic for the first time four years ago (in a two-handed race, teamed with veteran Yves Parlier). This summer she impressively won her class in a thirty-six hundred-mile, solo transatlantic race.

I find her in Newport, on the eve of sailing the *Kingfisher* back to the United Kingdom, accompanied by two others. Soft spoken to the point of incomprehensibility, the five-foot-three-inch MacArthur is Kingfisher's first big sailing sponsorship. After winning her class in the Route du Rhum race in 1998 she approached them with her dream of racing the Vendée Globe.

"Anyone can do it," was her main selling point. "About half of the Vendée Globe starters will be first-timers," she counters when I broach the subject of her inexperience. "Of course some of them have done the

Whitbred." She broke in her new high-tech boat by sailing it from the shipyard where it was built in New Zealand thirteen thousand miles to the United Kingdom. She shared the first half of the trip with a crew, then pulled off the second half solo. "The worst weather we had was a gale wind at the beginning. We didn't plunge deep down south and the weather was very stable. It was a good break-in, but the conditions weren't anything like I know I'll see in the Southern Ocean.

"In my own defense, I guess all I can say is that you can never learn everything in advance. I know I'll be learning a lot during the race." Her team has already forced her to practice righting the boat once it's been knocked upside down. "It was quite violent, actually. I feel ready for the worse conditions, but I won't know until I'm there."

I relay my anecdote about Titouan and his preprepared casts. She says that sounds pretty extreme. I ask her if she's ever been scared on the water. She lingers a long time, then changes the subject. Not wanting to jinx her, or force her, I drop the question. When she says good-bye, I can't help but wonder if I will ever see her again.

• • •

Pete Goss was the hero of the last Vendée Globe. His heroism surfaced in the wildest seas of the Southern Ocean. A nine-year veteran of the British Royal Marines and one previous round-the-world race (crewed, with thirteen others) Goss is not one of those poetic French navigators. "I'm not going out there to change myself, or dig deeper, or any of that shit," he says. "I simply love to sail." In 1996 he was honored by the governments of both France and the United Kingdom for his rescue of Rafaël Dinelli. About the rescue, today Goss will only say, modestly, "It was both the worst and the best moment of my life." His written memory of the rescue is hair-raising:

The wind was blowing at hurricane strength—sixty-five knots and over—and increasing in the gusts to eighty knots. Rafaël's boat was surfing on waves high as six-story buildings. He was trapped inside the upturned hull after being capsized by a huge wave which crashed across the boat, flipping it on its side and turning it upside down. The mast broke and was pile-driving through the hull—water poured in through the holes it made. The diesel tanks were leaking and the fumes were making him violently sick. He clambered into the cockpit, which was awash, clipped himself to the submerged hull, faced the fifty-foot seas and fought it out. Each wave that struck choked and froze him. . . . he could feel her begin to settle lower under his feet for her final trip . . . to the bottom.

When he finally found Dinelli—like the proverbial needle in the haystack—it was forty-eight hours after Dinelli's boat sank. The French sailor was frostbitten and hypothermic and clutching a bottle of champagne. I find Goss at the shipyard outside London where he is repairing the one hundred and twenty-foot-long, super-catamaran *Team Phillips* he intends to sail in another round-the-world race scheduled to take off on December 31. (Dubbed simply, "the Race," its claim is "no limits," that is, any size boat, as many bodies on board as you like, may the deepest pockets win.) He insists he doesn't think back too often to his Vendée experience, which he eventually completed in one hundred and forty days. "It's basically 'Been there, done that, moved on.' It was the best race I've ever done. I had a brilliant time, really enjoyed it. It was a real adventure, everything I could have dreamt of.'"

He pauses, reflects for just an instant. "And I mean real adventure, in the sense that you design the boat, build the boat, work out all the systems, maintain all the systems, then do the physical act of actually sailing around the world."

To me, the notion of rolling a sixty-foot sailboat in the middle of the ocean seems the scariest thing that could happen on any body of water. Goss is typically nonplussed; he withstood dozens of such knockdowns in the Southern Ocean. "It's a risk, certainly, but you have to embrace it, be prepared for it. You can't go into such a race naively. You go to the Southern Ocean prepared for it, hungry for it. It's fantastic sailing down there, really amazing. Once through the Southern Ocean, the Vendée Globe sailors are hardly on easy street as they round Cape Horn and head back for les Sables d'Olonne. As they close in on Africa and Europe they are often greeted by more head-on, gale-force winds. I'm just thankful I completed my first Vendée so that I'm not driven to go back and do it again," says Goss.

The same can't be said for his soulmate Dinelli (Goss was recently best man at his wedding). "I'm afraid it's a piece of unfinished business for Rafaël. I would never discourage him from doing it again. He deserves to finish the race." I ask Goss if he's ever scared when he's on the water. Surprisingly, his reply is candid, less hard-boiled soldierboy than I expected. "The ocean is a funny thing, isn't it? Even if people are frightfully scared of being on the ocean they'll still go on holiday to the beach and then spend days on the water's edge, staring out at the sea. I'm not scared of the sea, never have been. Certainly I have a healthy respect for it. But if you're scared of the sea, you shouldn't go out there, should you? I read about one guy who was learning self-hypnosis to help him be less afraid of the ocean. . . . I mean, if you feel like that you'd have to be bonkers to ever leave shore. You've got to cross the finish line to get it out of your system. That's why I'm so glad I made it the first time. Otherwise I'd be back there again."

• • •

I ask Jeantot what motivates people to attempt his race two, three times. "After you've done it once, you want to do it again because you want to prove the things you learned the first time. You're sure you can do it better the second time out. I've done it four times and never was it boring. It's something new each time. When you have the opportunity to do it several times I think it's great luck." I tell him I am reminded of something Moitessier wrote in his book *The Long Way:* "There are two terrible things for a man: not to have fulfilled his dream, and to have fulfilled it." Jeantot thinks about that for a minute. "It's incredible, because when you are living that race you say to yourself, never again. But two months later you want to go back. Maybe sailors have no memory. Maybe they need time to understand it. As I did. I needed to go four times around the world before I understood that it was safer on shore. At the very beginning we had no limits. We were able to go as far south as we wanted. In the first Vendée I went with some of the other competitors to sixty-six, sixty-seven degrees south, deep into the Southern Ocean, into the middle of dangerous ice fields, groaners everywhere, everywhere, for ten days. That certainly was the worst *souvenir* from my twelve years of competition. Now the limit is fifty-seven degrees south."

Before each race the rules of the no-rules Vendée Globe get a minor tweaking. This time out the focus has been on making sure each boat is truly self-righting. Last time, though the boats were required to be so, there was no prerace testing. This time Jeantot is asking all boats to arrive in Les Sables a month early where they—and their skippers—will be pushed over and expected to bob quickly back up. "The boats have to be unsinkable," says Jeantot. "The keels and bottoms must be painted bright red and their decks painted in Day-Glo colors. They have to be able to come up from a one hundred and eighty-degree knockdown. They must have five watertight bulkheads. Masts must be secured to try and avoid dismastings. Skippers must provide written plans detailing how they would get in and out of an inverted boat and collect their 'panic bag' and life raft along the way." It weighs on Jeantot's mind that in each race he has lost a competitor. Justifiably, he doesn't feel responsible. "That would be too heavy to bear," he admits, "so I won't allow it. You will never be able to make a 100 percent safe boat. At sea, everybody knows that once you go out, you are at risk.

"If a guy falls overboard, we'll never know exactly why, or what happened. Nigel Burgess? We never understood why he went overboard wearing his survival suit with two Argos beacons around his neck. We found his boat and it was fine. As for Gerry Roufs, we have no idea what happened to him, he simply disappeared. What improvement in the rules can we make from that? The last thing I say to each racer before he or she leaves is simply, adventure begins here."

HAS THE GREAT LAMAZOU
MISSED THE BOAT?

"*It is good to ride the tempest and feel godlike. I dare to assent that for a finite speck of pulsating jelly to feel godlike is a far more glorious feeling than for a god to feel godlike.*

—Jack London, *The Cruise of the Snark*

At three o'clock on a February morning, deep inside the smoky Haig's Bar in Venice, French sailor Titouan Lamazou is holding court, entertaining a hundred of his best friends and family. To his right at the bar stands Fernando Sena, director of Tencara, Italy's best-known boat-builder. To his left, Christian Veros, president and CEO of the Swiss watchmaker Tag Heuer. Nibbling on the long-haired sailor's ear is a long-limbed movie starlet. The mood of the disparate international contingency packing the joint is joyous fatigue—the night of revelry follows a day of toasting, highlighted by a luncheon at the French Consulate hosted by France's ministers of Overseas Territories and sports.

No one is higher than Titouan. Just beyond the door of the bar, floating on the moonlit canal, sits a shiny new, $18.5 million, ultra-high-tech racing schooner, the boat he hopes will take him around the world in eighty days or less. The French government helped him finance the craft; Tencara built it; Tag Heuer has promised $6 million to support his dream; the blonde, well, she too comes with being one of France's best-known adventurers. Who could fault the guy if he was feeling a tad swelled-headed?

Titouan's claim to fame is having sailed around the world faster than anyone: He did it solo in 1990, in one hundred and nine days. His next, widely publicized project is to lower his own mark by taking on one of the world's most formidable challenges, a feat dreamed up more than one hundred and twenty years before by another Frenchman, Jules Verne.

As the blonde whispers into Titouan's ear, I'm in his other, asking him how it is possible to keep his ego in check given all this adulation, all this attention, all this, well, nibbling.

He pauses, arresting me with crystal-blue eyes, exhales a stream of smoke and lifts a tumbler of grappa. "You cannot get caught up in ego," he contends. "I have ego, sure, and I know the importance of media and sponsors. But the goal is not to be famous, the goal is not even to have the 'best' boat. What is important is saying you'll do something, then doing it."

Okay, I'll go for that. But just for fun I ask him to dig out his business card. We check out the logo together. It is a self-portrait of a handsome, long-haired, seemingly godlike man kissing the moon and sky. Is this self-presentation not evidence of a healthy ego? "Okay," he laughs, "maybe I may have a small ego. But I know I can't walk on water."

It is nearly sunrise when the room begins to empty. As we head out the door someone asks Titouan what he's going to do in the morning, just a few hours away. "I think," he says, "I will go for a sail. By myself. But not until I have a small sleep."

The Venetian night is bathed in fog. I'm not quite ready to retire. Neither is the man from Tag. As we stroll across the brick walk to the Hotel Gritti, he elaborates on why his company believes in Titouan and his dreams. "It's not about selling watches, really. It is about beauty and freedom. It is about image." He pauses, looks skyward. "But we better sell a hell of a lot of watches."

Sailors with logos? Egos bigger than boats? Retail sales versus big dreams? Is this what adventuring has come to?

Perhaps. But for Titouan Lamazou—and the other top dozen French sailors, including Bruno Peyron, Florence Arthaud, Philippe Poupon, Olivier de Kersauson, Alain Gaultier, Yves Le Cornec, Gabriel Guilly—big egos, slavering sponsors, and adoring bimbos may be deserved. France produces the best sailors in the world. Twenty-one of the sixty World Sailing Speed Records maintained by the International Yacht Racing Union are held by French—from the twenty-one thousand-mile "Round the World Non-Stop Single-Handed" to the three hundred and fifty-five -mile "Plymouth to La Rochelle." It has been this way for decades and their countrymen love their sailors for their successes and panache. (When I asked one sailor about his crew, he said without fanfare that it included a painter to document the adventure. A painter? Only the French.)

When Titouan set his round-the-world mark he was feted with a ticker-tape parade down the Champs Elysées. Florence Arthaud, the only woman at the top and perhaps the best known of all French sail racers, must change her phone number every six weeks to elude the myriads who want her to christen boats, open stores, send them photographs. After Philippe Poupon won the thirty-seven hundred-mile Route du Rhum, every bus stop in Paris featured an ad campaign starring his larger-than-life mug. In other countries such receptions are reserved for returning war heroes, or Michael Jordan. Stop any Frenchman, ask them to name a great sail racer, and they'll rattle off ten.

By comparison, in the United States the only time a sail racer gets attention is when he or she dies, preferably tragically. This year for the first time, America's Cup champ Dennis Conner has entered a boat in the quadrennial, nine-month-long, five-stage Whitbread round-the-world race. Yet even as he signed up, Conner confessed there was no way he was going to personally sail the five legs. "This is a young man's deal," said the chubby fifty-year old with a penchant for five-star meals and hotels. When you get down to the Roaring Forties you're cold and wet, and there are no showers. There is no way to get out." French sailors would never allow such sentiments to cross their lips. They live for such punishments.

There are a few explanations for why France breeds such great sailors and fervent fans. Go into any little village on the country's three thousand miles of coastline and you'll find a sailing club. Everyone from five years old and up is out on dinghies. These are not yacht clubs, available to only the well heeled or aristocracy. They are open to everyone. It's kind of like

Little League in the States. Thus the grocer's son has as much chance of becoming an international top sailor as a blue blood.

The French also have a different relationship with summer leisure time than most nations, which can be traced to 1955 when by law French companies were commanded to give their employees thirty-two days paid leave between June 15 and September 15. As a result, the entire country goes on holiday at virtually the same time, most to the coasts. There, they sail. Back in Paris each fall the annual boat show fills eight buildings and attracts more than four hundred thousand. They don't just come to look; they buy boats. Saltwater is in their blood.

As for the cult surrounding champion sail racers, one man deserves credit for creating the Frenchies' romance with racing. I met Eric Tabarly in the elegant bar of the Hotel Gritti Palace in Venice. He'd come to wish Titouan, one of his protégés, well. Wrapped in a worn leather jacket, his sea-worn face a matching hue and texture, the sixty-two-year-old Tabarly had made most of the young sailors who are now grabbing records and headlines. Titouan, Jean-François Coste, Yves Le Corne, de Kersauson, the Poupon brothers—all learned to race by crewing aboard Tabarly's six *Pen Duicks*. During the 1960s and 1970s he set virtually every speed sailing record and became France's most-famous adventurer. When he broke the transatlantic record in 1968, one hundred and eighty thousand people turned out along the Champs Elyseés to welcome him home.

I approached Tabarly hoping he might give me some insight into what makes French sailors tick, what makes them better than the rest. "These are not golfers," he said, looking around the crowded bar and pointing out some of his one-time students. "They risk their lives, they go out there and do something which is the most dangerous sport. When they go off into the Southern Ocean there is no one on the sidelines who can help them, no helicopter that can save them. They cannot be rescued. If they go over down there, it's over, they're dead. That makes them different from other sportsmen.

"Why are they so popular? The French love somebody who does something unusual. And sailing around the world in eighty days—this would be truly unusual."

Ever since Phineas Fogg's 1872 race by train, boat, and elephant to round the world in eighty days, a variety of adventurers have considered the possibility of it actually being accomplished under their own steam. It's been done by jet, hot-air balloon, combination of boat-bus-plane, et cetera. But when Titouan launched his boat in February no one had come close by sail alone. If he—or any of his peers—were to break eighty days it would mean shaving one month off his existing record. That would be like lowering the record for the twenty-six-mile marathon from two hours to an hour and a half.

Despite the seeming impossibility of breaking eighty days, a pack of the world's best sailors—most French—actually cooked up a competition, complete with a revolving trophy and prize money. They did it in part because they were bored. They'd sailed across the Atlantic and the Pacific in faster and faster times, around Europe, the United Kingdom, Australia, from New York to San Francisco, Marblehead to Halifax, on monohulls, catamarans, and trimarans, with crews and solo. What was left? Only to conquer the last of the great romantic adventures: Around the World in Eighty Days.

The organized race traces to a night in 1985, when Florence Arthaud, Yves Le Cornec, Gabriel Guilly, Yvon Fauconnier, and Philippe Poupon were sitting around a kitchen table after the Whitbread, drinking and talking. It was Le Cornec—veteran of several round-the-world races—who suggested they make a race of eighty days. At the time it seemed unthinkable, even to these guys. The first Vendée Globe Challenge—the single-handed race around the world—had yet to be held. The Whitbread—the crewed, five-stage round-the-world race—had only been run four times. The record for racing around the world nonstop was three hundred and thirteen days (Britain's Robin Knox-Johnston, in 1968).

Two years later, future Whitbread champion Peter Blake—a New Zealander by birth, but an honorary Frenchman given his sail-racing expertise—mentioned he might like to try an eighty-day race. In 1990 he and Arthaud met in Freemantle and the subject was raised again. Later that year—on a barge on the Seine—a half dozen sailors met with the goal of formalizing "the race."

"While everybody had a lot to say, there wasn't a lot of agreement," says self-confessed sail-racing groupie-turned-promoter/race organizer/babysitter Jane Redford. "Nobody yet had a boat for such a race, but everybody had an idea of what they wanted to do. Blake and Lamazou envisioned building big, classic monohulls. Arthaud and de Kersauson and Bruno Peyron envisioned huge multihulls."

Over the next year the details were hammered out in Paris, between Arthaud's living room and Lamazou's office. Officially organized as "L' Association Tour du Monde en 80 Jours," the "Trophée Jules Verne" was announced on October 20, 1992, by Arthaud, Peter Blake, Jean-François Coste, Yvon Fauconnier, Gabriel Guilly, Robin Knox-Johnston, Titouan, Yves Le Cornec, Bernard Moitessier, and Bruno Peyron, under the patronage of the French Ministry of Culture and several sailing organizations and with permission from the Jules Verne Society, whose grandson was present at the announcement. They wrangled a $60,000 grant from the Minister of Culture and the Peter Stuyvesant Foundation to have a trophy built. (American sculptor Tom Shannon won the contest to construct it.) A cash prize of one million dollars was sought. (The French betting organization PMU initially promised the prize, but backed off after being criticized for touting Arthaud and Lamazou's names in advertisement without the sailors' permission.)

The rules were simple: Go around the world as fast as you can without stopping, on the boat of your choice, with the crew of your choice, leaving from an imaginary line stretched across the English Channel between the lighthouse créac'h on Ouessant Island in France and England's Lizard Point. All boats must pass the capes of Good Hope, Leeuwin, and Horn to port and then recross the same imaginary line across the English Channel. Propulsion was to be solely by natural forces of the wind and of the crew. The entry fee was 80,000 FF ($16,000). You didn't necessarily have to join the organization to make an effort, but it was strongly encouraged.

"What made this race different," says Jane Redford, who acted as liaison between the sailors, a necessity since some of them are not on speaking terms, "was that for once sailors got together and organized their own rules, their own association. The Trophée Jules Verne was conceived by sailors, for sailors, to be administered by sailors."

According to Redford, Titouan did most of the organizational work. "He probably did 60 percent of the groundwork, while simultaneously financing and building his own boat. It made sense—it was his record that was at stake."

Once the trophy was announced, the hard part began: Raising money, building boats, then racing them around the whole damn world. Even Redford, who knows these sailors well, doesn't quite understand the motivation. "It takes a certain amount of courage or folly to do something like this," she admits. "It's not just seamanship—you've got to be half crazy. I wouldn't do it if you paid me $10 million. What's so fantastic about what these guys do is they make our dreams for us. They are our modern-day Shackletons."

Hmmmm.

The February morning after Titouan's big day in Venice, we drift away from the dock in a thick fog, into the Adriatic Sea. He's taking the boat (dubbed the *Tag Heuer*) out for its inaugural sail. He is at the wheel after his "small sleep," shouting out commands as cranks and winches fly and the green-coated crew spreads out along the one hundred and forty-three-foot-long ship. Curious *battello* taxis roar up alongside, honking their horns at the spectacle.

Of all the French sailors I have met, Titouan is by far the most intriguing. In part that's because he has interests beyond sailing. A loner, an accomplished painter, he has published a novel and a book of photographs and sketches of Moroccan architecture. He is part owner of his own boatyard (Capitaine Flint) and is a skilled politician (he played a big role in convincing the French government to allow investors in his new boat to write-off their investment).

He did not come from money, nor from Brest, where the best sailors in France begin competing as youngsters. His grandparents were farmers in the south of France; his father an engineer in the oil business. His mother, also an engineer, was killed in a car accident just last year. Titouan credits her with encouraging him to be a painter, the career he chose for himself at age eleven. "She was a dreamer and she encouraged me to dream," says Titouan, looking up at the off-yellow sails of his new ship. "Perhaps most importantly she encouraged me to take my heroes from novels—not the writers, but the characters." His favorite fictional heroes? Blackbeard and Tom Sawyer. (His novel, *The Treasure of Atlas*, carried an epigraph drawn from Huck Finn, perfectly matched to a Frenchman's sensibilities: "We did it and we did it elegant, too.")

In the early 1970s an art teacher in Marseille pushed Titouan toward sailing. He made his first crossing of the Caribbean when he was seventeen; his two-year military service was spent aboard Tabarly's legendary *Pen Duick VI*. But when he was twenty-five he gave up sailing and moved to Morocco, to write and paint. That lasted two years. "I went back to the sea because I realized I didn't finish what I started," he says.

His first big finish was a second in the 1987 BOC Challenge, a solo round-the-world race. He followed that with races across the Atlantic, from Quebec to Saint Malo and Lorient–Saint-Barthélemy—Lorient before winning the 1990 Globe Challenge in record time. In 1990 he was named World Champion of Sea Racing, 1986–1990.

His intimates are few and include the designers of his boat, his lawyer, and his meteorologist ("He and I have been around the world together already many times—on computer," laughs Titouan). Members of his family remain his closest confidantes. Brother Josie helps design the boats and organize the office; his father, Jean, is his money man. "His biggest advice—after years of being in business and in debt—is keep no debt and don't sign your name too many places," says Titouan.

His detractors, including peers like de Kersauson and Bruno Peyson, see Titouan as taking himself too seriously. For his record-setting Globe race, Titouan was so obsessed with winning he consulted with doctors and had plastic molds built for his arms and legs: If broken, limbs could be bound in plastic casts so he could continue. During the race he was heard over the radio telling his onshore team: "If I don't win, I'll shoot myself." One result of his obsessiveness was that he took the lead from the first and never lost it. Afterward he admitted, "It's an illusion to think that a boat is a synonym of happiness or dream. A boat is a source of colossal trouble.

During a race, happiness is rare. It does not involve being serene or calm or relaxed even for one moment."

Perhaps the greatest testament to his skill and place in the French sailing community is the crew he's assembled to man the *Tag Heuer*. Fifteen men, including some of the best skippers in France, like Yves Le Cornec and Jean-François Coste. Why would they sign on with Titouan rather than sail their own boats? "It is an adventure they would never have the energy or the know-how to pull off," says Redford, "but they would hate to miss out on the adventure of a lifetime."

Titouan's lawyer, Marc Frilet, insists Titouan is "a natural leader."

"Many racers turn to Titouan for advice. He is the 'authority' among top sailors because he takes the most responsibility. Florence Arthaud is an employee of her sponsor, same with Bruno Peyron and Olivier de Kersauson. Titouan is a partner. He goes to them with a plan, they arrange a contract, and then all the sponsor worries about is whether he lives up to the services contracted. He gets the ship built, hires the crew, arranges everything. He is very organized—something not all French sailors are."

Right now his biggest responsibility is justifying the $25 million to be spent on his latest dream. There are still many hurdles. The hi-tech boat must be fully shaken down before he takes it on a rigorous sail. And he's still looking for sponsorship money. Then there's the slight challenge of actually sailing the boat more than twenty-one thousand miles around the world. I ask what he expects will be the most difficult part. "On a good boat there is no difficult part. The most immediate one is the Roaring Forties off Antarctica, with their cold, rough seas. But with a good crew, even they should be okay. I am much more afraid of doldrums. Right now eighty days is quite difficult to do; seventy days is impossible. We are confident it will be possible for us to do it in seventy-four days. By the end of the century eighty days will be nothing."

As the big boat cuts through six-foot swells, Titouan leans against a four-foot-tall steering wheel. If it takes him eighty-two days, will all his efforts have been for naught? "You cannot say it is a success if you miss your target," he says. "But for me, the adventure must be part of the rest of my life, not the only part. With the boat built the hard part is finished. Now all I have to do is sail it around the world. No problem."

"The event is the boat, the event is the boat." This seems to be Titouan's mantra. I wonder if he is saying it because he truly believes it, or if because by repeating it over and over it takes the focus off the eighty-day mark—which many believe impossible aboard a big monohull.

Everyone knows multihulls are faster than monohulls. Thus logic would have it they have a better chance of breaking any record. But few believe a multihull—invariably lighter, flimsier, more susceptible to technical breakdown—can endure the rigors of a superfast, round-the-world sail. Titouan is convinced the best combination is his lightweight monohull.

Constructed by Tencara, best known for building the America's Cups *il Moro de Venezia,* the *Tag* is the biggest all-composite boat ever built, from materials previously used primarily for fighter jets and rockets. It weighs fifty-five tons (the bulb alone weighs ten tons) and can put up 1,930 square meters of sail on twin 33-meter masts. Aboard will be the most advanced computer system carried on a private ship. No one doubts the boat will be fast. But is it tough enough? Much of the race will be set in the harsh Southern Ocean; can this new boat manage the necessary high speeds in fifty-foot seas, while sailing into seventy- and eighty-knot winds? During his one hundred and nine day sail, aboard the sixty-foot *Écureuil d' Aquitaine II,* Titouan averaged 9.48 knots an hour. To make it in eighty days, this boat will have to average 12.8 knots.

The day before we sailed I spent an hour talking with Frederico Sena, director of Tencara. He was quite open about the boat's experimental construction and about how it had been modified after Mike Plant's high-tech *Coyote* appeared to fail, resulting in tragedy.

"This boat is by no means an extreme boat in regard to safety," says the Portuguese-born Sena. "The technology has been applied to other boats. The America's Cup boats use carbon fiber, Nomex, and other sophisticated products. Many boats built out of composite materials have gone round the world in the Whitbread race. What makes this boat different is its size.

"We were very, very careful. That's why we are constantly watching smaller boats now racing, that are using the same technologies. The issue of the keels in the Globe is one instance. We had three or four weeks of intense recalculation just after Plant's accident, to try and understand why his boat had its problems. It could have been for stupid reasons, or a miscalculation. If it was miscalculation, we didn't want to make the same mistakes. Our designer spoke with virtually everyone in the world who has designed keels, to try and understand what had happened."

I ask if they changed anything based on what they learned about Plant's boat. "Yes," he admits, "we built a new keel, of slightly different alloy and shape. We had an aluminum blade that had been cut; now we have an aluminum blade made of sheet, glued together by machines."

Our conversation took place in February, nearly a year before Titouan was scheduled to set off around the world. In a statement that would come back to haunt him, Sena told me, "The fact is, we don't expect the boat having a major problem." Titouan, sitting beside the boat builder, added: "If these boats were totally safe they would never win."

One subject studiously avoided during those celebratory days in Venice was that even as Titouan's boat was being christened, three others—captained by two Frenchman and a Kiwi—had the jump on him. Bruno Peyron, Olivier de Kersauson, and New Zealander Peter Blake were attempting to break the one hundred and nine-day record and making a run at eighty days.

Frenchman de Kersauson—a veteran sailor, perhaps best known for his five-years as host of a popular radio show, *The Big Heads*—took off first. An antiestablishmentarian, he purposely ignored the rules of the Trophée Jules Verne and its association. His departure on January 22, aboard an eighty-one-foot catamaran, was kept secret and was not from the imaginary line drawn at Lizard Point. When he did report back to shore, he gave false positioning.

When two-time Whitbread champ Peter Blake heard de Kersauson was setting out after the record he hustled to ready one of his old boats, sponsored by the New Zealand apple company Enza. He hoped to raise money to build a One hundred and twenty-five-foot monohull for his round-the-world attempt. Instead he refitted a nine-year-old, eighty-five-foot catamaran and invited the first man to sail solo nonstop around the world, Britain's Knox-Johnston, to join him.

Bruno Peyron's reaction to de Kersauson's effort was similar to Blake's. He rushed to the start line aboard an eight-year-old catamaran. The current Transatlantic record holder (six days, thirteen hours) and veteran of twenty-seven Atlantic crossings—eleven of them solo—Peyron is a formidable skipper. He and Blake left from Lizard Point within hours of each other, on January 30. The irony to the departure of all three was that despite any prelaunch bragging, none really believed they would break eighty days. To a one, they were attempting to steal some of Titouan's big press, to break the one hundred and nine-day record.

Twenty-four days after departing, de Kersauson quit just above Cape Town. After twenty-six days at sea, in the middle of the Indian Ocean, Peter Blake gave it up. Only Bruno kept going.

No one, least of all Peyron, though he'd make it around the world. He left deep in debt, on an aged boat. The best thing in his favor was experience; his four-man crew had more than one hundred transatlantic crossings among them. That counted. In the Southern Ocean, sailing into eighty-two-knot winds, they were making twenty-eight knots per hour—without a sail up. For a full week the boat was readied for capsizing. They almost called it quits off Brazil after hitting two sperm whales, cracking the boat's port hull. Crewman Olivier Despaigne spent two days inside one of the hulls essentially rebuilding the boat from the inside out, with epoxy. Video taken in the Southern Ocean shows Bruno, hands on the computer below deck, asking out loud, "What the fuck are we doing here?"

Ultimately they survived the winds, the whales, fifty-foot swells and even the doldrums. At 9:18 on the morning of April 20, Peyron's eighty-six-foot *Commodore Explorer* completed the circumnavigation of the globe in seventy-nine days, six hours, fifteen minutes, fifty-six seconds. He'd averaged 13.98 knots and his multi-hull had not flipped, cracked, or sunk. In somewhat understated fashion, Peyron had accomplished what Jules Verne could have only dreamed: He had sailed around the world in less than eighty days, under his own steam.

A month after his return, I find the thirty-five-year-old Peyron in his hometown of La Baule, on the Atlantic coast. He'd been front-page news since his return; his hometown had swelled with crowds when he sailed into port. He was hardly prepared for the onslaught of media attention and admitted he was having a hard time coming down. "I could never have predicted this," he says, tousling the hair of his ten-year-old daughter, Alexandra. "That's probably why we made it."

The son of a captain in the merchant navy, Peyron is hardly foreign to the sea. Bruno is the eldest of three sailing brothers—Loïc once held the transatlantic record, Stéphane has windsurfed across the Arctic Ocean. As we speak Bruno is in the midst of writing the inevitable book about his adventure, as well as planning a movie about the feat. When those are complete he plans to find a sponsor and build a one hundred and thirty-foot catamaran. Then he will try and lower his record.

"I wanted to make the first attempt so I could learn for the second try, the big one," he says. "I was really just trying to beat Blake, and to maybe make a new world record. Unlike some of the others, like Titouan, I refused to say 'It's easy, we're going to make it and so on.' We were not so sure."

I ask when he knew he was going to break eighty days. "The last day. That's no joke," he says. "The two or three days before we arrived there were no winds at all in the Key of Biscayne. We were totally becalmed. So we just waited, and waited." He credits the good humor and skill of his crew—three Frenchman and American Cameron Lewis—for the successful voyage.

Already Peter Blake, Florence Arthaud, and Titouan are promising to lower the new mark. Does he think his new record will be broken soon? "Of course. Somebody will go faster. But we'll tell them it is very dangerous. It is the ultimate challenge on the sea, that's for sure."

Before meeting Peyron I had spent an afternoon in Paris with Florence Arthaud, who is also trying to raise money ($20 million) to build a one hundred and thirty-foot trimaran so she can take a run at eighty days. Her boat designers and their computer assure her the boat they have planned can round the globe in sixty-nine days. Just how fast does Peyron think his new boat, when built, can make it around? "I should say in about sixty days. I think that will be the maximum."

Back in Paris, Titouan and his team were shocked by Peyron's sail. "No one is more amazed he won than Bruno," says Marc Frilet. He then launches into spin control, French style. "That Peyron beat eighty days by just a few hours is good; if he had done it in seventy days, that would have been big trouble. Titouan and the designers of his boat think he can do it in eventy-five, seventy-six days. Plus everyone knows multi-hulls are faster. So if Titouan can beat Peyron's mark aboard a mono-hull . . ."

The new record is heightened by the fact that Titouan and Bruno Peyron are hardly close friends. But in the spirit of the Trophée Jules Verne, he showed up at the finish to congratulate the new record holder.

"It would have been better if he didn't break the record," Titouan tells me afterward. "But now he has set a new standard. It's good for the media. Now there is a real race. For us, it changed not much. For us the most important thing is the creation of the boat."

Titouan's five-room office, early in July. Ornate scroll embroiders the ceiling. Black metal balconies look out over Clichy. Marble fireplaces anchor each end of the main room, which is otherwise dominated by a pair of easels. One holds work in progress, a painting of a twin-masted red sailboat on a black sea. One long table in the conference room holds only models of the *Aquitaine* and the *Tag Heuer*. The bookshelves are filled with the works of Klee, Hockney, Gauguin.

Titouan is red-eyed. The day before he'd been in Venice, tomorrow it's to Nice for a boat show. Last week it was Japan, lining up a crew member and publicity, looking for sponsors, arranging for TV coverage.

Much has happened since that glorious weekend in Venice, even worse than Peyron breaking his record. On a Saturday evening, March 27, a storm whipped the Adriatic off the coast of Yugoslavia/Albania. The crew was sailing the *Tag Heuer* back to Venice for a prescheduled checkup— Titouan was in Paris—when the boat, sailing into fifty-knot headwinds, hit a still-unidentified floating object, ripping a hole as big as a semitruck in its port side. It began filling with water.

Quick-minded crewmen rushed below to close the watertight doors, saving the boat from sinking. Instead it floated like a cork, its aft out of the water. A trio of Navy ships from the United States, Italy, and France circled. Due to the high winds and swells it took twenty-four hours before crew members could be transferred and towing lines attached. On Monday morning, thirty-six hours after initial impact, the boat was safe in the Italian port of Brindisi.

Three months later Titouan still has no idea what the boat hit. His best guess is a container or a sunken ship. "Whatever it was, it was something strong," he says. "That is the last time I'll not be on the boat."

Though the boat is in dry dock at Tencara he is still hoping for a January departure. Pressures are mounting. Lloyd's of London is threatening not to pay for the boat's estimated $2.5 million repair, contending the damage was due to "faulty design." Tag is threatening to pull its sponsorship if the boat is not back in the water soon. To top it off, the boatyard co-owned by Titouan has had to be closed. "We had to fire everybody," he says. "The economy in France is very bad; nobody is buying big boats."

Jane Redford articulates what others in the French sailing community are saying only to each other. "When Titouan's boat broke up it demanded a lot of reevaluation. Is it tough enough? The bottom line is the bigger the boat, the bigger the screw-ups. A little hole becomes a big hole, a little money becomes a lot of money. But it's too late for him to change now." Meanwhile others prepare to challenge the eighty-day mark. Specifically, Peter Blake's planning another try, scheduled to depart in December or January. So is de Kersauson.

I see Titouan several times over the next few weeks and he seems to be reevaluating the whole effort, even as he struggles to keep his project moving forward. One night he suggests maybe he'll just rerig the boat so that he can sail it himself. Another day he laughs that sometimes he doesn't even like sailing that much and imitates a bored crewman pulling in a sail. One day he insists what he really wants to do is paint ("Sketches bring me more powerful reward than sailing"); the next he admits right now he would not be wholly satisfied just sitting at a table painting ("I need to go and I need to arrive").

"Nobody has built a boat like this before, so of course it is a risk," he says in July. "Isn't this true: Some things have to be unknown, they have to be risky, or it's not adventure."

Three months after it was launched, the Tag Heuer *limped back to its shipyard in Venice, never to sail again. Titouan never raced again either. Instead he turned his energies to painting and writing, and is now a best-selling author in France of exotic travel narratives, which he writes, illustrates, and photographs.*

BREAKAWAY SURVIVAL

The commuter train from Birmingham to Hereford is standing-room only, making the last leg of the twelve-hour schlep from Paris to the English countryside tedious, exhausting. I do my best to hang onto a strap, suck in stale cigarette smoke and avoid the stares of the homebound wage slaves. My weariness is compounded by the knowledge that the weekend ahead does not promise rest and relaxation. I am slated to join a "team" of laymen—lawyers, from a London insurance company—in learning survival techniques in the hills of Wales.

The teachers? A band of rugged-if-slightly-bent former British Special Air Service Commandos (SAS), the Green Beret of the United Kingdom. Though physically frayed, I am mentally alert enough to recognize immediate trouble when I step off the train in Hereford and am met by a pair of the former elite Army boys grinning big, hardly sober. My new buddies, who introduce themselves as Mick "Ginger" Tyler and "Able" Frank Able, literally stumble over each other as they explain that those liver-bellied lawyers from London have bailed out. One feebly citing a broken leg as an excuse!

Truth is, I was it, the only survivalist to show. This is not good news; I had hoped for company in my misery. Nor was I particularly thrilled when I threw my bag into the back of the car and caught sight of the provisions the boys had packed for our weekend: A steel pot filled with live rabbits and eels, several cases of Heineken tallboys, and an already cracked bottle of malt whiskey. While I had been hesitant about the weekend, now my eyes quickly scanned the train schedule to see if I could get back to London this night. Staying put took on even more frightening proportions when I climbed into the front of the Citroën wagon for the hour drive to the Welsh border and the Brecon Beacons hills, where I was to spend five days sleeping under wet leaves, eating fungi, and harpooning trout. As I pulled on my seat belt, I spotted a box of cassettes between the seats—everything the Carpenters had ever recorded. As we pulled away from the rail station, "Able" Frank, whose military reputation was earned for blowing things up in the jungles of Borneo, was taking a long pull off a bottle of whiskey, which interrupted his humming along with Karen Carpenter's "Rainy Days and Mondays." At that moment, my survival looked bleak.

• • •

Over the years a variety of friends in the United Kingdom adventuring community—mountaineers, polar men, pilots, sailors—had shared stories with me about an eccentric former SAS commando, a twenty-seven-year veteran of the British Army, they all claimed was the toughest guy any of them had ever met. His name was Ginger Tyler and he was now imparting the knowledge he'd gained in a dozen years spent behind enemy lines in secret jungle and desert insurrections around the globe to insurance executives, surgeons, and secretaries willing to fork over $100 for three days or $250 for five. His Breakaway Survival School was teaching civvies how to live like killers: How to scavenge for edible foliage, skin rabbits, and gut eels, how to find their way up and down darkened hills in freezing fog and rain, how to sleep under leaves and hide—if absolutely necessary—in pools of freezing water.

Motivated by the wild stories I'd heard about Ginger Tyler, I had signed on for one of his five-day excursions. When I arrived in Hereford to discover I was the lone guinea pig my lightly considered lark quickly seemed a big mistake. Ginge, while offering his apology for my lonesomeness, was quick to remind me that adaptation was what survival was all about.

And I was quick to gather that my solitary presence was fine with the half dozen other former SAS veterans Ginge had assembled to help with the weekend's "class." Thus my first lesson in survival turned into an advanced class in pub crawling. In the hours after I wearily descended from the train, we traveled—lager by lager, pint by pint, shot by shot—through a seemingly never-ending string of seventeenth-century pubs that line the road from Hereford to the Welsh border.

(Ginge Tyler's Survival Lesson #1: In a strange pub, always order your lager with a 'lemon tops'—a dash of lemonade—to ward off any unpleasant bitterness.)

I barely survived that first long night, spending the wee hours propped in a corner, nearly comatose. The night was followed by a morning of more of the same—another five-hundred-year-old bar, more war stories ("Tell 'im about the time you got shot in the ass, Jordy!" "Or the time, Ginge, we had to drag you three miles with a broken leg?").

(Survival Lesson #2: Always buy a round for the locals. You never know whose field you may be crossing the next day.)

After one last round, the late-afternoon drive to the Brecon Beacons through the lush, rolling patchwork fields that are trademark Wales, offered necessary relief from the industrial grit and the smoke-filled pubs. Pheasants darted across the narrow tarmac, buzzards and green woodpeckers sat in the trees. The meadows were dotted with sheep and cows. The now-sobering crew had, thankfully, traded the Carpenters for the slight improvement of "The Bolero." The only disturbing visuals were the road signs. The hills come with indecipherable Welsh names, like Gwaun Taf and Twyn Mwyalchod. "Outdoor Education Center" translates to "Canolfan Addysg Awyr Agored."

By nightfall of my second day in-country, we reached the hillside encampment Tyler uses as his base. It was pouring rain. After making camp beneath parachutes dragged from under wet leaves we ate our first meal of the day—boiled rabbit. "Consider it an honor that you're alone with us, mate," confided Ginge, ripping into a sinewy leg. "It's like private lessons."

My companions, when sober, couldn't have been a more happy-go-lucky band of fifty-year-old former killers. Their motto (actually just one of several they would trot out over the weekend) was "Once a soldier, always a soldier." The hills and valleys where we were camped were the very same they'd survived to pass muster and join the elite SAS three decades earlier. They—Jordy, Frank, Mush, Bobby (who's still in, currently guarding the

Sultan of Brunei) and Ginge—relished coming back to the Brecons, no matter the excuse. Over the years they had survived many tough spots together, covering each other's backsides while instigating, spying, and wreaking havoc behind enemy lines, on behalf of "democracy."

They liked returning to the site where those most formative years began. Ginge's weekend survival school was an excuse for them to get back to the only life they'd ever truly loved. A little history. The SAS was first formed in 1941 to raid behind the German lines in North Africa; in the fifties it was reformed to fight Communist terrorists in Malaya. Headquartered in Hereford since 1960, its presence is still felt today, if surreptitiously, in coups and secret wars around the world. Once in the British Army any soldier may apply to join the SAS. The first step to qualifying is a nine-week training and elimination course, in these very same Brecon Beacons hills. Its tests include a "Speed March" (twelve miles up and down three thousand-foot peaks lugging rucksacks, rifles, et cetera, which must be covered in four hours), followed immediately by the "Endurance March" (forty to forty-five miles over similar terrain in thirty-six hours).

The next test is a four-week course in every kind of parachuting, including crashing through trees (you aim for the tallest tree, desperate to cling to its high branches and then lower yourself to the ground with two-hundred-foot nylon webbing). Only the toughest survive. Those that are chosen to join the SAS instantly become equals: Rank is stripped, pay is reduced to that of a private (a "financial disincentive" they call it), discipline is no longer an issue—it is expected. There are no drill parades, no fancy uniforms, few direct orders. You are expected to know what is expected of you. Dropped behind enemy lines, you live on short rations. Your clothes often rot off in the jungles just before you're reassigned above the Arctic Circle. A knowledge of the local language and medicine is essential. So are hand-to-hand combat and demolitions. Officially the SAS motto is: "Who Dares Wins." Its unofficial credo? "The man who cannot look after himself is no use." Newspaper accounts from the sixties dubbed SASers as "the James Bonds of the jungle." The average stay in the elite unit is six years. But once an SAS man, always an SAS man. I quickly notice things about my new pals that separate them from the ordinary. Like they don't leave a pub, no matter how many pints they've thrown back, without stopping at the door, ever so briefly, and surveying the street. Once headed down the sidewalk they stay close to one wall, one eye constantly peeled on the buildings and rooftops across the way. In the morning, no matter how hungover, when they first open an eye they give the room a quick inspection. What exactly are they expecting? "The goddamn enemy," Ginge explains. "And you never know who that might be."

• • •

Tyler's Breakaway is one of just a handful of survival schools in the United Kingdom, which are becoming increasingly popular among the outdoor cognoscenti and day hikers alike. His is known as the most informed, the most rigorous. "This is not a glorified camping exercise," he warned when we crawled out of our leaf beds our first morning. "I'm going to teach you how to take care of your frigging self." He said he'd teach me mountain rescue, orienteering, night navigation, how to improvise weapons, trap rabbits and pheasants and catch trout by hand, how to exist on plant life, make shelter in the middle of the forest, and start fires in freezing rains.

All for a mere $250. "I'm not about making money," admits Tyler, "I'm about living."

(Survival Lesson #3: The red berries of mountain ash are too bitter uncooked, but can be boiled down to a jelly. They make especially good seasoning for venison—or rabbits, if that's all you've got.)

Our first hours in the woods are spent hiking into the tree-covered meadows Tyler uses as his training grounds. Wielding machetes brought back from the jungles of Thailand, we set to building a fire, skinning rabbits, gutting eels, and fashioning bows and arrows, snares, and fish harpoons from local trees.

(Survival Lessons #4 and #5: The key to starting a fire in the rain is dry kindling: Look first for dead branches under pine trees, birch bark, or birds' nests. Young rabbits make for the best eating; the first thing to do after they are dead is squeeze the urine out of them so it doesn't contaminate the meat.)

Ginge and Frank then shoulder the responsibility of taking me on my initial six-hour march, to test my mettle and teach me some of their tricks. As we walk away from the fire I swear a couple of the others are humming, "We've Only Just Begun," in unison. After an hour's fast-paced hike the lessons come fast and furious. We stop by a quiet pool. Mick lies flat on the ground and plunges both hands quickly, quietly into the icy water. I watch silently as he literally tickles a trout from behind a rock into his hand. Back on his feet he plucks dandelion roots and puts them carefully into his pocket; we would boil them later for a hot drink instead of coffee.

The most abundant food source in these woods, I quickly learn, is bracken, or ferns, which we also pick to boil. Burdock leaves can be munched raw, as can those from hawthorn bushes and nettles, though boiling reduces their bitterness. The leaves of rose bay willow make for good tea. When it comes to mushrooms, Ginge's advice was simple: "Never eat anything you're not 100 percent sure of and avoid anything with white gills, the ribbed part on the underside of the cap. Watch out for the *Amanita muscaria* (fly agaric), the red-white toadstool pictured in fairy tales—it'll kill you." Standing atop a cliff overlooking the misty, green valley he assures me that "puff balls are edible, too, as long as you clear them first of slugs or snails. Although slugs are certainly edible, they can eat fungi which are poisonous, which will kill you."

After hearing my stomach grumble Tyler admits that on his five-day courses some of his clientele tend to get a bit hungry. But he claims the toughest part of his course is not the diet but the mountain rescue, which involves rappelling (or abseiling, as the Brits prefer) and hauling "the injured" up and down steep cliffs. "It's most often dangerous for the guinea who volunteers to get strapped on the stretcher," says Tyler. "They're the ones who get banged up as they're drug up the hills, then carried—or dropped—back down."

(Survival Lesson #6: When hauling a stretcher up a hill always assign one person to keep watch on "the injured's" head. No sense beating them senseless as you try and save them.)

• • •

After the boys settle into their outdoor routines they prove to be excellent guides and companions. Particularly Ginge. I'd had my doubts soon after we met, during our long pub crawl. Especially when I found myself helping to stuff him—this toughest of all commandos—into the back of a hansom cab while he drunkenly tongue-lashed its driver for every sin from pulling too close to the curb to having sex with sheep.

(Survival Lesson #7: "Night Navigation" means finding your way back home from the nearest pub without a flashlight.)

That initial evening had been exuberant, excess heaped upon excess. At each new pub Ginge quickly became the focus of the room as he regaled listeners with bad jokes and war stories, ordering ales and whiskeys faster and faster. At each stop the tough guys put the lone American— me—on the spot, insisting that I explain, if not defend, what they'd heard about Bill Clinton's decision to formally allow pooftahs into the U.S. military. To a soldier they agreed this was a bad thing. (Ginge: "You hear about the young pooftah who goes into be interviewed for a command? The officer in charge asks, 'So, do you think you could kill a man?' He thinks for a minute before replying, 'Well, yes sir, I think I could. Eventually.')

As the night wore on Ginge took on comic perspective. His face is a caricature when he's sober, his thinning red hair (the origin of his nickname) connected by a solid bushy eyebrow wrapped across his face. His countenance became ever more ruddy and cartoonish as he told joke after joke, laid insults on total strangers, bussed them with great apology, then insulted them all over again. By midnight he was speaking in tongues even while offering to buy yet another round. But I shouldn't have been concerned for him—he's apparently well practiced at such debauchery. Barely able to stand at midnight, he was up and out for a jog at seven the next morning, then home to cook eggs and bacon and beans for breakfast.

Born in 1939, Mick Tyler grew up poor in Kent, one of seven kids. His first familial responsibility was pinching eggs for the table. While he did poorly in the classroom he excelled in sports. On May 3, 1955, at age fifteen, he joined the Boys Army and moved to Hereford. He took to military life instantly. "It wasn't much different than I'd been living," he laughs, "and they fed me." A battery commander's report in 1956 dubbed him, "A really promising and courageous boy NCO. Pleasant to work with and reliable." In 1957 another year-end report said he was, "One of the first to choose as a campaigner in times of stress."

During his twenty-seven years in the British Army he served with the Para Brigade, Commando Brigade, and the 22nd Special Air Service Regiment in Cyprus, Jordan, Kuwait, Aden, Norway, Germany, Denmark, Singapore, and Borneo. In the SAS he was one of a four-man team engaged in secret wars, "hearts and minds" missions. Though skilled as a medic, linguist, and demolition man, Ginge's expertise was weaponry. After six years with the SAS he signed on as a Special Forces Survival Instructor, teaching new troops jungle and desert survival techniques, medical assistance, parachuting, and snow, rock, and ice climbing. In 1968 he was awarded the Commando Medal, the highest honor in the British Army.

Though he left the army in 1982, he is still all soldier. Adorning the walls of his two-bedroom suburban Hereford townhouse are pictures of him and some of the boys—Paddy Winters, Spud Murphy, Tanky Smith, Alec Spence—posed in the jungles of Malaysia, Thailand, Cambodia. He is proud of a thick scrapbook from those days (His mates jokingly call it his "I love me" book). "Unlike me, Ginge can't leave the life behind," confides best friend Frank Able, now a copier technician who on weekends serves as Ginge's daytime aide-de-camp and nighttime babysitter. "Today when people ask me I refer to my twenty-three years in the army as 'my last job.' Ginge, he still talks about that life, incessantly. Because he misses it, compares everything to it." When Tyler quit the army he came back to Hereford. He'd married a local girl and they'd had three daughters. He tried working as a roofer, a carpenter, even selling dogs, anything to make a buck. Then his wife got breast cancer, which moved quickly across her chest and to her brain. Horrified by her sudden death in 1989, Ginge retreated to the job skills he knew best, teaching people how to live. It was what he'd always wanted to do.

"My wife, as good a mother as she was, never understood soldiering, never understood what I did away from home," he says over a plate full of beans. "She didn't understand that after I'd been home for a few days I had to get out, either back to the wars, or to the pubs, to be with my mates. That was my life. She got the checks, raised the kids, did a good job. But she never really understood me." Today he lives with a young Thai woman, a bank clerk. "We're just mates, that all," he says.

Tyler's favorite words are two: "Bollocks" and "lovely," the latter used as an exclamation at the end of virtually every sentence. His hobbies are squash, metal detecting, and local history. For fun he is a "fell runner," a kind of marathoning over mountaintops. For example, the Peaks-of-Snowdon Race is a twenty-five-mile footrace up a fifteen thousand-foot mountain. He's done that eight times. The Manx Mountain Marathon is thirty miles long, ranging over twelve mountain summits. He's done that nine times. When we finally made it into the hills I remembered something Ginge had told me the night we first met, not long before he collapsed, dead drunk. Maybe he had spoken the whole truth about himself in that one beery breath: "I am the most real bloke you will ever meet," he had slurred. Now, after less than forty-eight hours in his company, I was tempted to believe him.

• • •

Our third morning in the muck began as had the previous two: with a downpour. Sopping wet and hungry, I found myself inspired by the calm that had taken over the others.

(Survival Lesson #8: The fungus of jew's-ear, found on dead elder branches, cures a sore throat.)

These were not the same war-weary clods I'd caroused with in Hereford; the more time we spent under the parachute, the more introspective they became, the more open. Gone were the bad-joke-telling, manly-man braggarts of the pubscene. Instead, they seemed truly at ease in the woods, much more willing to impart what they'd seen, and learned, during their combined years of espionage and fighting.

That's not to say they didn't get a big laugh out of watching me slide on my ass down a wet embankment or chuckle at my attempts to start a fire from wet leaves. They were men after all. By midmorning the fog was lifting and Ginge took me out on his own. We clambered up muddy footpaths and over wide fields, through freezing fog and rain, bumping into the occasional sheep marked by spray paint, which has apparently replaced branding as a mark of ownership.

After slip-sliding down a steep hill of wet grass we paused for a drink behind a tall waterfall. Ginge pointed out the spot in the pool below where we'd jump, if we had to, if, say, we were being chased by a squad of VC. I promise Ginge Tyler has never heard of Robert Bly, yet his outdoor teachings smack of some of the same manly "finding yourself" blarney. Yet for all its hairy-chested maneuverings and skills-testing, Breakaway is still a business, which Ginge is just now starting to get comfortable with. His brochures read like late-night infomercials. Officially the classes he offers are called "Management, Initiative, Motivation, and Team-Building Courses."

From his photocopied brochure: "Our Aim is to (1) Combat stress (2) Develop resourcefulness (3) Encourage teamwork (4) Bring out leadership (5) Develop self-reliance & confidence." Some of the biggest companies in London apparently go for this kind of stuff. Citibank, Lloyd's, Marconi, and more have all sent managers out for weekends with Tyler and his boys. Individuals come by word of mouth initially, and many come back. On training civilians, Ginge is politic, businesslike. "I get these blokes out here who during the week might address each other politely around the office as, 'Hello, Mr. Jones; Hello, Mr. Smith.' But they never really know the man, or the woman, they work next to, which inhibits their ability to work together as a team.

"Well, they come out with me and I force them to jump into icy rivers, build shelters, scrounge for food, and save each other's ass. All the time they're watching me saying bollocks to every obstacle. The next Monday they're back in the office, and instead of 'Hello, Mr. Smith,' it's 'Bollocks this, bollocks that.' They watch me and get tougher, I guarantee. I don't mind teaching them, even the whiners. I've nothing to prove anymore—I've done it all. Now the challenge is passing information along. The more of a problem the people are, the better the challenge."

After several hours in the hills I'm drenched in sweat from desperately trying to stay on Tyler's heels. When we arrive at the Blue Pool he and the boys have been warning me about since I arrived it is almost with relief. "It'll make your nuts jump into your throat," they had cautioned. It was February after all. While we strip to dive in, Ginge puts his most important rules of survival in succinct order: "Make the most of any situation. Size it up. Undue haste makes waste. Remember where you are. Vanquish fear and panic. Improvise. Value living. You only pass this way once—so get on with it." With that, we plunged in . . . and the boys were right.

(Survival Lesson #9: Before diving or jumping into the blue pool, or any unknown waters, cup your privates.)

In the army Tyler got ahead mostly on physical skills. Sweet and charming when sober, he was always one of the most popular of all "the boys." Since he's retired, say his friends, he's been a tad lost. After all, his expertise was big guns, a skill he rarely calls upon these days. His post-army life is filled with conundrums. He can't figure out how to program the clock on a VCR ("It's not me style, mate"). The electricity in his apartment is pay-as-you-go and he often forgets to plug a shilling in the meter in the downstairs loo, and off go the lights. His favorite talk remains of the past. He is unwilling to give up those days, or not ready at least, and that's why he so loves going back into these hills each weekend. It helps him relive that life. It helps him survive.

• • •

After burying the parachutes under deep beds of leaves and hiding as best as possible any evidence that we'd been there at all, we slog through the muck, back to the cars. Muddy, cold, and hungry (despite all the foliage tips and all those delicious rabbits and eels, I was starving) we stopped at the New Inn in Ystradfellte for dinner.

(Survival Lesson #10: The skin of rose hip contains more Vitamin C than oranges. It can be eaten raw or fried—just scoop out the seeds and pith, which can irritate the stomach.)

Inside Ginge picked up the Sunday papers and quickly zeroed in on an account reported from these very hills. Apparently late on Friday night a lawyer who had gone out with one of Ginge's competitors ("on a so-called Management Course," chided the news account) had suffered a fatal heart attack while slogging his rucksack up to two thousand meters. ("He wasn't overweight," the story quoted his wife of six months.) Mountain rescue was called and his stiffening body carried down in the dark. The story went on to criticize such survival schools for taking out-of-shape folks into the woods and pushing them too hard.

Setting the paper down, Tyler is at first contrite, then angry. This kind of thing is definitely not good for business. "That's exactly why I gather the people together the night before we begin, right here," he says, pounding his fist on the seventeenth-century wooden bar. "I buy them some drinks, feed them dinner, and suss them out pretty quickly. I can tell who's talking big, who seems a little scared. I pay close attention, so that when I do push them, I know when to pull back. But some guys, obviously, don't know how to suss people out, they don't know what they're doing." He picks up the paper and turns to the sports pages. "Another pint, Ginge?" asks Frank Able, serving his customary salving role.

"Well, yes, I think I will. Lovely idea Frank, lovely." In the background, I promise, one of the boys is singing along loudly with, "For All We Know."

A NEW CROATIA

A light blanket of new snow covers the fields south of Karlovac. This Croatian valley of travertine barrens, nestled between the Mala Kapela and Licka Pljesivica mountains, was the front line during the five-year civil war that split the former Yugoslavia. Today, two years after that war ended, every neat, two-story house we can see from the road is pocked by hundreds of bullet holes. Most are abandoned forever, the rest are slowly being repaired, missile holes and burned-out roofs patched with new cement and shiny red bricks.

Zeljko Kelemen drives the burgundy van. A big man with the body of an aging athlete, his sad eyes slope across a square face. He pulls over and we climb out to look down onto the Karona River, near the town of Slunj. Serb rebels had dynamited tremendous cliffside rocks into the river, an effort to destroy a Croat's mill. Amidst the detritus of the dynamiting Zeljko points out a wire hanging across the river, a reminder of prewar whitewater slalom kayak races.

"When I think of the war I am very sad, angry," he says as we walk along the river on a cold, January morning. "I never had any prejudice against anyone. Neither did most of my friends." Employed these past eleven years by Croatia's largest tour agency, he volunteered to fight, but was not called. Introduced to paddling by an older cousin in 1969, rivers have long been the most important thing in his life. He spent the war years exploring in Slovenia, Croatia, Bosnia, and other Eastern European countries, looking for raftable runs.

In 1989, the year before war broke out, he founded the Riverfree Club in Zagreb. Its mission is to preserve rivers in their free-flowing condition by proving their commercial value as tourist and recreation resources. Postwar he is an intriguing mix—part promoter, part conservationist, with the soul of an entrepreneur trapped in the body of a former-Communist-state citizen. A trained pilot who majored in English during his school days, he is a worldly forty-seven-year-old. During three days we spent touring Croatia he amazed me with such non-Stalinesque witticisms as, "Advertising without marketing is like winking at a girl in the dark."

Standing above the Korona river, reminders of war abound. Many of Zeljko's are river-related. When war first broke out he had tour groups returning from river trips whose route was blocked by skirmishes between Croat regulars and Serbian rebels. During the war he loaned rafts to the Croatian army, just before the war-ending Operation Storm. Bridges destroyed by rebel bombs, the rubber boats were used by soldiers to cross the Korona into Serb-occupied territory and then ferried the wounded back. "I never saw those rafts again," murmurs Zeljko.

His most dangerous river trip had little to do with rapids or undercuts. Last June he and friends made a first descent of the Una River, tracing the Bosnia/Croatia border. "We knew the roads, bridges, and railroad were damaged or destroyed and that some land by the river was not yet cleared of land mines," he says. Reaching the river was easy, by following the local fishermen's trail. What they did not expect was to have to portage around a twenty-meter waterfall, which led them through a field laced with mines.

"The mines were marked, but grass had grown up over the markers," he says. "Nobody said a word as we tiptoed through the grass, rafts balanced on our heads." Their trip got the attention of the local media and soon afterward Bosnian Army units cleared the remaining mines and rebuilt the road. Last August the first Una Regatta was held, with three hundred participants. Thanks to Zeljko's efforts to publicize the river, discussions of damming the Una have been taken off the agenda of Bosnia's electric company.

• • •

The day before, we sat in a Zagreb restaurant near Croatia's Parliament. During the war, bombs had landed just one hundred meters away, hitting the presidential palace. Polka music played over loudspeakers in the background as we talked.

Neither environmentalism nor river running are common pastimes in Croatia. Zeljko knows he's a bit of an odd fit, but he's used to that. As a teenager he chose a high school that specialized in languages ("Because I was better at English than math") and because it was near an outdoor hockey rink. When it came to university he started out studying English then, with the encouragement of teachers, switched to aeronautic school ("Mostly they trained people to work at airports"). Pilot courses followed. Still, all he wanted to do was paddle. (Fittingly, he never considered following in his father's footsteps, since he worked for a company that made parts for dams.)

Brought to his first canoe club by his older cousin when he was just six years old, he began competing in canoe and kayak races at fifteen, on the Sava River, which flows through Zagreb. "For ten, fifteen years that club was my second home. Every day I would spend the whole afternoon at the club, then go into town with my friends. Our passion was competition. But if there was a good disco nearby, I would do very bad in the race because I would have stayed in the disco all the night. We weren't getting any money for it, we just did it for fun. We built our own fiberglass boats, made our own sprayskirts and paddle jackets. It was more recreation than sport."

After a mandatory year in the army he needed only fifty more hours to obtain his commercial pilot's license. But it was winter and the flight school was closed because of bad weather. To earn his beer money he took a job at a travel agency. "I liked it and forgot about the flying," he explains. Since then he's worked around tourism, though never giving up his love of paddling. At one point he took a job with a hotel in Karlovac so that he could be near the confluence of four rivers and paddle every day. Sheepishly, he admits his passion for rivers cost him his first wife and occasionally makes it hard on his second. He lives with her (and a second daughter) in his mother's Zagreb house. The small yard, garage, and even its rooftop balcony are filled with canoes, kayaks, and the detritus of a commercial rafting business. For the past decade he's run the "adventure" desk for Atlas Tours—Croatia's largest travel agency—focusing on canoe and rafting trips across the former Yugoslavia.

"I was lucky," he says, sipping a Coke. "The same cousin that introduced me to canoeing and to adventure also introduced me to *Huckleberry Finn* and *Robinson Crusoe*. Those things changed me forever."

• • •

Plitvica Lakes National Park is Croatia's largest, at fifty thousand acres, established fifty years ago, on April 8, 1949. On a cold, clear day Zeljko and I hike among its frozen lakes and waterfalls. He has been trying for years to convince the park's managers let him run canoe trips on the upper lakes, so far without success.

It's a big job he's taken on, requiring him to be equal part salesman, promoter, and educator. At every turn he finds himself talking until he's blue in the face, trying to explain how protecting rivers really is both good for the environment and for tourism. He delivers his mantra to politicians, government ministers, electric company managers, the man on the street. Everyday is a new challenge: "One of biggest educations we must make is for people not to use the river only for washing their cars, or changing their oil, which is quite popular." Even the river guides he himself trained sometime need reminders, like dynamiting rocks out of the way or cutting down low-hanging trees may be expedient but not environmentally sound.

Though his message is slowly being heard, he gets little help, especially from the government, which would prefer he not even use the English word "raft" in his promotions. "They would prefer I use the Croatian word, which of course no one understands, and makes my message even harder to get across."

His biggest fight at the moment is trying to prevent a second dam on the Dobra River, sixty miles outside of Zagreb. He first ran commercial trips on the Dobra in 1989, with great success. Using information generously passed out by electric company workers, he coordinated the day trip with releases from the existing dam. Now, thanks to his high-profile campaign against new dams in Croatia, those once-friendly electric company employees are forbidden from giving him any information. Which makes it difficult to schedule trips on the Dobra.

"Now that tourists are coming back to Croatia, it would be great to get back on the Dobra. Before the war we'd made contracts with people who live near the top of the river to help them develop camps, to build rooms, to expand their farmhouses to accept tourists, all with support of the National Tourism Board. Which means there are more and more people against the industrial use of the river."

But his opponent is sizable, the national electric company—HEP—a powerful monopoly.

How powerful?

"This congress gave them a concession to use rivers to make and sell electricity. They are supposed to pay 1 percent of the money they make selling energy to the state. Out of arrogance, they never signed the contract and refuse to pay the 1 percent. But no one can tell them to stop producing electricity, because then we have no electricity.

"There are sixteen thousand people working for HEP and I'm not fighting all of them, just a few top management who don't care," says Zeljko. "These managers make like $9,000 a month; the average salary in Croatia is $400 a month. They can't possibly understand how a raft guide who makes $40 a day feels about protecting the river."

The Dobra's twelve-mile raftable stretch is close to Zagreb and its citizen and tourist base. Ironically Zeljko and his then-novice guides perfected the run during the war years. "There were thousands of United Nations troops stationed in Zagreb, with nothing to do," says Zeljko. "There was a U.S. MASH hospital at the airport, with hundreds of doctors and nurses just waiting in case they were needed. Most of the injuries they treated were for basketball injuries. A Finnish construction battalion spent its time building a bridge, and a sauna for themselves. Canadian and French soldiers were stationed near the airport. They were all looking for some recreation on their time off. I offered them rafting trips."

"They were all young people, trained and fit," says Zeljko, and he used them as guinea pigs as his guides learned the river. "It was easy to bring them to the river with beginner guides because if the boat flipped they were happy. We put in just below the dam's power plant. When they release water we had fifty cubic feet per second for the first two, three miles. There's one big hole that can flip boats easily, and lots of big waves. It was the biggest thrill most of them had during their service here.

"We did those trips in May and June of 1993. Then Karlovec was attacked by rockets and we could hear bombs falling around Zagreb. After that they were not allowed to leave their stations, so it was a short season."

Those trips generated a lot of local media interest and the following year hordes of locals sought out Zeljko to organize more rafting trips. "People had heard about rafting, seen it on television in places like the Grand Canyon, and now it was here in their country. I figured I should concentrate on them, because the more local people I brought to the river, the more people there would be against building new dams."

With Atlas's help he bought five Avon rafts and organized a race on the Dobra, garnering even more attention. ("It was beautiful weather, with sponsors providing beer, Coke, we all got sun tans, it was great.") Now all of Zagreb wanted to go rafting.

Despite initial skepticism from his bosses, in the waning years of the war, canoe and rafting trips became a boomlet for Atlas, selling out weeks in advance to tourists from Germany, Italy, Scandinavia.

"The hardest part was that 99 percent of the people had never been in a canoe before," remembers Zeljko, "and it was very difficult for them just to go straight."

In the last two years he and Atlas have expanded to several rivers near the Dalmatian coastline, where thousands of tourists flock to the beaches every summer. But Zeljko's favorite rivers are inland, particularly the Una and Mreznica, each featuring dozens of beautiful waterfalls and difficult rapids.

His campaign to keep rivers free of dams continues. "The only problem is that now I'm wasting 90 percent of my time on things I shouldn't. Now I spend a half hour each day organizing trips and five hours writing letters to ministers.

"Just today," he details, "I sent a letter to the Ministry of Environment. I need his help if I'm to do canoe trips in the national parks. I sent him statistics that I picked up in Denver last summer that show the incredible economic impact rafting has on that state. How many people it employs, that kind of thing. River rafting in Colorado generates $100 million a year, which a country like ours—in big economic trouble, where unemployment is a big problem—needs to seriously think about.

"What reaction will I get? Probably nothing. But I have to keep trying."

• • •

Asphalt turns to gravel, then mud and snow as we wind downhill toward the Mreznica River and the home of Zeljko's friend Milka Smokjanovic. Serbian, she is waiting with Christmas Eve dinner for us—the Greek Orthodox Christmas is celebrated early in January. The two—Croat and Serb—met a dozen years ago when he canoed upriver during an exploratory trip and stopped to visit her small mill. "I told her right away that we could start tourism on the river and that she could make money renting out her beautiful meadow to rafters and canoeists," laughs Zeljko. "She thought I was out of my mind."

"But after one season she became a believer. Thanks to money she made renting her field and selling cheese and bread and meals to rafters, she was able to buy a little color TV, a small car for her son. She became one of the richest women in the area. The meadow was so nice, people didn't want to leave."

Their small enterprise was halted after just two seasons, thanks first to invading Serb rebels joined with the Yugoslav Army, then the Croat Army, as it reclaimed the area. During the height of the fighting she moved to Serbia. When she returned she found her home destroyed; in the past year she has rebuilt the roof and interior walls and her mill is operating again. People come from twenty miles away to grind flour for animals and bread. But things are a long way from back to normal. The bridge at end of her road was destroyed; virtually all of her neighbors, their homes destroyed, will never return. To use the phone she must hitchhike into town, past burned-out homes, schools, and shops.

Widowed, with two grown children, Milka is in her fifties. She wears multicolored moon boots, thin navyblue pants, a black wool vest over a thick navy blue sweater, and a small orange scarf around her neck. Thin salt-and-pepper hair is pulled into a short ponytail. She is excited to have company, greeting us on the road below her stone house with a firm handshake and three kisses each.

After a tour of the mill we watch the winter sun set over the green-blue river that drops through a small rapids directly in front of her house before bending into a small eddy in front of her meadow.

With a bright smile and twinkling eyes, the only English words she knows are "cheese" and "thank you." Thanks to Zeljko she has become an ardent believer in ecotourism. On the wall of her simple kitchen is the new 1999 Atlas Adventures calendar, next to pictures of her son and daughter. Thanks to her daughter, now living in Italy, she has a few pieces of furniture. Electric lines were knocked down by rebels. She heats with wood; a propane canister sits in one corner for a hot plate. Batteries power a small radio, candles are her only lighting.

Rubbing cold hands before the woodstove we talk as she prepares a Christmas eve dinner of freshly slaughtered pork shank, raw onions, fresh bread, and homemade cheese. She offers an aperitif of home-brewed plum brandy. In the candlelight she searches for and finds a simple silver tray. Placing two glasses on it and a big bottle of beer she invites Zeljko and me to sit.

They reminisce about the summers she played host to passing groups of rafters. "She's a great cook," says Zeljko "We'd have fresh, hot bread every morning. Fantastic thick bean soup with macaroni and sausages for dinner. For big parties she would grill a lamb or a pig. They were some legendary parties. When we camped here nobody wanted to go to sleep.

"And she loved it. She made many friends, from many different countries. It was a great example of ecotourism at work, because it didn't change her, or her place. She earned some money to buy a small tractor, some better clothes, some furniture. I made a contract with her to use her meadow and paid her three years in advance. That way she could build some toilets and improve the road. It worked well, until the war."

In 1990 all travel through the region ended, except for tanks and military transports. "We had good bookings, but it was clear the country was not going to be safe anymore," says Zeljko. Electric lines were cut, garbage was thrown into the river. During the first two years of fighting, Milka refused to leave.

Eventually word of her business and cooking skills leaked, specifically to a camp of UN troops stationed nearby, mostly Czechs and Poles. "They discovered this beautiful place by the river, and that she was a good cook, always willing to sell them some wine or beer," explains Zeljko. "When one of the officers had a birthday they would come to her and ask 'Can you make us a special meal, some drinks?'" In order to make "reservations," they gave her a military field telephone.

Jealous, Serb neighbors accused her of being a spy and the phone was taken away. A land mine was thrown onto her roof, one of several efforts to scare her away from her valuable land. There was an obvious profit motive behind efforts to chase her out—she had a contract with Atlas to use her land. Her neighbors, a mix of Serbs and Croats, were savvy enough to understand that whoever occupied her land after the war could eventually go back to collecting rents from passing rafters.

Now that she's back home, and back in business, she and Zeljko are anxious for the rafting season to begin. They make plans to meet again soon to talk about schedules. "I am ready," she announces emphatically.

After dinner, the night sky filled with stars, she bids us goodbye on the icy road, with kisses on each cheek. As Zeljko and I cross over the just-rebuilt bridge he is silent, thinking about Milka and what lies ahead for them both. Unprompted, he speaks out of the darkness.

"You know, I've got enough to do to last the rest of my days. It's a good thing I like what I'm doing."

These pieces appeared, in slightly different form, in the following publications:

"A Shagbag's Journey," *previously unpublished*

"Desert Wanderings," *Men's Journal,* April 1999

"Wild Man in Africa," from *The Adventures and Misadventures of Peter Beard in Africa,* Bulfinch Press, 1993

"The End of the World," *Men's Journal,* May/June 1993

" The Colca Plunge," *Summit,* September 1994

"Thirteen Things Cubans Love about Cuba," *National Geographic Traveler,* March 2004

"Inside Guatemala," *Diversions,* February 1994

"The Nine Lies of Hector Villaseñor," *Sports Afield,* October 1998

"Rapid Descent," *National Geographic,* September 1994

"Big Chop on the Yangtze," *Adventure Journal,* Fall 1998

"Murder in the Karakoram," *Outside,* October 1998

"Air Antarctica," *Men's Journal,* August 1992

"On Thin Ice, One Last Time" *New York Times Magazine,* February 26, 1995

"The Iceman Turns to Water," *National Geographic Adventure,* Fall 1999

"Sacrificial People," *Condé Nast Traveler,* May 1993

"Postcards from Newfoundland," *Mungo Park,* September 1997

"Alone against the Sea," *National Geographic Adventure,* November/December 2000

"Has the Great Lamazou Missed the Boat," *Outside,* October 1993

"Breakaway Survival," *previously unpublished*

"A New Croatia," *River,* April 1999 and *Salon,* September 1999